The Strength to Let Go

A Mother's Journey Through Her Son's Addiction

Jo Henry

iUniverse®

THE STRENGTH TO LET GO
A MOTHER'S JOURNEY THROUGH HER SON'S ADDICTION

iUniverse books may be ordered through booksellers or by contacting:

iUniverse
1663 Liberty Drive
Bloomington, IN 47403
www.iuniverse.com
1-800-Authors (1-800-288-4677)

ISBN: 978-1-4917-6147-2 (sc)
ISBN: 978-1-4917-6148-9 (e)

Library of Congress Control Number: 2015902635

Print information available on the last page.

iUniverse rev. date: 03/10/2015

Contents

Foreword

*I*n over three decades in the chemical dependency treatment profession, I've witnessed the devastating impact that addiction has on scores of individuals and families. One of the great tragedies of this disease of addiction is that so many of those affected by it never recover. What Jo Henry's book gives, besides an intimate walk through the garden of her heart as she struggles with her child's affliction, is the realization that it takes a myriad of concerned friends, loving family members, and a few dedicated professionals to achieve the miracle of recovery.

If you, or someone you care for, has a loved one who is struggling with drugs or alcohol, then *The Strength to Let Go* is a must read. Jo's willingness to share her experience is both a blessing and a gift. I encourage you to take *The Strength to Let Go* home, find a quiet place to read uninterrupted, and open this gift.

John V. G. Mayton, retired program administrator of the DART (Drug and Alcohol Rehabilitation Treatment facility) Cherry Program, Goldsboro, North Carolina, is a master of sacred ministry (MSM), certified employee assistance programmer (CEAP), certified alcohol and drug counselor (CADC), and certified substance abuse counselor (CSAC)

Preface

It has taken years to put my thoughts and feelings together to tell this story. For a long time it just hurt too much. But I made a commitment to a very special young lady that I would try, and, to that end, I will tell you how love and faith and a strong will gave new hope to a situation that looked hopeless.

For those of you who love someone who is on the threshold of the hell that is addiction, we probably stood where you are now at some point on our journey and, like you, desperately needed to believe we would come back from the edge of absolute disaster—one I was told repeatedly would end in prison or death. Hopefully you will see our story as one of encouragement and understanding.

This story is based on real people and events that did indeed happen, though I changed some names and locations. Some of it is how I wished it had happened, and much of it I wish had never happened. This is my honest attempt to tell the story how I saw it and lived it and felt it. The order in which the boulders fell on our broken road is probably not important, but eventually it felt like a never-ending avalanche. Just as we crawled out from under one rock and dusted off our hearts, we were hit by another, bigger, boulder.

Millions of families are impacted by drug and alcohol abuse every day. We are one of those families. We are your neighbors, we attend your church, and we shop in your grocery store. We are rich and poor, and come from every racial background. I share my story so perhaps you will understand how a loving mother can unwittingly enable her son and at the same time continue to ask, "Why is this happening?" Perhaps walking in my shoes through these pages will prevent you from falling into the same hole I did.

Part of the irony in this story is that my training in family counseling and community drug awareness programs didn't prevent disaster in our own family. I want you to get to know us from the beginning, especially our son, Mike, and perhaps that will help you understand the full range of emotions we experienced.

What went wrong? There are endless possibilities. I still don't fully understand how we got into that horrible and dark, scary place that surrounds addiction. This is not about blame, mine or anyone else's. Hopefully it's a celebration of the beautiful journey we call life that inevitably ends in death. Someone I loved dearly died way too early on this journey but not in vain.

Fear gripped my heart as I desperately wanted to save our son. Sitting at my computer one night, I finally understood I couldn't do that, but it took a while longer to understand that letting go was not giving up. I could hold on to hope and love, but I wasn't in control Mike's life. I had to find the strength to let go. I had to let him confront his issues on his own. As an enabling mother, I was delaying a positive future.

I hope you find encouragement to believe in the miracle of ongoing recovery in these pages. I invite you to celebrate with us as we as we live forward, grateful for each new day.

Jo Henry
Johenry1445@gmail.com

Life can only be understood backwards; but it must be lived forward.
Soren Kierkegaard

Chapter 1

I Had a Plan

*D*o we ever really know the path our life will take, and looking back, would we change it if we could? I only know we wouldn't be where we are today if we had taken some different paths on our journey. Mike would tell you everything happens for a reason.

I don't know when a plan for my life started to form. Maybe it was when I was a little girl as I sat in the middle of my bed playing with paper dolls, a favorite childhood pastime. I just know at some point I had a hazy road map for the journey I thought my life path would follow. I would grow up, get married, and have some kids—two or three—and several grandchildren.

There were pictures in my mind of family gatherings—warm, fuzzy feelings with the smell of baking chocolate chip cookies wafting in the background. And I suppose I thought we wouldn't have any worries and would all live happily ever after. I was a naive little child, and I've never been good with maps. About the only thing that became a reality from that lovely picture I dreamed up were the chocolate chip cookies, and they were usually burned on the bottom.

My life didn't unfold according to any plan with all the pieces falling into place. When I played paper dolls, I was in charge of everything

1

and everyone in the story I created. If I have learned one thing in life, it is this: I am *not* in charge of some master plan, a hard lesson for a controlling, Type A woman. Life is nothing like playing paper dolls. Thus I have come to believe my challenge is to have the strength, the resilience, and the flexibility to adapt to God's plan on this journey. It was never easy for me to figure out where the road was going. There were so many twists, turns, bumps, and forks in the road.

We have lots of choices along the way, and some decisions are much more important than others. I believe if we take too many wrong turns, we are apt to find an obstacle in the road that should prompt us to change directions. We must have slipped way off our path because we hit some big boulders on our journey. And then—and then, there was an avalanche.

Looking back it all seemed to start out right. I grew up in the average all-American Midwest family in what I thought was the perfect hometown, Jefferson City, Missouri. Both sets of grandparents were there plus all of my aunts, uncles, and cousins from both sides of the family. We actually had those wonderful family holiday gatherings where we all crowded into my grandma's little house to laugh and share stories and eat cookies and blackberry cobbler.

My only sibling was my little brother Russ who was born when I was in high school. He graduated from kindergarten when I graduated from college. There would come a time when my baby brother, Russ, would be my pillar of strength in the middle of the worst storm of my life. But I couldn't see that far down the road.

I had a wonderful and normal childhood growing up in the fifties and sixties. Our high school football team had the longest winning streak in the country, the majority of my classmates were planning to go to college and life was good. Even though we were in school during that time of national upheaval and rebellion, we were definitely not a part of the drug or hippie scene. For us, drugs were aspirin and Midol. We didn't even think about drinking or smoking in high school. We were just "good kids." That made parenting a lot easier for our parents, but it did nothing to prepare me for dealing with drug or alcohol issues when I became a mother.

The week after graduating from college, I married Ben, one of my best friends from high school. We moved to south Texas, where Ben had taken a job as a chemical engineer, and I would be teaching high school English in the fall. That was the first move of what would turn out to be a dozen moves as Ben moved up the corporate ladder of success. We experienced hurricane Bertha early in the fall of that first year in south Texas. Bertha was the harbinger of many more storms to come.

A year and a half later, Ben got a big promotion to the home office in New York City. Our move to the Big Apple in 1969 was not without excitement. We got stranded at the entrance to the Lincoln Tunnel for hours in a record-breaking snowstorm the night we arrived. We finally got across the snow-mounded streets of Manhattan to the hotel and parked the car as close to the curb as we could. We were so exhausted we just grabbed an overnight bag, locked the car, and went into the hotel. That first night, our car was broken into, and everything in it was stolen. We filed a report at the police precinct, and I asked them, "When do you think I will be getting my things back?" The officer just looked at me, laughed, and shook his head. *I told you I was naïve.*

Amid all the stress of that move, I looked at the calendar and realized I might be pregnant. I needed to establish a doctor anyway, so thought I might as well make an appointment. The "highly recommended" doctor took my history, examined me, and told me I wasn't pregnant, but he could help me with my infertility problem.

What? Who me? *Infertility?* Had I heard him correctly? My mind was racing, and I'm sure my heart was too. He went on to explain that with my history of irregular cycles, it would probably be very difficult to get pregnant. We hadn't been in any big hurry to have a baby, but as of the moment he used the dreaded word *infertility*, it was my goal in life, my quest, to have the children I desperately wanted. I had always known having children would be a big part of my life. I was meant to be a mother. Now I <u>desperately</u> wanted a baby.

Motherhood was a huge part of what I thought was in my life plan. I left the doctor's office in shock followed by tears, lots of tears. I had to tell Ben we had a problem—of all things, an infertility problem. Another book could be written about that ordeal.

Chapter 2

Take a Different Road

My quest for motherhood had hit a roadblock. Two years into our efforts to become parents, we moved to Bay City, Texas, and four years after that move, we still had no baby. After two surgeries and a lost pregnancy, fertility drugs and additional doctors did not prove successful.

We had a big decision to make. We could try to accept not having any children, or we were going to have to take a different road to parenthood. After much discussion, adoption was our obvious next step. I had no way of knowing that the struggle we had endured to become parents was a walk in the park compared to what was to come later.

We settled on an adoption agency in Houston and started filling out the paperwork. We were told the process would probably take at least eighteen to twenty-four months. That sounded like a long time, but then we had been on this road for six years, so maybe two more wasn't so bad if we knew at the end we would finally have our baby.

We were staying busy during those years and made some great friends. We helped start a community theater, and I left teaching and was employed at a family and individual counseling agency while I worked on my master's degree in psychology. I received additional training in creating community drug awareness programs. That was my first real introduction to the perils of substance abuse, and I thought I was well informed after that extensive training and field experience, but it didn't help later when the problem was under my own roof.

We had only one step left for final approval from the adoption agency, the home visit. Out of the blue, Ben was asked to do a special six-month project in Canada, and then we would come back home to Texas.

I talked to Betty, our case worker, and she assured me if we returned for the home visit and moved back in June as scheduled, it would in no way hold up the process.

We flew back in March for our long-awaited final visit. The azaleas were blooming, and everything looked so green compared to all the snow in Montreal. I made sure the house was spotless and decided to bake a quiche for our caseworker, who would be visiting through lunchtime. Quiche was as popular in Montreal as tacos were in Texas. As much as I wanted to impress her, I wasn't going to make my own crust, so I bought that in the store. I carefully chopped and mixed the ingredients and stuck the mixture in the oven to bake as she arrived. Betty was a wonderful woman who put us at ease and laughed easily. That was a good thing—especially on that day.

She was seated at our little breakfast table, and we were chatting away. My quiche had cooled just enough, and I went to cut it into serving-size pieces. *Something was wrong.* Something was definitely wrong. I couldn't get the knife to cut through to the bottom. *Keep smiling.* I got the spatula to see if I could get the first piece out. *What was this?? Paper?* Oh my God, there were *two* crusts in that pan separated by a piece of paper.

Oh crap! I didn't say that out loud did I? *Now what should I do?*

"Can I give you a hand there?" Betty said. It must have been obvious by the look on my face that there was a little problem.

"Uh … well …" *This can't be happening! Not on such an important day!* I bit the bullet and confessed. "I screwed up," I said, shaking my head.

"Well, it smells great. It can't be too big a problem," Betty said with a smile on her warm face.

I started laughing. What else was there to do in a situation like this? The bottom crust on my quiche was barely cooked, but the one under the paper was perfectly done.

She had to know I was just dying of embarrassment, and she totally took all of the tension away with her hearty laugh. "We're going to have to get you a pretty sturdy little baby," she said with a twinkle her eye.

"Does that mean we passed?'

"Of course you passed," she said with her arm on my shoulder. We were both still laughing as Ben came through the back door to join us for lunch and the remainder of the visit. Luckily the chocolate chip cookies were great, and the bottoms weren't even burned that day.

I looked back on that visit many times with a smile. From the very beginning of my efforts to be a good mother, starting on that day of final approval, I had a plan that just didn't go as I had envisioned.

We went back to Montreal for the remainder of Ben's assignment, but I was anxious to get back home and get ready for our baby. Ben was offered a full time position in Montreal, but he turned it down. We returned to Texas, and I went back to my job at the counseling agency. We worked with school-aged children and their families, as a nonprofit agency in an informal setting. That was back in a time before everyone who walked in the door had to have a diagnostic code. Our intervention had some very positive results.

While I was busy helping other families, I was so anxious to start our own. We were just waiting for the phone to ring. Several weeks later, in October, at five o'clock in the afternoon, the phone finally rang. I answered, and it was Betty. Her first question was, "Is Ben home yet?"

"No, but I expect him any minute. Is everything all right?"

"Yes, everything is just fine. How's your weather down there?"

Now why in the world was she asking me about the weather? *It wasn't much different than the weather in Houston … hot and humid.* "Hot and humid," I replied.

"Have you baked any more quiches with two crusts lately?" she asked and then started laughing.

"No, I always check how many crusts are in the pan before I put the filling in now." I heard Ben in the driveway. "Ben just pulled in the driveway. Did you need to talk to him?"

"Actually I want to speak to both of you." My heart was beating fast, and I was starting to think that this could really be *the* phone call. Ben came in the door, and I yelled at him.

"Ben, come here right now. Betty is on the phone, and she wants to talk to us."

"Are you both there?" she asked.

"*Yes*, yes we're both here." I think I was shouting as I held the receiver between us.

"Hi, Ben, this is Betty."

Why can't she just say why she called? Is she going to ask him about the weather too?

"Hello, Betty," Ben said in his normal, calm voice.

"I have some news for you two. We have your baby. It's a boy."

"Really? Oh wow, it's a boy, Ben." I was jumping up and down and waving the phone around and hugging Ben all at the same time. "*Wow*, we have a baby. We have a baby boy!" Then I heard Betty saying something else. "What? I'm sorry. What did you say?" I was so excited I almost forgot she was still on the phone.

"I said I hope you don't have plans for tomorrow, because you can pick up your baby at one o'clock tomorrow afternoon here at the office." She gave us all the vital statistics on our baby and instructions for what to bring with us. I was writing notes and laughing and crying all at the same time. We were going to get our son the very next day. I was finally going to be a mom!

I got very little sleep that night. I selected a tiny pair of green terrycloth footed jammies and a green blanket I had made with a green frog on it to go pick up our baby boy. It had been such a long road to get to this point, but at that moment all the pain and agony melted away in the blissful anticipation of getting to hold our baby in a matter of hours.

We were up bright and early for our drive to Houston. The door opened, and Betty came in holding a tiny bundle, and she placed him in my arms. "I'll leave you alone to count his fingers and toes," she said with that familiar smile.

I pulled back the receiving blanket, and there he was. He was a precious, beautiful baby. He blinked and looked back at me. He had something wet on his little cheek. I took my finger to wipe it away, and I realized it was my tear. I handed him to Ben to hold for a minute, and then I took him back in my arms. We had waited so long for this, and it was all I dreamed it would be and more … to hold our eleven-day-old baby boy in my arms.

We had overcome a bump in the road on our journey by seeking a different path, and I finally had Mike, my precious baby, in my arms, and I was holding on tight. It would never be easy to let go of this precious little boy.

Would we be good parents? Would motherhood be the joyous journey I had always dreamed about? *Who is this little person we just named Mike? Will our son grow up to be successful and happy?*

It's nearly impossible to see the picture in the tapestry as its being woven. It becomes clear only when you step away and look back at it.

Chapter 3

Becoming a Working Mom

After the phone call in October, in November we took a trip to Missouri to show off our new son. Our families were delighted to welcome a new addition. The fact that Mike was adopted was never an issue with any of our family. We had waited so long, and it all felt so right.

When Mike was eight months old, Ben got a promotion, and we moved to Corpus Christi, Texas. It was difficult to leave that little Texas town we had called home for five years, but moving was just a part of corporate life back then. I loved being a mom and spent hours playing and reading to Mike and teaching him things. He was a very smart and pleasant little boy, and there was no such thing with him as the terrible twos. I guess he was just saving all that for later.

When he was three, Mike was in day care two mornings a week, and I was finishing my master's degree in psychology. Other than the six-month hiatus in Montreal, I had worked as a teacher or counselor up until the day the phone rang telling us to come pick up our baby. I had to admit I was missing work, even though I adored spending time with Mike.

I had an opportunity to take a part-time sales job with a division of Ralston Purina. Ben was not excited about my venture. Early on I met Joyce, and she joined my sales group. It turned out her husband was also a chemical engineer, who worked for a different company than Ben. We had a lot in common and Joyce and Dwight became our new best friends.

About a year after I had started this part-time job, I got a call from the area manager asking if I would take over the full-time job as the center manager. Ben was not happy with my decision to become a working mother, and I have asked myself many times if that could have been a contributing factor to Mike's issues later. No doubt other working mothers have asked that kind of question of themselves over the years. Many women have no choice, but I did. I didn't have to work, but I chose that path.

I had a journal that I wrote in from time to time. Even then, writing out my thoughts and feelings was a sort of therapy. An entry when Mike was four reflected some of the frustration and guilt I felt surrounding my decision.

Nov. 19, 1980

My frustration continues as I try to juggle my work and home and family. I ask myself the same questions over and over with no satisfactory answers. Am I wasting Mike's most precious years? Am I cheating Ben out of my time and energy that he deserves? What am I striving for? Are my priorities wrong? I continually consider quitting my job and then reason out why that's not the answer. I feel guilty for working when I said I wouldn't till Mike started school. I feel angry that Ben reminds me of that at every opportunity. And sometimes I feel very alone.

If I wasn't working would I really do better with all those little things that frustrate Ben? Would I pick up my shoes, pair his socks, never run out of milk, lose 20 pounds and get the bills paid on time? I don't think I did a very good job with those things BEFORE I took this job.

Then if all that isn't enough to put me in the pits, I envision Mike terminally ill, emotionally warped or run over in the street and point an accusing finger inward. Yuk! How miserable!

Time to get my head on a positive track. One good course in time management would certainly help … but then I don't have time to put that into my already overcrowded schedule. Hooray for my sense of humor. This will get better.

It was almost like I had a premonition that trouble with Mike was in our future. Looking back, it certainly might have been a mistake for me to take that job. But on life's journey you don't get to go back and take a different path. You go forward and hopefully learn, so at the next fork in the road you will make a better decision. Or not.

I went on to become a full-time regional manager, and I had two other sales centers that reported to me. That was even more time consuming and required some travel, but I was excelling in that position too and winning national sales awards. If taking the job in the first place was a mistake, I certainly managed to compound the problem.

What was happening to little Mike during those years? Mike went to preschool and then all-day kindergarten and was a thriving, well-adjusted little boy. We had a woman that came in to stay with him and clean house during the time he wasn't in school. Her name was Maggie, and she loved Mike. I still spent lots of quality time reading and playing games with him and delighting in my role of motherhood, even if it was as a "working" mother. And I pushed my guilt to the edge of the road.

We told him he was adopted from the very beginning, earlier than when he could even understand what that meant. When he was two and three, I would tell him his "Doption Story," about us waiting a long time to get him and how happy we were. He would ask a few questions along the way, and we always answered them honestly.

Were there signs way back then of the trouble that was to come with our son? If so, I didn't see them. He had some strong personality traits that were obvious early in his life, but I saw those as mostly positive.

He had gotten a bike for Christmas when he was four. We tried to convince him to let us help him learn to ride. After all, it had training wheels. He just wasn't interested. We tried on several occasions to encourage him and offer our help. Nope, he just wasn't interested. Then one day, he got the bike out of the garage, asked Ben to remove the training wheels and said he was going to ride his bike. Ben helped him get started a few times, and he kept at it until he was off riding easily up and down the street that same day. He did it his way and only when he was ready. Perhaps that was an omen.

Chapter 4

Logic Doesn't Always Work

Mike finished first grade, and my job was still causing stress at home. That summer, Ben got another promotion that would require us to move to Dallas. That was a chance to change directions. I was not going to be working, and Ben was happy about that.

While Ben and I had the luxury of growing up in one hometown and finishing high school in the same system where we started kindergarten, our son did not. We would end up moving a total of five more times during his school years.

Mike was happy in school and had some little friends in our neighborhood. More personality traits were emerging in a series of incidents. He sold peeks at his Dad's *Playboy Magazine* for a nickel a page to some neighborhood kids. I got a call from the "mother of the year" PTA lady who probably never burned the bottoms of her cookies, letting me know about Mike's business deal with her child. *I didn't even know he knew where those magazines were.* I decided I would let Ben handle that one. I smiled thinking maybe Mike was going to be a great salesman.

I hadn't been one to push the idea of forcing Mike to take three bites of everything. We had been through dinners with kids that cried and whined and argued over that issue the entire meal. However, I asked him to at least taste new things to see if he liked it or not. I had made some homemade chicken noodle soup, and he refused to taste it and wanted some Campbell's from the can.

"How do you know you don't like this if you don't try it?"

"I just know." There was that defiant streak.

"That doesn't make any sense." I thought I could just appeal to his logic and intelligence. "You might think you won't like it, but you could be wrong, and you won't know till you have some facts to base your judgment on." *How could he possibly deny that logic?* "You have to at least taste it. Then if you don't like it, you don't have to eat it, but you have to taste it." Ben and I continued to eat, and Mike continued to sit silently.

We finished, and he started to get up from the table. "No you haven't tasted your soup yet. You have to at least taste it before you are excused." This was really not working out well. He picked up a cracker and started to eat. I cleaned up the kitchen and watched as he munched on all the crackers beside his soup bowl, but no soup. I sat down at the table and tried again.

"Mike, this is made from all fresh ingredients. It didn't have to sit in a can on the shelf in the store for who knows how many months. If you would just taste it, you might like it." I smiled sweetly and handed him the spoon.

"I won't like it, so why do I have to taste it?' He did not smile sweetly and proceeded to calmly put the spoon back on the table beside the bowl.

"Because if you don't at least taste it, you could sit here all night!" I let that soak in as I walked out of the kitchen. I had always believed logical reasoning could and should win out. I had been the captain of my college debate team, but that wasn't helping in this situation.

After another hour of sitting at the table, he finally put a small amount in the spoon and put it in his mouth. Predictably, he started gagging, probably before any taste buds had a chance of tasting anything! For the rest of his life, Mike would not eat homemade chicken noodle soup, mine or anyone else's. *Strong-willed kid.* I needed to pick my battles carefully before I dug in my heels. In hindsight, it was probably more about a power struggle than it was about logic, at least from Mike's point of view.

It should have also been a lesson to me that kids, no matter how smart, are not always responsive to logical reasoning. It didn't work so well when Mike was at this age, and it certainly didn't work at all in our struggles that followed later. However, I suspect that part about *trying everything* kicked in when it came to alcohol and drugs. Sometimes the lessons we tried to teach didn't have the impact we intended.

Chapter 5

Finish What You Start

*M*ike made friends quickly and settled in to the new schools and neighborhoods as Ben's career continued to move us around the state of Texas. I was amazed at how adaptable he was. Looking back, it couldn't have been easy to be the "new kid" over and over. He managed to get involved in sports and activities easily, and that helped.

Shortly after one of our moves, he joined the neighborhood swim team. They practiced at the neighborhood club pool, and the swim team coach was also the lifeguard. Any time the boys on the team went to the pool to play and swim, the lifeguard/coach would instruct them to swim laps, tread water, or do some other training drill. Mike thought he did enough of that during team practice time, and he wanted to be able to just play. He came home one day and announced he was quitting the swim team.

We had established a policy with Mike—what you sign up for, you have to finish. You don't have to sign up again, but you complete what you start. Thus ensued the lecture on not quitting. When Ben got home, young Mike came to present his case, and he did a good job. His gift of persuasive oratory was developed early and served him well. We

17

were left with one good argument on the table—don't waste money by signing up and then quitting.

"How much did it cost for me to join the swim team?" Mike asked.

Ben thought back, "I think it was thirty dollars."

"Well, Dad, you've got a good job. Can't we afford thirty dollars? And the season is half over anyway," he pleaded.

"Yes, Mike, we can probably afford thirty dollars, but that's not the total point," Ben was trying to drive his point home to our young son.

Mike went back and ticked off his earlier arguments that we had already more or less accepted as valid. "So actually, this time it pretty much just comes down to the money, right?" he asked.

"Well, yes, but don't underestimate the importance of hard-earned money. It's easy to do, Son, when it's not your money," Ben told him. Mike excused himself and said he would be right back. We looked at each other, and, quite frankly, I was ready to tell him he could drop the team. Even then I was always the first one to want to give in to Mike.

Mike came back and sat at the kitchen table. "You agreed the season was half over, right?"

Gee this tenacious kid was just not going to give up. Was this a product of our lesson coming back to haunt us already? We agreed that yes it was indeed half over.

He proudly counted out fifteen dollars from his saved allowance and Christmas money, handed it to Ben and said, "Now, I'm off the team, and I didn't waste your money." With that he got up and went out to play. We found ourselves smiling. We shared a moment of amusement, and, more importantly, we felt a moment of pride. And, yes, we kept his money.

Before he started the fifth grade, he was tested and qualified to attend an advanced placement school for the exceptionally bright students in the district. I was opposed to segregating the smartest kids from the rest, so we didn't choose that option. Instead he applied for a fine arts school. He was selected and was there for fifth and sixth grades and did very well. During that time, I was a volunteer in a community drug awareness program, and went to his classroom among others, to make a presentation about the negative effects of using marijuana.

Chapter 6

Growing Pains

Mike attended junior high school in the affluent Plano, Texas, school system. Ben's position with the company required a great deal of travel, much of it international. It was not unusual for him to be gone for the entire week. Mike and I fell into a routine of being relatively laid-back when Ben was gone. When he returned, it was a different story. Ben had pretty high expectations and was not into my style of negotiating most decisions with Mike. We hit some rocks in the road as Mike was hitting that age of breaking away from Mom and needing his dad around more. The timing was definitely not good. Even when he was home, often it felt as if Ben was still mentally connected to work.

As Mike became a teenager, life didn't get any easier. We would get entangled in endless verbal wars. I tried to pick my battles carefully and stay laid-back when possible. The only one I felt like I made any headway on at all was the choice of radio stations in the car. My car, my choice. *Don't touch that dial!*

Then Ben would come home and be angry at Mike for not doing his chores and angry with me because I hadn't made him get them done. I tried to explain to Mike how this was going to work when he didn't do what was asked of him. I think this is when we started referring to Ben's karma. "Don't upset Dad's karma!" became a sort of mantra.

Mike changed the phrase a bit to, "Don't mess with Dad's karmals." That stuck with us forever. Ben can laugh about it now, but he did *not* find it funny at the time.

Journal entry, May 1990:

Mike continues to defy me every chance he gets. I know it has a lot to do with his age. Fifteen is quickly becoming my least favorite age for boys! What happened to my sweet, well-mannered little boy? He is a challenge! Ben is not exactly a big help, and I definitely need his help. This crap about not disturbing his Karma is getting a little old. Give me a break. I asked him to take over dealing with Mike on just one issue—ONE. I said I would stay completely out of it and he could handle it from beginning to end. He can pick it—taking out trash, cleaning the pool, keeping his room straight, or feeding the dog—his choice. I was so angry when he refused. His role is to sit on a pedestal and judge my inadequacies as a parent, but he can't find the time or the inclination to administer just one chore. He really has no idea what I am dealing with. It's much easier to evaluate and criticize than "to do."

Looking back, I probably didn't grasp the amount of stress Ben was under with his job and providing a nice income for us. I was focused on my need for his help with Mike. Yet I was allowing Mike to manipulate me on a regular basis and getting in the way of some of Ben's ideas on discipline.

Mike was having a better time being fifteen than I was having learning to adjust to his emerging manhood. I tried to use my sense of humor whenever possible, a form of maintaining my sanity. Mike seemed to be a great organizer of all sorts of activities, including a fantasy football league, a backyard boxing club, and a football betting pool that we squelched as soon as we found out about it.

One of his best friends went on vacation with us to Missouri. Doug's dad was Jim Cummins, the southwestern regional news director for *NBC Nightly News*. Mike highly respected this man and was fascinated by his career in television news.

Another man he respected and loved was my dad. Over the years, when I traveled with Ben on business trips, my dad would come and stay with Mike, and that was a treat for both of them. Dad set firm boundaries, and Mike followed them without question. He adored his Papa. And the feeling was mutual.

Not long before his sixteenth birthday, we were moving once again. This time Ben was going to the corporate office in New Jersey. He had some reservations about taking that job, but in the end decided to do it. I hoped that meant less traveling, and so did he.

Mike's friends gave him a surprise going-away party. Mostly he was surprised by many very flattering things some of the girls wrote on a big "good-bye" poster. He confided in me after the party.

"Dang, why didn't they tell me those things sooner? If I'd known they felt that way ..."

Life is just like that sometimes. People don't say the things we want to hear until it's too late.

This time we would be leaving Texas, the only state Mike had known as home. Actually, Clinton, the little town in New Jersey where we found a house, was beautiful and reminded me of our hometown in Missouri. There were hills and trees, and everybody went to the high school football games on Friday night. Before school started, football practice began, and that kept Mike busy as the junior varsity quarterback. He started dating a girl, and that kept him even busier. He had his sixteenth birthday in the fall, but the driving age in New Jersey was seventeen—a fact that did not make him happy.

During his Christmas vacation, he made a visit back to Plano to stay with Nate, one of his best friends, and visit his other buddies. I had no idea then, but during that visit was the first time he got drunk. And he liked the way it felt. I had no clue he had taken his first step on a very treacherous path.

In late February, Ben came home with totally unexpected news. He was going to be promoted to president of a company within the corporation, and we would be moving again. *Seriously?* We had only been in New Jersey for nine months and there were still boxes I hadn't unpacked. Ben needed to take over the position right away, and I didn't want us to be separated for three months, but we had never moved Mike in the middle of the school year. Mike insisted he was ready to go, so that's what we did. We took a house hunting trip to North Carolina, bought a home in a neighborhood with its own marina, and came back to pack up the house for yet another move.

This time we were moving to a beautiful southern town on the Atlantic Ocean. As a special treat we bought ourselves a boat, since we would be living on the waterway. Mike was excited about the boat and delighted we had agreed to get him a car. He had been driving with a permit just before we left Texas, but that had not been allowed due to the later driving age while in New Jersey. This was going to be an exciting adventure! I had no idea what kind of adventure we were in for.

Chapter 7

First Meeting in the Marina

It was one of those picture-perfect Saturdays in April. It was 1993, and the world seemed like such a perfect place. There wasn't a cloud in the Carolina blue sky, a light breeze blew in off the ocean, and you could smell the salt in the air mixed with sea grass and the aroma of the wetlands. I had walked down to the marina with Mike with a book in my hand. I was going to take a little time to relax and read, even though there were still boxes to unpack. In all honesty I had a hidden agenda to keep an eye on him, as he was going to "practice" with our new boat.

The nineteen-foot Grady White sat in the first boat slip in the neighborhood marina. I watched Mike jump down into the boat, and a smile lit up his entire face. The truth was we had never had a boat before and didn't know a thing about boating. He was sixteen, a sophomore in a high school he had entered only a week earlier when we had moved once again due to Ben's career. We arrived in North Carolina in March, and Mike was going to finish the school year in the new location. I had some concern about how that would go, but he had accepted leaving friends and homes behind as a normal part of his life.

Maybe this move to the Carolina coast would turn out to be his favorite. He had access to a boat, lived five minutes from the beach, and was now driving his new SUV. The Low Country house we bought had a suite on the ground floor that was designated as Mike's room. The rest of the house was up one level with a large wraparound porch in the front and a big deck in the back. We had provided him with all the material things that would be a sixteen-year-old's heaven on earth. On this glorious day at the marina, I really had no idea how that heaven could become such a hell. Perhaps we would have done some things differently had we known what was to come down the road, but we had no idea. To paraphrase a popular Garth Brooks song,

If we had known how our child would fall, then who's to say, we might have changed it all.

That song came to mean so many things to me over the years. But I have jumped ahead, so back to the beautiful Carolina day when all was right with the world.

I was sitting in the gazebo in the little neighborhood park next to the marina just soaking in the scenery when I heard the sound of flip-flops on the dock and the unmistakable chatter of young female voices. I watched as Mike moved to the back of the boat and tried to look like he knew what he was doing. The girls approached, and he looked up.

"Hey," the brunette with the big eyes said. We had already learned that's how they say "hi" in North Carolina. "Nice boat."

"Thanks," I heard Mike say. The girls were all just standing there looking at him. "You gotta boat?" he finally asked.

The girls sat down the cooler and bags they were carrying. "Yeah, and a couple of wave runners. You've got a great slip ... easy to get to.

We have to haul everything across the last dock to get to ours. It's the red one." She pointed across the marina to the last slip.

"Oh." Mike looked across the marina at her classy red inboard. She had a much longer walk on the dock to get to her boat. "Yeah I see what you mean. I guess we were lucky to get this slip," he smiled. There were about thirty slips for residents of Magnolia Hall, our new coastal neighborhood, just minutes from the bridge to the beach.

"I'm Peyton. I live a couple of houses down and across the street from you. I saw you moving in last week. These are my friends Sara and Caroline. Sara lives in the house on the corner."

Both girls gave a kittenish "hey" greeting.

"Oh yeah ... Hey. I'm Mike." He had to squint his eyes as he looked up at the girls, backlit by the bright sunshine. *Where were his sunglasses?*

"Are you at Coastal High?" the thinner girl, named Sara, asked.

"Yup, enrolled last week. Do ya'll go there too?"

"Of course," Sara put her hand on her hip.

I sat totally still hoping the girls wouldn't see me. It felt a little like I was spying. *But moms like to know their kids are getting socially "settled in" to the new place.*

"Well, see ya around," Peyton smiled and gave a little wave.

"Uh, yeah." Mike looked like he was searching for something else to say. "See ya."

Peyton and her two friends walked off lugging the cooler and bags with bright-colored beach towels. He could have offered to help them carry the cooler.

He had planned to practice backing the boat out of the space and docking it again, but with the girls around, I suspected he might postpone that attempt. It was a little windy, and it was a challenge to maneuver in the small space. It wasn't like it was a big boat, but it was tricky. Ben and I had each given it several tries and found the wind and tide frustrating factors. When Mike had asked if he could go give it a try, I said yes. But then I came up with the book excuse so I could lend a hand if he needed it—another example of my need to be in control. I looked over to see what he was doing.

He watched as the girls loaded stuff on the red inboard speedboat at the other end of the marina. It was an impressive boat. It didn't appear they were paying him any attention at all as he fiddled around in our boat. I could see he kept stealing glances in their direction. I knew he was postponing starting the boat because he was still unsure of his ability to maneuver it in and out of the slip.

Mike knew he needed to get this boat docking thing figured out so he could demonstrate his skills to Ben. Ben wasn't too keen on letting him take the boat out anyway. Just then the inboard roared to life, and Peyton easily maneuvered the big boat out of the slip, through the small neighborhood marina, and out into the Intracoastal Waterway. She gave Mike a wave as they passed.

"See ya" Peyton called as they sped away. Mike waved and smiled.

She looked like a natural behind the steering wheel of the bigger boat. I couldn't get out of the slip without my heart pounding and my knees shaking. We hadn't even taken the boat out of the marina yet.

All alone in the marina, it was time for Mike to practice getting in and out of the slip. Mike started the motor and carefully, very carefully, put the motor in reverse and backed the boat out. And then he carefully tried to pull it back into the slip—and whack, it hit the dock. I opened my mouth to shout at him but closed it. I think he had forgotten I was there watching. He backed up again and continued to practice—getting in and out of the small space.

How bad was this? We owned a boat, and we couldn't even get in and out of the boat slip. How were we going to take it out into the intracoastal canal? We needed to figure this out soon because we had used most of the gas with our practice sessions.

"Hey, Mike, can I give you a hand?" I had visions of all the paint getting knocked off the front of the boat.

"Sure. Come over and just try to keep the bow from hitting the dock when I come in."

I smiled. It was nice to know he still needed good old Mom to help him. It was predictable that Mike would be the one to master navigating the boat around. It became his favorite toy for the next several years—when he wasn't grounded from using it.

Chapter 8

Meeting the Parents

A few weeks later there was a neighborhood party at the little gazebo park adjoining the marina. It was a casual early summer affair with most of the neighbors and kids of all ages. Early summer for this part of North Carolina started in mid-April. The dogwoods and azaleas were flourishing in their multitude of colors. Moss swung from tree branches in a sensual dance on the salty breeze. The hotdogs were cooking; some kids were tossing a Frisbee while a dog barked and tried to intercept it. Several neighbors were drinking beer and casually talking in small groups. I watched as Peyton arrived with her parents and spotted Mike gazing out over the boats in the marina.

"Hey. How's it going, Mike?"

"Hey," he replied with a smile. The southern greeting came naturally for him now. He walked over to where she was standing by the cooler filled with soft drinks and beer. He reached down and grabbed a coke and wiped it on his shorts.

She already had a great tan, shown off nicely in her lemon yellow shorts and white scoop neck top. She had a full but athletic body, not skinny like so many of the girls Mike's age. I thought she was a very attractive young lady. Her best feature was her big dark eyes. A close second was her heavy mane of sun-streaked honey brown hair. You couldn't miss her infectious smile and bubbly personality.

"These are my parents, Mark and Liz," she introduced him. "This is Mike. You know, they moved into the house down the street a few weeks ago."

Mark looked Mike up and down for a moment and then said, "Man, you got some skinny-assed knees," and he chuckled loudly. I could see the expression on Mike's face change as his cheeks reddened. I saw him force a tight smile. It was true that Mike had long, slim legs, and he had been teased before about his knees … and he didn't like it.

"Dad!" Peyton reproached him. "Don't pay any attention to him, Mike." She gave her dad a reproving look, which he seemed to totally ignore as he looked over the crowd.

"So, I understand you moved here from Texas with a short stay in New Jersey," Liz interjected. Obviously she was trying to steer the conversation in a more positive direction. She seemed to move easily into the role of peacemaker.

Mike was probably grateful for the change of subject. "Yeah, we lived in Texas my whole life before."

"Oh, a cowboy in our midst," she said with a smile. "How are you liking the real South?"

"I love it." His face lit up.

"Well, hell, what's not to love?" Mark said as he spread his hands wide.

Actually Mike *was* loving his new surroundings. He missed his pals in Texas, but after the first week, he told me of all the moves we had made, this looked like the place he could really love. I found that especially comforting since I had feared we would never settle in one place long enough for him to feel like he had a "hometown." Hopefully we would stay here for him to finish high school and for it to become the place he could call home.

Peyton's dad moved away, happily greeting some other neighbors. *Well he was certainly a gregarious guy.* Mike visibly relaxed as Mark walked away.

"Peyton told me you're on the track team and doing well," Liz commented as she continued to smile and focus on Mike.

"It's fun. I really like it." Mike had a natural talent for distance running. When he had played football, his favorite part was running laps at the end of practice. His friends on the team never understood his passion. When he had registered for school, the counselor asked him about his interests and got him signed up for the spring track team. He had already made his mark as an integral part of the 4 x 400 relay team and running the mile.

So Peyton knew he was on the track team? And mentioned it to her mom?

"Well it's great to have you here. The neighborhood can use a few more guys, right, Peanut?"

"Yeah, right, Mom." Peyton sighed and rolled her eyes.

"Okay, I get the message—time for Mom to move on. Anyway, it's nice to meet you, Mike."

"Yes, ma'am, you too." Mike replied. He was so handsome with a smile on his face.

I realized I was smiling too. I could feel the warmth of this lady and sensed a great relationship between mother and daughter. Once again, I had been the unnoticed observer as Mike interacted with the young lady named Peyton.

I looked around and felt this was indeed one of those Norman Rockwell scenes—Americana at its best, and the setting was a postcard. I met several other neighbors and ended up by the gazebo chatting with Ben as the sun started to set. Orange streaks splashed across the blue sky mixing with the azure water. I looked over and once again saw Peyton approach Mike. I didn't mean to be eavesdropping, but I didn't avoid listening either. *Okay, I was straining just a little to hear.*

"Hey, a bunch of us are heading down to the south beach tonight. You wanna go?" Peyton asked.

I saw Mike hesitate like he didn't know what to say. He had met a few people at school and made a couple of friends on the track team, but his social life was not overbooked. *Of course you want to go, Mike. Just tell her yes. Stop kicking the grass with your toe and look at her!*

"Sure, I guess."

"We go to the south end, where you can drive out on the beach and party."

He hesitated like he hated to say the next line. "I'll have to check with my parents."

Good boy!

"Okay. We're gonna leave here about nine or so. Can you take some more kids in your car? You have four-wheel drive, right?"

"Sure, I guess," he stammered. "I mean, yes ... I have four-wheel drive."

"Great! Let's go tell your parents."

Come tell us? What happened to ask us?

"They're over there, by the gazebo," he motioned. He had that look of dreaded hesitation. He had just gotten his black Isuzu Rodeo four-wheel drive when we moved here. He had been totally shocked when we took him car shopping, and he got exactly what he wanted, and it was brand new! I had argued that his first car should be a used one, but out of the blue, his dad had been insistent that we go ahead and get him a new SUV. I felt strongly we should wait and hold the new car as a graduation gift or some other "reward" occasion. Ben argued that he didn't want to be bothered with constantly having to repair an older car, and newer models had more safety features. Mike had taken drivers' education in Dallas, but then the move to New Jersey with the older driving age delayed his getting a license. He had been anxious to get some wheels of his own. I finally gave in on the new car, and we all came home from the car lot happy—especially Mike, who was obviously stunned. I admit, it was great to see his excitement. We had let him drive it to school, but he hadn't been out at night with it by himself, so I knew he wasn't sure how we would react to this request.

"Nothing ventured, nothing gained. Come on," Peyton said as she grabbed his hand and pulled him in our direction at the wooden gazebo.

"Excuse me," Mike said. "Mom, Dad, this is Peyton. She's a neighbor … the one with the red boat," his voice was covered by Peyton as she jumped right in.

"Hey, welcome to the neighborhood," she bubbled. "I love the big front porch on your house. Don't be surprised if you find me swinging on your porch swing."

"It's nice to meet you Peyton," I replied. "No problem. Swing away." Ben just smiled and nodded.

"We'd like to help Mike get more acquainted … with the area … and … some of us are going out tonight … to the south end of the beach and wondered if it would be okay with you guys if he joined us." Peyton had on her best smile.

"Well, I guess it's okay," I said. Mike flashed an appreciative smile, and then I turned to his dad, "Ben?"

"No problem." Ben took another sip of his beer.

"Just be in by midnight," I said.

"And it's okay if he takes his car, right?" Peyton had zoomed in on Ben.

Ben frowned slightly. He hadn't realized this was part of the request. He rubbed his beard, a frequent habit when he was thinking. Mike was holding his breath.

"Well …" I watched as Ben thought about it. And it struck me how handsome he looked in his late forties with his thick shoulders and well-trimmed beard.

Peyton turned on her feminine charm. "We'll take good care of him. I'll ride with him so he won't get lost, and we will definitely be home by midnight, I promise," she batted those eyes and gave a little salute.

Ben chuckled, "With an offer like that, can I go along too?"

"Sure, come on," she kidded with him.

"Okay, Son, but be careful." Ben was usually pretty reserved, but Peyton had warmed right up to him, and I could see he was at ease with her. Sometimes it's hard to find the fun and warm side of Ben until you get to know him well, and Peyton had immediately tapped into his warmth that he didn't easily share. The only other person I knew that had that effect on Ben was my brother's wife, Jackie. For the most part, he was all business. I, on the other hand, was mostly into Mike's business, or so it seemed to Mike. I'm sure he knew I would have a million questions about Peyton … even if there really wasn't anything to tell … not yet anyway. We would have never guessed at this point what an important role she would play in Mike's future.

Chapter 9

The Wreck

The first trip to the south beach had obviously been fun. Two weeks later, Mike had a car full of kids and headed that direction again. Peyton was not along on that trip. When he was not home by midnight, I knew something was wrong. He had been so good about keeping to his weekend midnight curfew. I was awake and having that terrible parental experience of not knowing where your child is and sensing something was wrong ... and not being able to do a thing about it. We didn't have cell phones out with every kid at that time. I lay there awake and tossed around and looked at the clock every five minutes. I turned on my bedside light and woke Ben up. He assumed Mike was messing around and missed getting home on time and would pull in any minute.

I tried to accept Ben's explanation, but in my heart I just knew something was wrong. Is that some extra sense God bestows on mothers? I called it mother radar. There would be no rest until I knew Mike was safely home.

That's when our phone rang, and I just knew it was bad news. I grabbed it, and I'm sure I probably yelled his name. "Mike, where are you? Do you know what time it is?" I started with the questions.

"I'm okay, Mom. I'm at the hospital, but I'm okay."

Oh my God! "Are you sure you're okay? Why are you at the hospital? What happened? Who's hurt?" I threw so many questions at him before I even gave him a chance to answer. Out of the corner of my eye, I saw Ben getting up to get dressed.

"I had a wreck. But I'm not hurt. Mom, the highway patrolman wants to talk to you."

I sat on the bed gripping the phone so hard my knuckles were white. Ben saw the look on my face and knew this was not good. I quickly whispered, "There was a wreck, Mike says he wasn't hurt, but the patrolman wants to talk to me."

"Mom, are you there?"

I shared the receiver with Ben. "Yes, Son, we're here," I replied. I heard him hand the phone to the officer.

"Ma'am, this is Officer *(Whatever he said his name was)*, and I wanted to reassure you that your son is unhurt." I took a breath. "He was not drinking, and we found no drugs involved. It appears he hit some sand across the road and went into a skid, which he overcorrected. It appears the vehicle flipped at least twice."

My heart might have stopped. The vehicle flipped at least *twice*? That sounded awful.

"One passenger was hurt and is being treated. It does not appear to be serious. There were a total of eight passengers in the vehicle, which may have actually saved them from injury as they were packed in there. Your son will be ticketed. That is typical when there is an accident resulting in injury. I don't believe he was speeding, but due to the accident you would have to say he was traveling too fast for the conditions. I suspect it was mostly a matter of inexperience in handling a skid."

I managed to thank the officer and asked him what we needed to do at this point. I guess that was a pretty dumb question, but I was a bit dumbfounded at the moment. He suggested we might want to come get our son at the hospital, because he obviously didn't have a vehicle to drive. *Oh, yeah … it flipped … as in* flipped over *at least twice.* My mind was racing.

Mike got back on the phone and in a small, miserable voice he said, "Tell Dad I'm really sorry."

"We're just glad you're okay. Is there only one person hurt? Are they going to be okay?"

"I think so. Are you coming over here?"

"Of course. Oh, which hospital?" I realized at the last moment I didn't know where he was calling from. There were two hospitals in town.

He told us, and we hurriedly threw on some clothes and started for the car when we realized we weren't sure exactly where the hospital was located. We grabbed the phone book and looked at the map. Ben told me to just bring the phone book along, and we would find our way, which we did.

Mike was fine but scared, mostly, I think, of how Ben might react. We were both very calm. We gave the young man who had a cracked collar bone a ride home and proceeded back to our own home and tried to get some sleep with what little was left of the event-filled Friday night.

We drove down to see the car the next morning. It was covered with a tarp. The man pulled it off, and there sat what had just yesterday been a brand new Isuzu Rodeo. It was dented everywhere. The front windshield was smashed, and a windshield wiper dangled from the shattered glass. My knees gave way, and I sat on the ground, and then the tears came.

Mike put his hand on my shoulder and said, "I'll pay you back, Mom, honest. I don't know how, but I'll try. Don't cry; please don't cry, Mom."

I finally managed to croak out, "It's not the money, not the car. It's you."

"I know, Mom. I didn't mean for it to happen. I'm so sorry."

"No, you don't understand. I'm crying because after seeing this horrible mess, I'm just so glad you're okay. My God, you could be dead!" In that moment I had sunk to the ground, it had really hit me that we could have been viewing the morbid wrecked body of our son rather than looking at the twisted metal and broken glass of the totaled vehicle. I just sat there and cried. Ben had been right about buying a newer car with safety features. I was so thankful only one young man had minor injuries.

That was the beginning of a long series of traumatic events that would wreck our lives in this lovely city by the sea we were going to call our hometown. The wreck was the worst thing that had happened to our little family up until then, and I couldn't imagine anything more frightening. I was so wrong.

Chapter 10

The Probe

$\mathcal{M}$ ike quickly mastered the intricacies of the boat, and by the beginning of that first summer, he was spending hours on the water, a great place to make friends, especially if you're the kid with the boat. He took up wakeboarding, and as a proficient skateboarder and snowboarder, it was an easy transition. We had been going to our timeshare condo in Lake Tahoe every winter since he was very young, and that's where he learned to snowboard. His skills learned on the mountain transferred well to the wakeboard on the water.

The road wasn't totally smooth, but I was assuming much of Mike's behavior was his age and hormones. He was still being defiant with me much of the time and insisting I was overly involved in his life. There may have been some truth to that.

He had gone without a car for almost three months. The SUV was totaled, and the insurance paid in full. Again Ben did not want a used car, and Mike had his eye on a little red Ford Probe. At least it would hold only four passengers. Once again, Mike used his persuasive skills in a note to us.

I am trying to see things more through your eyes and I probably wouldn't consider getting my kid another new car if he behaved like I have been. I appreciate you are going to get me a car in a week or two and I am finding the error of my ways much too late. Now I can only start to turn my ways around. I hope you can see this and see that I will be responsible, mature and respectful. There is no way I deserve that Probe. In fact, I don't deserve any car, but I can dream.

Save this note and keep it as a receipt. Watch me grow in maturity before your eyes. I'm ready to be a man and I'm going to start acting like one. You will see change. There is no way I can apologize enough for my actions. I can only stop and turn it around. I love you.

He got the new red Probe. There wasn't much he asked for that he didn't get. We were making his life very easy.

Nathan, his friend from Dallas, came to visit toward the end of that first summer after his sophomore year, shortly after Mike had gotten his dream car, the red Probe. We had reluctantly agreed to let them go for the day to Myrtle Beach, and then that evening Mike left a phone message to say they were going to spend the night there. We were definitely not happy, but we would have to deal with that when he got home because we had no way to contact them.

I got a call very early the next morning asking if I had heard from Mike. It sounded like Nathan, but he hung up as soon as I said I hadn't heard from Mike. *Why would he be calling for Mike when he was with Mike?* With no way to contact Mike or Nathan, I knew something was definitely wrong.

I waited and paced the floor. I was so angry, and most of the anger came from my fear. When I couldn't stand it anymore, I called the hospital. *Thank God he wasn't there.* Then with dread I called the police department. I gave his name, description, and what kind of car he was driving. The clerk remembered him. Mike had spent the night in jail. *What? What had he done?* For urinating in an alley. *What? Why in the world would he do that?*

"Is he still there?" I asked with a mix of horror and anger.

"Let me check. No, his bail money was wired in a couple of hours ago, so he's gone," the clerk replied.

"Who wired him the money?"

"Someone named Kate, and I can't read the last name. Look, ma'am, kids get locked up here every weekend. We're just trying to keep it safe and clean out there. No charges are filed, but it's a never-ending job," he told me, like this was so routine.

This was not routine for our son. I had never dreamed he would spend a night in jail and certainly not for peeing in an alley. "Thank you," I said and hung up. I didn't even know who Kate might be. Ben came in from his tennis match and knew immediately that I was furious. We had already discussed grounding Mike and taking the car away for staying overnight in Myrtle Beach in the first place. Now he might be grounded for life.

Mike came in about an hour later with a story about having to go to the bathroom … and there were no public restrooms … and they were caught in a traffic jam on the strand … and he just jumped out to relieve himself rather than wet his pants in the car. He had been arrested and taken to jail, and Nathan had slept in the car in the parking lot of the jail, not knowing what to do. Nathan, as I had suspected, was the one who had called our house that morning to see if Mike had called us—which he hadn't. He had been afraid to go in the jail and ask when Mike would be released. He had no experience with jail either.

Mike was grounded, and the car was parked until school started. He was not allowed to use the boat until further notice, and that probably hurt the worst. And we let him know we did *not* expect him to ever spend another night in jail. Little did we know what the future held for our son. So much for holding on to that note he had written as a promise for his more mature and respectful behavior.

He hadn't bothered to mention that he and Nathan had also been drinking on their little excursion. That was information I learned much later. I marvel now that it didn't even occur to me to ask. I was so blind.

The summer had been filled with drama. I was taking acting classes and had a leading role in a local play. But most of the drama was going on at home. I had caught Mike in more than one lie; his belligerent attitude was grating on me, and our attempts at discipline were irritating him. We were running out of privileges to take away as punishment for his bad behavior and failure to follow our rules. Ben and I were trying hard to be a unified parenting team, but that was a struggle too.

After Mike's eventful summer, it was time to start a new school year. He had done so well in spring track that Coach Roberts had recruited him for the cross-country team. We were happy to see him so involved with a sport he was growing to love. He quickly became one of the fastest runners on the boys' team. At his school, the girls' team had excelled for the past few years, but the boys' team had not. That was a challenge to Mike, both as an individual and as a member of the boys' team.

I had high hopes things would calm down with the start of school. He had made a lot of friends, several of whom spent a great deal of time at our house … or should I say down in Mike's private suite below the main level of our Low Country style house. To get to Mike's room, we had to go out on the porch, down the stairs, and across where we parked cars under the house. There were no indoor stairs connecting his room to the main part of the house. *What were we thinking when we decided to let a sixteen-year-old boy have that much freedom?* Obviously we hadn't been thinking clearly. We did put in an intercom.

Peyton and Mike stayed good buddies, but she had her own circle of friends from her class a year younger. Colin's best friends, Brad and Audrey spent almost as much time on our boat as Mike. They were a cute couple, and I adored them. Audrey would sometimes come upstairs and we would sit and talk and she would let me know what was going on in their young world. They were all good kids, and I loved having them at the house. I became "Mama Hen" to them, and the name stuck and spread to other of Mike's friends. It was not unusual for me to fix fifty or more chocolate chip pancakes on a Saturday morning as kids would appear for breakfast. I honestly never minded one bit. They also liked my chocolate chip cookies, even if they were sometimes burned on the bottom.

I still had no reason to believe our son was headed for such serious trouble. And he was often his old lovable and respectful self. I had taught high school and been a counselor, and he appeared to be a pretty typical, sometimes moody teenage boy at this point. At least that was what I told myself.

Chapter 11

The Fall Begins

en had a business trip early in the fall, and wives were included. I had Debbie, a friend and acting coach, come stay at the house just as a precaution. Mike had a curfew and was instructed to have no parties while we were gone. There were to be no more than four friends there at a time. I didn't want Debbie to have to deal with the larger groups that gathered at our house so frequently. I called her to check in and knew something was up.

"I'll let Mike tell you about it when you get home. Everything is fine though. Nothing to worry about," she told me on the phone. That meant I was going to worry till we got home. When we got back, Mike admitted some friends had dropped by after the first football game.

"We told you no parties while we were gone, Mike. No more than four friends here at a time. So you had to have had more than that. So how many were here?" He just bit his lip and looked away. "Were there more than ten people here at the house?"

He looked down at the floor, put his hands on his hips, and hesitated. "Uh, I guess I would have to say yes." He looked up with a crooked smile.

We proceeded to lecture him and let him know we were disappointed. He was also grounded until further notice. The next morning he came upstairs to breakfast in a better mood than I expected.

"Mike, honestly, how many people were here after the game?" I asked.

"Mom, since I'm grounded forever, will it make any difference how many were here?" he asked, as he forked another chocolate chip pancake.

"No, I guess not, but I would like to know." The house sitter had been very vague about the size of the party and assured me that Mike and his friends had cleaned up afterward. That got me wondering just how big the party might have been.

"The punishment won't get any worse? Promise, even if it was a few more people than you might think." He was being his most charming self. He knew exactly how to disarm me.

"Okay, fine. I promise. Surely there weren't that many." He just smiled and looked at me. "Over fifty?" I was just picking a big number out of the blue.

"Maybe more," he said quietly.

"More than fifty kids were here after the game?" I asked incredulously.

"Mom, I don't really know how many were here, but it was probably over two hundred. There were cars parked for blocks." Now that he had opened the door to the truth, the story came pouring out. Kids had just kept coming. He said he had just mentioned at the game that we were out of town, and the word spread quickly. And by the way, yes, there had been beer. He and Brad and some other friends had gone around the neighborhood and picked up cans and bottles, and Audrey and the girls had cleaned his room and around our yard.

Good grief! I was stunned.

"I swear, I don't know how it happened. The numbers just got out of hand, but nothing bad happened, and Debbie said everyone had to be gone by midnight, and they were. I'm really sorry, Mom. I knew you'd be upset, but the crowd just kept growing, and I don't even know who brought the beer. Could I have another pancake? You're the best, Mom."

"I might ground you for life plus a few years," I said as I shoveled another big pancake onto his plate full of syrup. He had my heart, and he knew it. He was grounded, but I wasn't angry. He definitely knew how to manipulate me.

About halfway through the year, I noticed Mike was keeping air freshener in his room that I hadn't purchased. That was unusual. My first thought was, *the kids are smoking down here in his room.* I asked Mike about it, and he laughed and gave me a story about the raunchy smell from his bathroom from some of the guys. I actually thought it was kind of funny that he had gone to the trouble to buy room air freshener for that reason, and we shared a laugh. I should have known he wouldn't have used his own money for that. But I bought into his story hook, line, and sinker. I even laughed about it. Mike was good at making people laugh.

We had a storage room under the main part of the house across from Mike's room and some extra trash cans sat over behind that room. We were doing some yard cleanup from an encounter with another hurricane a few weeks after I had asked him about the air freshener, and Ben went to get one of the big cans. When he took off the lid, it was at least half full of empty cans of air freshener, all the same brand and fragrance. Now I knew boys could have some raunchy trips to the bathroom, but this was something else. Mike was out on the boat when Ben showed me the cans.

"What the hell is this?" he asked.

"I don't have a clue, but something is definitely going on here. What would he use this much air freshener for?" I told Ben about finding the first can in Mike's room, but this made no sense.

When he came back in from the boat, he had a friend spending the night, and there wasn't an opportunity to approach him without the friend. Finally we decided to ask him to come upstairs later that evening. He didn't answer on the intercom. When I went down to knock on his door, it was locked. That was unusual.

"Mike, unlock the door, hon. I need to talk to you."

"What do you want?" he asked from behind the door.

"I want you to unlock the door and come upstairs for a minute."

"I'm busy."

"Mike, open the door right now." No response. "Do you want me to go up and get Dad or are you going to open the door *now*?" This was unusual and not acceptable behavior. What was going on?

He cracked open the door. "Mom, I've got company. Can this wait till in the morning?"

"Actually, no, it can't. We want you to come upstairs for a few minutes." *What was that sweet smell coming from his room?*

He reluctantly followed me upstairs. When we asked him about what we'd found, he adamantly denied it. "I have no idea where those cans came from. Why are you asking me?" He actually came up with some good lines and I might have bought one, but my mother radar was pinging loudly.

Remembering the sweet smell from his room, I suggested maybe we should go downstairs and also talk with his friend who was spending the night. That did it. Mike never wanted to be embarrassed in front of his friends or get his friends in trouble. He was a fiercely loyal friend.

"No, don't say anything to him. He doesn't have anything to do with this."

"With what?" Ben asked. "What are you doing with this stuff, Son?" Ben is a chemical engineer. Mike's answer stunned us both, but Ben most of all. He admitted to "huffing" air freshener. By spraying a large quantity on a towel and then inhaling it, you could get a quick temporary high. I had no idea that sticky sweet, flowery smell could get you high. *I swear I would puke!*

Ben was appalled and explained to Mike how ridiculous this was and then started on the dangers of inhaling large amounts of chemicals that you knew nothing about. Mike swore he would never do it again. I asked if that was what he had been doing when I knocked on his door. He readily admitted that was the case, so I said we needed to call his friend's parents. He pleaded with us not to do that. He swore he was the guilty party and knew his friend's father might kill him if he thought his son was involved. He was in the military. We spoke to the friend, and he also swore never to huff again. With hindsight, I definitely should have called his parents. I would have wanted to know. I was so wrong not to call, but I let the boys talk me out of it.

We did our research and found this was a current craze around the country. Why had we never heard of it? I felt so dumb when I remembered how readily I had accepted Mike's explanation of why he bought air freshener. I called the drugstores and large chains like Kmart and alerted them to kids buying large quantities of air freshener. Most of them were as ill-informed as we were, but some acknowledged noticing a trend in increased sales.

To the best of my knowledge, that was the end of Mike's huffing air freshener. It was a very scary incident for all of us, but we dealt with it. I checked Mike's room for the next few weeks, but found nothing suspicious. I was happy to have Ben so involved. Maybe his knowledge of chemicals had helped frighten Mike as he made him aware of the danger.

We had one other incident that year, and it was our second encounter with Mike and the law. He was picked up for buying a six-pack of beer, under age. When he admitted where he had purchased the beer, the policeman let him go with no charges. They had the location under surveillance for selling to minors, and that was their target. Again he was grounded after another talk about obeying the law.

I started trying to be much more observant, and I asked lots more questions. Mike saw this as nagging and being on his case. I saw this as better parenting.

Mike started dating Missy, the head cheerleader, and in the spring of his junior year he ran for senior class president ... and won. He was running track and cross-country, serving as a peer counselor at his school and was a member of the Fellowship of Christian Athletes, and his world looked good ... from the outside anyway.

The summer after his junior year, Mike convinced his high school cross-country coach that the boys' team should all go to a camp at Appalachian State in Boone, North Carolina. The top runners had already decided they wanted to go, so the coach agreed to accompany them. The girls, not to be outdone, signed up to go too. Mike could be a very persuasive young man. Too bad he never had any interest in the debate team, although Coach Roberts probably felt like from time to time he was debating Mike. It was going to be a good fall season his senior year.

Everything appeared to be going much better with Mike. I thought he was as happy as I had ever seen him. Ben was immersed in his business, and that was going well. I had gotten very involved with the acting community, was serving on the board of a small theater company, and was a volunteer with the Festival of Trees, the major fund-raiser for the local Hospice. We had joined a golf and country club, and we were playing a lot of tennis and golf. Peyton's parents belonged to the same club. We had no reason to think things were not going well. Our life was a little like my chocolate chip cookies. It looked good and sweet on top, but it was getting burned on the bottom part that we didn't see.

Chapter 12

Mike's Senior Year

*M*ike entered his senior year and I had no reason to think it wouldn't be a fantastic year for all of us. He was president of his class, surrounded by lots of friends, and still dating Missy. He was excelling on the cross-country team that he captained and had finished with his best grades ever the second semester of his junior year and had gotten the coach's award for most valuable team member, even though Mike had been a force to reckon with for Coach Roberts.

The previous summer, Mike and his friends did some drinking that we were aware of. It seemed that was the norm for high school boys in North Carolina—not legal but accepted. We warned him to always have a designated driver, and he and his friends were very good about that. Was that the right thing for a parent to do? We were in essence condoning his drinking, his breaking the law. We thought it was just a little beer on weekends. If we had forbidden him to drink, would that have changed anything? Would that have stopped him from drinking?

On a shelf in his room, he started a collection of empty liquor bottles. I asked him about it, and he laughed it off as, "Just thought it looked cool."

"Where do you get them?"

"Oh, people give them to me." I assumed he would not be drinking hard liquor. Really I didn't know where the bottles came from. He was so dedicated about training for cross-country, there was no way he was drinking hard liquor. *Seriously? Yes, I was that stupid!*

Something was starting to go wrong, but I couldn't put my finger on what. For one thing, I never knew which Mike was coming through the door when he came upstairs. Sometimes he was so happy and silly and playful, and other times he was silent and moody. I recalled from my teaching days that boys and their hormones could be unpredictable, and I tried to be patient. I got the brunt of his grouchy side as he knew not to mess with Ben's "karmals."

Then on his eighteenth birthday that fall, we had a huge blowup. I honestly don't recall how it started. But I do know how it ended. I think I went down to his room to ask him to come upstairs to have some birthday cake, and he didn't want to. He was yelling at me for no apparent reason; at least it wasn't apparent to me. He started throwing stuff in a duffel and said he was leaving home.

"Leaving home? Where do you think you're going? You can't do that. My God, it's your birthday. You haven't even had cake yet!" How had a request that he come eat some of his birthday cake escalated into this declaration?

He was serious. He was going to leave. I went outside and yelled for Ben to come downstairs. Mike had taken out the intercom when he figured out I could set it to "monitor" and listen to what was going on in his room. As Ben was finally coming downstairs, Mike was going out his door. I was in tears and wanted Ben to stop him. Mike was yelling some things I probably want to forget, having to do with not being able to stand living in the same house with me. *Me? Why me? What the hell had I done?* I wanted to shout, *I'm the one who goes to every cross-country meet, feeds your friends chocolate chip pancakes, and* smooths things over with your dad! Why is all this anger directed at ME?* I really didn't understand. I just knew I did not want my angry son to leave home. I was sitting on the steps that went up to the main part of the house crying and pleading with Ben to please stop him.

"What's the problem, Son?" Ben had walked into a hornet's nest and was lost. Well, so was I!

"I have to leave, Dad. I just can't take it anymore. She's driving me nuts." He was throwing stuff into the back of his car.

"Why are you doing this? Where are you going?" I asked through my tears.

"I don't know, but I'll let you know." And with that he got in the car and drove off, and the tears really broke loose as I sat on the steps. It would not be the last time I had a meltdown on a set of steps.

"What the hell happened down here?" Ben asked with this puzzled look on his face. "What did you do to piss him off so much he had to leave home?"

I exploded. "I can't believe you asked me that! You are not going to sit on your pedestal and criticize. Not this time. Don't even think about going there!" All of my emotion was going to get directed at Ben. I wasn't going to take his undeserved criticism, not this time. He just turned, walked around me, and went upstairs. I was shaking with emotion. My son and then my husband had just trampled my heart, and I doubt they even realized how devastated I felt. I don't know how long I sat on the steps, trying to understand what I had done to bring all this down on my head. *What just happened?* I didn't understand. I was so lost!

When those you care about keep insisting that you are to blame, pretty soon you just have to start believing you are the cause. And that is a heavy dose of guilt that does not go away easily. I knew I had good intentions and acted out of love. However, that doesn't mean my actions weren't overbearing to our son. I honestly didn't know what had triggered his leaving.

About two hours later, I was scraping Mike's birthday cake into the trash with tears still streaming down my cheeks, when the phone rang. "Hell-o," I said, trying to keep the quaver out of my voice. By this time, my head was so stopped up, it would be obvious to any caller that I had been crying … or I was dying with a head cold.

"Hi. I'm Kate's mom."

"Yes?" *Why was she calling? I didn't feel like talking to anyone.*

"Mike asked me to call you and tell you he's here. He asked if he could spend the night, and I told him that would be okay. I hope that's all right with you."

I opened my mouth, but no sound would come out over the lump in my throat. "Thank you so much for calling. I'm really sorry." I felt myself choking up again. There was silence on the line. I guess neither of us knew what to say. "I … uh … hate to ask you this, but did he say anything to you about why he left?" I honestly had been thinking about it and could not figure out what had prompted his extreme reaction. It was almost as if he had been looking for an excuse to leave, which made no sense to me. I would have loved to discuss this with Ben, but I was so angry with him I wasn't about to talk to him at the moment.

She paused before she answered my question. "Actually, he said he had gotten kicked out of his house."

"Oh, that's not true," I told her. "He just got so angry with me and said he was leaving." *What was going on here?* There was silence on the phone. I guess she really didn't know what to say at this point either, so I said, "Of course it's all right if he stays there tonight, if it's okay with you."

Kate was a very nice young lady and a friend of Mike's that was seldom with the group at our house. She was the "Kate" he had called to send money to get bailed out of jail the year before in Myrtle Beach. "Yes, that would be just fine," she assured me. "You know we think so much of your son. He is a fine young man."

"Thank you," I managed to reply. "If you get a better idea of what is going on, will you please give me a call?" I was asking this woman that I barely knew to tell me what was going on with my son. That was just sad. She said she would, and I thanked her again, and we hung up. At least he had asked her to call and let us know he was safe. That trait would stick over the years.

"Who was that?" Ben asked.

An answer would mean I would have to talk to him, and I was still angry and hurt over his accusing question.

"Kate's mom." I answered without looking at him. He would have absolutely no idea who Kate was. He just wasn't involved enough in Mike's life to know. If I was overinvolved, surely he was under involved! "She called to say Mike was spending the night there."

"Who's Kate?" *Well damn, at least he had asked!*

Mike stayed gone for almost a week. During that time he had a cross-country meet. After thinking long and hard, I went that afternoon, and he was there but did not run well. After the meet, he walked by me and said, "I'm quitting the team."

"Really? Why would you do that?" I asked very calmly. Mike simply kept walking. Something was definitely going on with our son, and I didn't know what was prompting his bizarre behavior. I didn't attempt to follow him or question him. If he was trying to give me the message I was too involved in his life, then I could give him space—up to a point.

His teammates were concerned, and some were angry. A few came to talk to me after the meet. Their leader was behaving strangely, and they didn't understand.

"Mama Hen, what the heck is wrong with him?" Josh asked. "He won't even talk to us."

"Join the club! I'm with you guys, because I don't know where this is coming from either."

I made the decision to give him some time to work out whatever was bothering him. Ben was in agreement, and at least he and I had resolved our anger with one another.

Mike moved back home just as suddenly as he moved out. He didn't quit the cross-country team. He just came home one day after practice about a week after he had left. The crisis that was plaguing him seemed to have passed, and he still didn't want to talk about it. I tried, but he didn't want to discuss it. I let it drop.

Later that fall, Mike hit another bump in his road. The junior girls played the senior girls in a powder puff football game. It was a tradition that the senior cheerleaders would pick their boyfriends to be cheerleaders for the game. Missy picked Mike.

The cross-country coach, Coach Roberts, announced none of his girls could play in the game because in past years, some of the girls had sustained some minor injuries, and he did not want to lose any of them with the most important end of the season meets left to run. Because he forbid the girls from playing, he thought it only fair to forbid any of his boys from being cheerleaders.

Mike was outraged, and he felt banning the boys was totally crazy. No boys had been injured dressing up as cheerleaders and clowning around. He also threw in the argument that as senior class president, he was expected to participate in the event in one way or another. Coach Roberts gave him a flat *no*, period, no debate. Mike was used to being able to negotiate, and there was no negotiating with Coach Roberts this time. I think they had a kind of love/hate relationship. Mike was one of his best runners and had been the spark plug that had elevated his boys' team to one of the best in the region. But Mike could also be a force to reckon with.

He came home in a rage about the ruling. Our usual position was to support the school, the teacher, and the rule. I have to admit I could see Mike's point, but we told him to do what the coach asked of him. Again, he tried to make his case with us.

"Hey, Mike, it's not our decision. We didn't make the rule."

"Well, you're right. It's my decision. What he's doing is just wrong. The girls agree. They think it's crazy that he's restricted us guys just because he doesn't want them to play. Some of them are even going to play anyway."

"I hope they're ready to take the consequences of their actions," was all I said.

The night of the game, Mike was down in his room putting things together while he was waiting to be picked up by some of his friends. They were all going to watch the girls stumble around the football field. Mike hadn't said much more about the restriction after that day he came home so angry.

Mike put on a wig, makeup, and an outrageous cheerleader outfit with knee socks. He must have gotten one of my bras and stuffed it, because he made a very busty cheerleader. I saw pictures of him in all his glory. He said later he was hoping Coach Roberts wouldn't recognize him. *Give me a break. What other guy in your class would dress up like that?* Mike was voted Most Creative, and Best Sense of Humor for the yearbook at the end of the year.

Mike, one other guy, and three girls from the cross-country team disobeyed the rule made by Coach Roberts. He had no choice but to mete out some sort of punishment. They would not be allowed to participate in the next cross-country meet, which just happened to be the conference championship. That was huge, not only for the five guilty kids, but for the whole team. Once again, Mike was outraged, not because he would be punished, but because the innocent team would suffer. Mike was always in the top three runners on the boys' team, usually first. He begged the coach to give him some other form of punishment, but the coach stood fast. They could not run and couldn't even ride the bus with their teammates. When he came to us for support, we took the opportunity to make a point, even though it was a painful lesson.

If you choose to break the rule, you better be ready to suffer the consequences.

How I wish that would have stuck in Mike's mind in the years to come. It could have made such a difference.

As a footnote to this story, I agreed to drive Mike and the other guy who was banned from running, to the meet. Mike thought it was extremely important that he be there to cheer the team on that day. I had mixed feelings. A little part of my heart still agreed that the coach had made a bad decision in forbidding the boys to be cheerleaders, but I didn't say that to Mike. Honestly, I was frustrated Mike had put his team in jeopardy by his self-righteous decision. But I drove them there anyway.

It was a great day for a run, and I could see the disappointment all over Mike's face at the prospect of not running with his team. The team had enough depth as far as good runners, so the chances were still very good his team would win and qualify for the regional championships, which I suspect Coach Roberts was well aware of when he determined the punishment. And in all honesty, it was a good lesson in suffering consequences for your actions.

On this particular course, shortly after the start, the runners entered a trail through a wooded area and would emerge not too far from the finish line, so it was not good for spectators. The other high schools from our town were competing that day also as they were a part of the same conference. The start gun fired, and the pack of runners took off. Three of Mike's teammates were in the lead as they disappeared into the woods. The key would be what position the top five runners from his team would be in when they emerged.

We waited and watched. It would take only fifteen minutes or so for them to reemerge. And sure enough, there were still three of his teammates in the lead, then several runners from other schools, then two more of his teammates. That had to mean they would win as the team score was determined by the cumulative times of the top five runners from each team. As we continued to watch and cheer on the other runners, it was obvious something was happening. Some of the parents were running *toward* the runners and into the woods. Word started to spread that a runner from one of the other schools was down on the course and obviously in some sort of serious trouble. Then the word got worse; he was not breathing. An ambulance arrived and rushed him away.

A somber mood settled over the runners and parents who were there to watch. And then the unthinkable happened. We started to hear that the young man had not survived; he actually had been DOA. All of the runners, no matter which high school, knew one another from competing at the same meets. Some of the girls were in tears, and the boys just looked dazed. It was very uncomfortable as we stood around not knowing what to say or do. *Was it really true? How could this happen?*

Finally, Coach Roberts suggested his team and parents gather for a few words. He confirmed the bad news. "Today is a bad day for cross-country. We've lost a runner." There was an awkward silence that seemed to drag on. And then he asked if anyone wanted to say a few words. Mike stepped forward, took off his hat, and asked all of us to join hands, and he began to say a prayer. On a beautiful fall day, under the golden trees with a slight breeze blowing his blond hair, our son had stepped up to the plate to once again lead his team. He was where he was supposed to be on that day.

Mike and his team went on to compete in the regional championship, where all five of the top runners were from his team and posted a combined score that still stands as the school record.

A few short months later, in the spring, we experienced a loss in our own family and once again, Mike was there with heartfelt words.

Chapter 13

Santa Is Gone

I had been involved with theater and acting since we moved to North Carolina, serving on the arts council and heading up a newly formed association of local theater companies. I had also done a little bit of film acting, as this part of North Carolina was a thriving film center. I had a few small roles in some television series, had filmed a TV commercial for the newly formed Carolina Panthers football team, and auditioned for a major motion picture to be shot in South Carolina. Ben and Mike were very supportive of my acting endeavors. I think Mike was happy with anything that distracted me from being in the middle of his affairs.

I got a call from my agent, and I got the role in the major movie, directed by Bruce Beresford, the director of *Driving Miss Daisy* and staring Sharon Stone. The role was very, very small but we were all excited about my opportunity. I was even able to get my friend Joyce cast as an extra as a special birthday surprise for her. She flew in from Pennsylvania.

While on the set in South Carolina, I got a call from my brother. It was not unusual to get a call that Mom was in the hospital with pneumonia, but this was totally unexpected—it was my dad. He had suffered a heart attack and was in intensive care. I was mortified. My daddy was never sick, so this was such a shock. I was in a horrible situation. The master shots had been done, so I really couldn't leave. I went to one of the assistant directors to explain my situation. We settled on doing an all-night shoot if necessary so I could get finished and leave, which was *extremely* generous given that my role was *extremely* minor. That decision involved a large number of crew members as well as actors.

I was taking Joyce to the airport that morning, and I was going to finish filming that night and leave for Missouri. I called Russ from the airport only to learn my mom had just been rushed to the hospital with pneumonia in both lungs. When I left the airport, I had to pull off to the side of the road, overwhelmed with emotion. I couldn't believe this was happening, and I was not there to help my brother and my parents.

I finished the filming that night and then flew to Missouri, where I would go from intensive care with my dad to my mom's room one floor up. I believed from the time I arrived my dad would survive. He was joking with the nurses and was in good spirits, except for the discomfort of the edema. His kidneys weren't functioning, and congestive heart failure was increasing. And then things got worse, quickly. Suddenly my beloved Santa Claus was gone. My heart was broken, but there was no time to mourn. That would have to wait because we had to think about dealing with my seriously ill Mom, and a funeral had to be planned.

I called to tell Ben and Mike the sad news that night. Mike had a state championship track meet the next morning. I suggested he go ahead and run if he wanted to, and then they could fly out later that day. Ben went with him to the championships. He was running the mile.

Ben said when Mike took off, he set a very fast pace, too fast. He collapsed in tears on the infield on the final turn. He had tried too hard, and the emotion of losing Papa was more than he could deal with. They flew in later that day to St. Louis and drove to Jefferson City. When he got to the house, he came into the kitchen and put his arms around me and just sobbed. My grandmother was sitting at the kitchen table. It was the only time I actually saw her shed tears, and she lived to be ten days shy of one hundred.

My mother got out of the hospital, still with pneumonia, the day after Daddy died. We did the obligatory night at the funeral home, and then the funeral was the next morning. After we got Mom situated in the limo, my brother Russ, his wife Jackie, and Ben and Mike and I remained in the visitation room long enough to place a few items inside Daddy's casket. He had always joked we should put popcorn in his casket so he would know whether he was arriving in heaven or hell. If it was popped, he would know he had arrived at a heated location.

As we were ready to leave, Mike went up to the casket, reached into his pocket and pulled out his track medal from winning the regional championships and placed it beside his beloved Papa. He cried quietly, and we gave him a moment. It was an extremely difficult time for our son, who loved and respected my dad with all his heart. The loss of his Papa, who had given him total, unconditional love his entire life, had a significant emotional impact on him.

Mike wanted to speak in honor of his Papa at the funeral, which I thought was a fine idea, if he thought he could hold it together. He assured me he could do that. He wrote the eulogy all on his own and did a beautiful job delivering it. My dad would have been so very proud, as was I.

A REMEMBRANCE

We are brought together today to pay our final respects to a wonderful human being whose wit, love, and strength was an inspiration to us all. But now instead of mourning his death maybe for the rest of the afternoon we can celebrate his life. To say that Papa's life was cut short and unfulfilled just wouldn't be right. My Papa did more with the life he was given than I could ever dream to do. And to his grandsons, Hunter and me, he was a hero.

As a boy, a visit from Papa was an exciting and jovial event. It meant late bedtimes on Tuesday nights when we would sit in front of the television, sharing a bowl of popcorn, betting nickels, dimes and quarters on boxers I had never heard of. And it was all his change. It meant learning a few new jokes to tell to my classmates, but never my teachers. It meant good times and good feelings. Papa could make anyone laugh.

My grandfather had a story or joke for every situation. Above and beyond all else I will miss his magnificent stories, those wonderful stories. They will serve as an excellent reminder of the great times we had.

One thing in particular about visits from Papa that sticks out in my mind was bed time. When I was a young boy, I always loved to sleep with Papa. We used to bet a nickel to see who would fall asleep faster.

I'd lay there under the covers as still and as quiet as a child could, never winning a single bet, but I think it was worth the five cents to get a very active child to lay still just long enough for him to finally fall asleep. Papa was a smart man. It used to seem silly to me, but I would lie there listening to Papa breath—in, out, in, out—slowly, steadily, calm and easy. Papa never knew this, but I would lay beside him listening to his breath and then breathing in tempo with him—in, out, in, out—slowly, steadily, calm and easy in hopes that breathing like him would make me like him.

Seems pretty silly huh, but my Papa was my hero. Then again any person who loved you like he did, made you laugh like he did, taught you things and gave you quarters like he did would have to be your hero. Maybe what this world needs is just a few more people like my Papa … people who'll make you laugh no matter how bad things seemed, more people to show you that the glass is really half full, not half empty, like my Papa did. More people who really cared about you, and let you know it like my Papa did. A few more people as dedicated to his family like Papa was. To a grandfather, his grandchildren can do no wrong, and to Hunter and me, Papa could do no wrong.

I know my Papa is on the way to heaven now and I guess nobody knows how long that journey takes. To close I'd like to quote one of this great man's funny sayings. Papa often said. "You know what they said when they cut off the monkey's tail—It won't be long now."

That Catholic church was filled with laughter and tears. Mike had paid a very personal tribute to my dad, his beloved Papa. He had felt the unconditional love I had also always known from Dad. We were both going to miss him so very much.

Chapter 14

The Prom, Peyton, and My "Kids"

en and I had agreed to prepare dinner for Mike and Missy and three other couples that were sharing the same limo for the prom. The table was lovely, the food was great, and the girls looked stunning in their prom dresses and fancy hairdos. The boys looked handsome but a bit stiff in their rented tuxedos.

I did indulge myself by using all eight of Mike's baby spoons when we served sherbet for dessert. The girls thought it was "so cute." Mike … well, let's just say he tolerated it with a smile. We were taking the obligatory prom photos when the doorbell rang. It was Peyton, her date, and six others sharing another limo. Being younger and less rowdy, Peyton didn't socialize frequently with Mike's group, but she and Mike were still friends.

"Mama Hen, I need to talk to you," Peyton said rather frantically. She looked so pretty in her formal, and her hair was beautiful in a sophisticated updo. The other girls were excitedly chatting away and complimenting one another on their dresses. There was some back slapping and awkward greetings among the guys.

"What's up, Peyton?" I asked as she moved me down the hall away from the others.

"Look at this garden I have on my arm!" Her wrist corsage did in fact reach almost to her elbow.

"Wow," was all I could say.

"You have to help me prune this thing. Please," she begged. "It looks ridiculous!"

"It is … uh … a bit much." I had to admit.

"But don't do it too much. I don't want to hurt his feelings. I just can't stand all these flowers growing up my arm."

I had to chuckle as I grabbed my scissors, and we set to work pruning the arm garden. It did look much better when we finished.

"I knew I could count on you. You saved me. I owe you one." She gave me a quick hug, and neither of us would have imagined at that moment how huge her payback would be a few years later.

She slipped into the living room and joined the others. No one noticed we had lightened her burden, small and sweet.

A few weeks later, there was a pre-graduation party, and most of Mike's friends were going. I dropped Mike and Missy off and was going to return to pick them up much later that night. And, yes, I suspected there would be alcohol there, and I didn't want Mike driving. That was enabling behavior on my part, but I convinced myself it was cheaper for me to drive than paying for another limo. I always had an excuse for what I did along the way. Should I have forbidden him to go because I suspected alcohol would be served to under-age students?

No more than an hour or two after I took them, the phone rang, and it was Mike. "Mom, can you come pick us up?"

"Well, sure, Son. Is everything all right?"

"Not exactly," Mike said quietly. "And you'll need to get my brother Brad too."

"Huh? What's the deal? I don't understand what's going on."

"Mom, the sheriff's department is here and kids are being released to their parents, so we need you to come get us now. Understand? Missy's mom gave permission for you to pick her up too." He was still speaking very calmly.

"Okay, I can do that," I responded just as calmly. This was strange.

When I went to get them, indeed there were several law enforcement vehicles and the gated community security cars parked by the party house. I walked up the driveway having no idea what to expect. An officer approached me and said, "Which one is yours?"

Suddenly I guess I had triplets. Brad, Mike, and Audrey all greeted me with, "Hi, Mom." They had that expectant smile and a pleading in their eyes. "These three blonds are mine, and the little dark-haired one is his date. I have permission to pick her up too." *Was he going to believe these three are all mine!*

I think he was just happy to have someone remove young people from the site, so we were free to go. The four piled into the car with shouts of gratitude.

"Way to go, Mama Hen," Brad yelped from the backseat. They were all full of fun and laughter and happy to be out of the hands of the law. Someone had reported the party, and the homeowners were going to be charged, but the kids attending were being released if someone came to pick them up. For one night, I was the mother of three ... sort of.

I thought the homeowners must have been be so embarrassed to have all those law enforcement cars and neighborhood security in front of their house. I had no idea I would find out how that felt later.

It was finally time for graduation. Mike was accepted at six of the seven colleges and universities where he had sent applications. He toyed with the idea of going to the University of Missouri, but we weren't keen on the idea of paying out-of-state tuition when there were so many good schools in North Carolina. That was just another example of a fork in the road. We will never know the outcome of what might have happened had we let him go to school in Missouri.

Mike had decided to attend North Carolina State University and major in communications. He had a very positive attitude about setting off on the college experience, and we shared those positive hopes.

Graduation was a happy time worthy of celebration. My mother along with Ben's mom flew together from Missouri for the event. It had only been a few short weeks since my dad's funeral, and this would be a good break for my mom ... or so we thought.

We all went to the large graduation and proudly watched as Mike along with more than a thousand classmates bid farewell to high schools days. We took lots of pictures and celebrated like families do. It was a moment filled with mostly happy memories of chocolate chip pancakes and cookies and fun times. It was not a time to remember the bad moments that had gone on during those high school days, and there had been more than a few.

Two days later, both grandmothers were scheduled to fly back to Missouri together. The morning of departure, my mom woke up not feeling well. I got the thermometer, and sure enough she had a temperature of 101. I knew the signs of her recurring pneumonia. She could be fine one hour and the next extremely ill. I helped Ben's mom get packed, and we made the decision Mike would take Grandma to the airport while I took Nanny to the emergency room. Her temperature continued to rise.

As I knew they would, they diagnosed pneumonia and admitted her to the hospital. Now it was me calling my brother in Missouri to tell him about Mom rather than the other way around.

She spent two extra weeks recovering at our house. Everything went surprisingly well. Mike was very caring with Nanny and spent time with her while she was there. He had such a good heart and was not afraid to show his love for her. In her eyes, Mike was a perfect grandson. Of course, she had no clue about some of his transgressions, because I made it a point to not share that information.

We finished off the summer by getting Mike ready for the move to NC State. I was a happy mama buying sheets and comforters and helping him get together the "stuff" college freshmen supposedly need. In August, we packed the car and off we went to deposit our son at NC State. I hate to admit, as he walked us partway back to the car, I choked up and felt a little like the day I had walked him to first grade. He was still my little boy, just a considerably taller version with a few more experiences under his belt. But again I was filled with emotion.

When I had walked Mike to school that first day of first grade so many years before, I was in tears as I walked back home. Even though he had been to all-day kindergarten the year before, my little boy was going to "real" school. When I got home I sat down and wrote my parents a letter, which I found in my dad's billfold when he passed away. It touched my heart that he had carried it with him all those years.

Dear Mom and Dad,

How I have surprised myself this morning: This is Mike's first day of first grade and I came home from walking him to school and cried like a baby. This may seem silly to you, but I feel so proud of him and proud of us and mostly proud of both of you. I guess seeing him getting so grown up and experiencing the joys and pains of parenting make me appreciate you even more. So, I just wanted to take the time to tell you how much I love you.

You have given me so much and there really isn't an adequate way to show you how much that means.

Perhaps by being the best parent I can, is all the repayment there is. If Mike can grow up and feel as good about himself and love life as much as I do, then I will feel successful as a parent. You have passed on to me a sense of humor, a concern for people, a driving spirit and a will to achieve whatever goal I set my mind to and an undying belief in ME. Lord if I can do that with Mike, you share the credit.

I believe children are little seeds that we are entrusted with for a while to nurture and care for. You water them and protect them and hope with all your heart the sun will shine down on them. You give them your care and wisdom and discipline like fertilizer to help them grow strong. Try as you will, there may be a few bugs and a weed or two and the winds are always trying to blow them around. But the true test comes if they can make it through that "growing-up" to be a solid plant that blooms and blooms. I just want to thank you both for having such a green thumb.

With love,

I was already questioning my own "green thumb" as a mother due to the issues we had already faced with our son. Several years later in the middle of the night I would sit down to write "Just a Story" that reflected how the sun had not shone down on Mike, and he was not blooming. Indeed I would spend many nights asking God for help. When you are asking yourself over and over, "Why, *why* is this happening?" all of the things you might have done differently come flooding back to you. And chances are, you will never have the answers.

Chapter 15

Off to College

Ben and I went home to our "empty nest." Our son was going to test his wings and gain some independence. It would remain to be seen how well he handled all that freedom. I was also going to find out how it felt to not be involved in his daily life.

Mike had strong plans to change his study habits once he became a college student. *What study habits?* Any study habits would be an improvement, as he did a minimal amount throughout high school. He was smart enough to manage that. Once he started at NC State, he made sure he devoted at least an hour a day to studying—not an hour per class, but totally an hour. He told us later, sometimes he would study even two or three hours—in one day. For him, that was such a drastic change from previous behavior, he was sure it would bring drastic changes in his results. When he got his first semester grades, he was honestly surprised and sorely disappointed. He had two Bs, two Cs, one D, and one F. He had convinced himself he would make no grade lower than a B. Rather than buckle down and apply more time to his studies, I think he used his disappointment as an excuse to go the opposite direction. He moved into a different dorm at the semester change and roomed with a classmate who had excelled academically in high school. He had also been a teammate on the cross-country team. We hoped this would be a good example for Mike. Best-laid plans ...

Shortly after the beginning of the second semester, I could see a change in Mike. And I didn't like what I was seeing. He came home occasionally on weekends and holidays, but he was more and more closed off. He had started smoking, much to our disappointment, but he blew us off with, "I only do it occasionally, and I can quit anytime." That was Mike ... thinking he could control anything right up until ... he couldn't.

The first major incident involving the law was a "lowlight" of his second semester. I'm not sure we will ever know the entire story, but as it unfolded for us, indeed it was bizarre. I was in Missouri, once again due to a health issue with Mom. She had surgery to correct a macular hole in her retina and had to keep her head down for two weeks. She could sit up to eat but had to keep her eyes cast down. She had a special chair to sit in and a faceplate like the one used on massage tables to insert at the foot of her bed at night to place her head in. It was a miserable recovery ordeal.

From Missouri, I would fly on to LA for the cast and crew screening of the movie I had filmed a year earlier in South Carolina. My friend Joyce was flying from Pennsylvania, and we would meet up at the Kansas City airport for the remainder of the trip.

About three o'clock that morning the phone rang at my mom's house. I got up and answered it, still half asleep. *This couldn't be good at this hour of the night!*

"Is this the uh ... has anyone there ... Could you get me in touch with Mike?"

"This is Mike's mom. He's not here. This is his grandmother's house in Missouri. Is there a problem?" *Of course there was a problem, or they wouldn't be calling here in the middle of the night.*

"*No*, no problem, I was just wanting to talk to him; sorry to wake you." And the voice on the other end went dead.

"Wait! What do you ... hello? *Hello?*" No one was there.

There was no caller ID, I had no idea who had called, why they would have Mom's number, and especially at this hour. I just knew this was not good. My "mother radar" kicked in instantly, and I needed to find out what was going on. I quietly went into the kitchen after closing the door to Mom's bedroom. I looked at the clock and tried to make sense of what to do next. Ben would be getting up fairly soon. Should I just wait and call him? Who else was I going to call? Mike had no phone in his room, and I didn't want to call the dorm phone at this hour. In fact I wasn't sure it would even be answered. *This was just like when Nathan called from Myrtle Beach after Mike was put in jail. Surely that was not happening again!*

I probably opened the refrigerator door ten times. That's what I did when I was nervous, especially at my mom's house. I think I grabbed a piece of cheese and ate it. I racked my brain for who could help me find out if Mike was all right. No answers came. Finally at four o'clock I couldn't wait any longer. I dialed my home number, pulled the phone into my bedroom and closed the door so Mom wouldn't hear me. It was five o'clock in North Carolina.

The phone rang several times before a sleepy Ben answered. "Hell-o?"

"Ben, I'm sorry to wake you up, but the strangest thing happened." I thought I heard him sigh or maybe groan. "The phone rang here about three and someone was asking for Mike. I don't have any idea who it was or how they had this number, but it was just very weird." There was silence on the other end. "Ben, are you there?"

"Yes, I'm here, but I don't know what to tell you."

"Should I try to call the school? I have to check on him to be sure he's all right. I don't have a good feeling about this at all." I was trying to be calm, but I was worried and scared.

73

"If all they did was ask for Mike, that doesn't sound like anything to be to upset about to me."

"Well how did they get this phone number, and why would they call at that hour, Ben?" I knew he would think I was overreacting. "I don't want to put a bunch of long-distance calls on Mom's phone or alarm her, so would you please call the school and see if you can talk to Mike?"

There was a pause before he answered, and I heard his frustrated sigh. "Yes, I'll do that in a little bit. Do we have a number here somewhere for the hall phone?"

I told him where to find the number. "Thank you so much, sweetheart. It will make me feel so much better, and please call me the minute you hear something."

"Okay, I will. How's your mom?"

"About the same. This is difficult for her, but it's almost over. Russ and Jackie are taking over tonight when I leave for LA." *That's assuming we don't have a real problem on our hands with Mike.* "Assuming everything's all right."

"I'll give you a call if I find out anything. And don't worry so much. Everything is probably fine. Love you."

"Love you too." We hung up, and I sat there in the dark on the floor of the little bedroom that had been mine and then Russ's. It reminded me of being in high school and the times I sat in this exact spot talking later than I was supposed to on the phone. *God, that was forever ago!*

Talking to Ben made me feel a little better. I closed my eyes, leaned back against the wall, and said a prayer. It was time to go check on Mom again and make sure she was still sleeping with her face down in the doughnut hole off the foot of her bed. I definitely did not want her to know if there was a problem. She had enough to deal with as it was, and so did I.

Later that morning as I was getting Mom situated, the phone rang. I moved quickly to answer it. "Hello." It was Ben on the other end, and the news was not good.

"I guess you were right. There's definitely a problem. Mike is in jail in Raleigh, and I'm going there to bail him out."

"In … for what?" I needed to get the phone back into my bedroom again. I didn't want Mom to hear this conversation. "*JAIL?*" It was a whispered scream if there is such a thing.

"Apparently, he was skateboarding in a parking garage and reached into a car and got a comic book."

I was waiting for the rest of it, but Ben had stopped talking. "So then what happened?"

"That's it, as far as I know. The campus police picked him up, but then he went to jail because reaching into the car is considered breaking and entering, or at least I think that's what they charged him with. I'll know more when I get up there."

I had a million questions now. This didn't make much sense to me. "How could it be breaking and entering if the window was open? Why was this such a big deal that they took him to jail? Who called me on the phone? What is going on up there?" *Again my habit of asking too many questions at one time.*

Ben couldn't answer any of my questions until he had more information. "Let me get off the phone so I can wrap things up here at the office and get to Raleigh. I'll call you when I know more."

"Should I try to come home?" I felt so helpless to do anything, and our son was in jail, for heaven's sake. "I can just change my plane tickets." I forgot about meeting Joyce.

"No, that won't be necessary. Just help your mom, and then go on to LA. There's nothing else to do right now anyway. I'll take care of this."

I was so grateful that he was ready to take charge of the situation because it was obvious to me I was in no position to help. All I could do now was worry, and we all knew how much good that does! *Thank you, Ben! Oh, thank you so much.*

Ben drove to Raleigh and posted bail, and Mike was released. The story Mike told was still very confusing, and we knew some details had to be missing. But Ben called to reassure me that the situation was handled at least for now, and there was nothing I could do. We would hire a lawyer before Mike's court date. Mike would go back to school. The school year was almost over. In reality, I'm not sure Mike attended another class after that.

I drove to Kansas City, stopped at Gary and Louise's house for dinner and to return the car they had loaned me to drive to Jefferson City when I had flown in the week before. It was so good to be able to just stop for a minute, have a cup of coffee, and talk to good friends. Gary had been my old high school boyfriend and Ben's best friend. We had all remained close over the years.

I hadn't slept much taking care of Mom for several days before this boulder of Mike's slammed into us. I had been up since the 3:00 a.m. phone call, and I must have looked like death warmed over. When it was time to head to the airport, my body felt like it was filled with lead, and my head was pounding. I took two Excedrin Migraine pills without realizing it had caffeine in it. That woke me up. Gary and Louise took me to the airport, and I hugged them both as I went into the terminal to find my best friend Joyce. I looked back to wave and could not miss their concerned look. I must have looked really awful. Well I felt pretty crappy too. *But I was awake now. Coffee and Excedrin. Wide awake!*

I met Joyce and filled her in on the details of what had happened with Mike, and we boarded the overnight flight to LA. This was supposed to be such a fun "girls' trip" to the city of angels and the glamour of the movies. Instead I was consumed with a very confusing story that was unfolding with our son. I was totally exhausted, but my mind was pumped on caffeine. I talked the entire way to LA. And my best friend Joyce listened. Friends are invaluable.

We arrived in LA, collected our luggage and got in the taxi line to head for Hollywood. Our turbaned taxi driver wasn't sure how to get to Hollywood. *Seriously? Unbelievable! I don't need any more troubles.*

The next night we went to the cast and crew screening. Sharon Stone was there, and much to my astonishment, she greeted me with, "I'm so glad you could be here. Did everything work out all right with your dad?" I told her no, unfortunately I had lost Dad. She expressed her condolences and gave me a hug. We had made that film a year ago, and I was astonished and moved that she had remembered my situation.

At least for most of that night I left my troubles behind and marveled at my surroundings. I just pushed the fear out of my mind … as much as I could, at least for a little while.

Chapter 16

The Nest Isn't Empty

$\mathcal{M}$ ike had finished his freshman year at NC State. I think we knew before we got the grades that it would not be good news, and it was worse than we imagined. Mike had failed three classes and would not be going back. He admitted that he had not gone to classes much after the incident with jail. We were terribly disappointed, but for Ben, I think it was beyond disappointment. Mike had wasted his opportunity. He was such an intelligent young man with so much potential. We knew he was capable of doing or achieving anything he set his mind to. We had always placed a high value on education and it felt like Mike was resisting us at every turn. I remembered back to the first time he came home in third grade with homework.

He announced at dinner that he was not going to do that homework.

"Well, of course you are. After dinner, you can sit at the dining room table, and I'll help you do your homework. That's just part of school, honey. It means you're growing up. It's a way to reinforce what you learned at school." *That sounded very encouraging and supportive.*

"But its stuff we already know," he protested.

"Homework helps you practice and remember what you learned," I patiently explained.

"Mom, it's just busy work," he stated firmly.

Where in the world had he heard that term? He finally did the homework under protest, but it became a struggle that went on throughout his school years. Our little boy was sometimes too smart for his own good and did not hesitate to challenge what he was being asked to do.

"Son, you need to get a job and figure out what you plan to do. Your gravy train is over. I'll be happy to support you in school, but if you think you're going to sit around here on your ass or on the boat all summer, forget it!" Ben meant business, and I supported him 100 percent.

We had hired a lawyer in Raleigh, and he had gotten the charges reduced. At first we were astonished to hear the charge might be a felony. *Oh no, not a felony! That would follow him forever.* We probably still don't know all the details, but basically Mike and his friends had been skateboarding in this parking garage even after the campus police had warned them on several occasions to stop. Someone reported them and also saw Mike reach in the car for the magazine. The campus police came and cited them. They were supposed to report to the campus security office by midnight. When Mike didn't show up, they turned the matter over to the police. If he had just gone in like the others, he would have never ended up in court. *Irresponsible behavior!* The phone call had been from a friend trying to find Mike to get him to the campus security office. I still don't know how he got Mom's phone number.

When he went to court, he was charged with a misdemeanor, and the judge assigned him 250 hours of community service. Even the lawyer was stunned at that amount of hours. The hours would be worked off back in his home county. Mike would not be spending any more time in Raleigh.

He did much of his community service with the Department of Parks and Recreation. They built a Frisbee golf course and did other projects. He also learned how to waste time, as the employee he worked with would frequently just go park the truck and smoke and listen to the radio. That was our county government at work. How to be irresponsible and waste time was not a lesson our son needed.

I was still doing volunteer work with a large fund-raiser for Hospice. The woman in charge was married to the station manager of WWET TV, the NBC affiliate. I mentioned that Mike was looking for a job, and she said he should go apply at the TV station. Mike had been outstanding in his high school videography class. The instructor had suggested he go to school at North Carolina School of the Arts, where they specialized in the media field. Perhaps life would have been different if he had taken that road.

I relayed the information to Mike about the job at WWET, and he wrote his resume and applied for the part-time job at the TV station and got it. He very quickly picked up the skills and loved his job. Now we were on the right road! At least I thought we were.

He was living at home, working at the TV station part time and trying to complete his community service hours. Much of his spare time was still being spent on the boat with his wakeboarding friends. He even put together some wakeboard competitions that attracted competitors from across the area. He was a natural leader and planner. He just needed to use those skills productively.

In December Mike applied for a full-time position at WWET.

December 7, 1996

Last week I was informed that the full time week night production technician job would be opening up

I assure you that I am capable of holding the full time position with an unmatched level of professionalism and enthusiasm. Five months ago I walked in to WWET with very little knowledge of how television production worked. In the last 20 weeks I quickly learned the skills needed to assist the director in nearly every aspect of news production including cameras, audio, and graphics. I did this missing only one scheduled work day. In my time off the clock I have also helped sports with cameras and have learned how to direct four second IDs and 30 second updates. This job is like no other I have ever had. I love coming to work, I love the challenge of performing difficult tasks under a rigorous time constraint. I actually feed on this and my performance level rises to the occasion.

Mike obviously had confidence in his skills and a passion for his work. He got the job and continued to work at WWET until 1999. People at the station became his friends and mentors. He earned their respect. The anchor of the evening news, Ann, became a fan of his work and a friend to our family. He learned almost every aspect of production. He was doing exceptionally well in his first full-time job.

Chapter 17

The Road Is Not Smooth

I suppose it's never easy to have your kids move back in after they have been off on their own. In our case, Mike had only been away for one school year, but he had an attitude and ideas about his freedom. His ideas and ours didn't match. Our approach was basically, our house … our rules. An attitude of entitlement did not sit favorably with us.

In the spring of 1996, as Mike returned home, Peyton graduated from high school and was going off to Auburn to major in music. She and Mike were still friends but saw little of one another. They seemed to be on separate paths heading in different directions and might likely drift apart forever. But life is not predictable.

Mike felt that I was constantly on his back, and I felt that he had no sense of responsibility. What I saw as encouraging him, he saw as nagging. I was trying to pick my battles, but I was overwhelmed with opportunities. I knew that Mike was drinking and that he was smoking pot. We warned him over and over of the dangerous path he was on and did everything we could think of to get him to change directions.

I gave him a copy of *Autobiography in Five Chapters.* I would end up handing him an additional copy many times on our journey. I should have read it more carefully for myself much earlier than I did.

There's a Hole in My Sidewalk
By Portia Nelson

Autobiography in Five Short Chapters

I

I walk down the street.

There is a deep hole in the sidewalk.

I fall in.

I am lost … I am helpless

It isn't my fault.

It takes forever to find a way out.

II

I walk down the same street.

There is a deep hole in the sidewalk.

I pretend I don't see it.

I fall in, again.

I can't believe I am in the same place.

But, it isn't my fault.

It still takes a long time to get out.

III

I walk down the same street.

There is a deep hole in the sidewalk.

I <u>see</u> it is there.

I still fall in ... it's a habit ... but,

my eyes are open.

I know where I am.

It is <u>my</u> fault.

I get out immediately.

IV

I walk down the same street.

There is a deep hole in the sidewalk.

I walk around it.

V

I walk down another street.

My efforts to stay vigilant were not taken well by Mike, who wanted to assert his "freedom" even if it meant falling in the same hole over and over. I can look back now and see I was falling in my own hole concerning our son. His attitude didn't seem to improve, and neither did mine. Yet, we still had our good moments from time to time … and then another twist in the road would throw us off balance again.

Mike,

Sometimes we definitely have problems discussing things. I found your attitude offensive and rude. It was not my intention to nag, but if that bit of nagging is just too aggravating, so be it. I think you'll soon find a little concerned nagging might be easier to take than some of the harsh realities of growing up and taking on adult responsibility.

Just so there is no misunderstanding about the use of the boat, I am totally serious when I say the boat is not to be used by you or your friends until your community service is complete. We told you time and again that you had to do community service to get boat PRIVELIGES and that we wanted it done by April 1. Your response has been, "No problem," so I hope it's not a problem to finish up. You had 36 or 38 hours left as of March 10. When you can show us some evidence of completing 250 hours we can discuss you using the boat. Don't ask until then.

If you want me to do your laundry, you have to bring it upstairs.

Mom

XXOOXX

Why was I doing his laundry anyway? Mike was working full time but not making enough to support himself, and he needed to spend several hours a week to finish the hours assigned by the court. I thought there was no choice but to have him live at home, but he certainly could have been doing his own laundry. I was doing nothing to force him to take responsibility at home.

Mike finally finished his community service hours, just under the wire of the deadline. That summer, he enrolled in the community college to begin taking courses again. We paid for his classes with the condition that he would make no grade lower than a C. I wasn't seeing any studying going on, and I thought I just had to step in.

Dear Mike,

I know you think I'm on your case lately—and you're right. But let me give it to you straight, from my point of view. As I see it, you made the choice to continue with school. We made it very clear that this was "Do It Right" time this semester or you are on your own financially. Don't blow this opportunity.

It kills me to see you go down that same street, heading for that same hole again. I know I can't do it for you. I even know that trying to warn you probably won't do any good. You have to see it for yourself. It's like I want to grab you by the hand and pull you to a different street—or at least away from the edge of the hole. We love you so much and want to help you. Dad can be quiet and let you try to grow up. He loves you quietly and I love you noisily. I know helping (interfering) doesn't work and it just makes you angry sometimes. Maybe you will understand when you are a parent. I hope so. Even then you won't be a MOTHER. We're different. I just don't want you to look back on this semester and wish you had made different decisions.

Love,

Mom XXOOXX

Storms of every kind were swirling around us, and our family was constantly engulfed in our own private turmoil.

Mike and his friends got stopped for having a small amount of pot on the boat. We paid for a lawyer, and the issue went away. Once again we were saving Mike from the consequences of his actions. Without a doubt, he was drinking more than we knew, and I honestly don't know what he was doing with other drugs, but certainly more than we could have imagined. We tried talking with him, preaching at him, and there was angry yelling from time to time.

My family in Missouri was not aware of what was going on with Mike at this point, and certainly my mother had no idea. She was continuing to have serious bouts of pneumonia, and I would fly home to help with her. We finally decided along with her doctor that it was time for her to move to assisted living, something she was not happy about.

I knew she was wondering why I hadn't suggested she come live with us. It was one of the most difficult moments of my life when I had to refuse her subtle request and not give her the honest reason for my decision. We were in the midst of dealing with Mike's drinking and drug issues and run-ins with the law, and I saw no reason to share that information with her. None of the rest of the family had any idea of his troubles except my brother. I knew I couldn't handle dealing with Mike and my mom in the same house. It was no secret where some of my "control freak" issues had come from. In that respect, I was too much like my mother. I felt bad about not asking her, yet I knew it was the right decision.

We encouraged Mike to find a way to live on his own. He asked if he could have a friend he had met at NC State move in temporarily, and then they would find an apartment and move out. We agreed. Conner was a nice kid, and after all, it was *temporary*.

In July we were hit by a hurricane named Bertha. In September, we were in the direct path of Hurricane Fran, a category 3 storm that did a lot of damage. Mike worked around the clock at the TV station and was congratulated for his efforts. He was excelling in his job at the TV station and getting lots of strokes for that. It was a very positive part of his life.

When we decided to sell the house several months later, we had to explain it didn't come with two guys living downstairs. *Temporary* had lasted until we moved into the gated country club community where we had been playing golf and tennis since moving to North Carolina. Conner and Mike rented an apartment, and once more we had an empty nest. Conner was going to school and wakeboarding, and got a part-time job at WWET. They were living "on their own," but Mike was still on that same street with the hole in the sidewalk. And we were right there on that same street, providing the financial support that was enabling him to stay right where he was, heading for the hole again.

88

Chapter 18

1999—A Year of Change

While so much of what was happening in our lives was centered on Mike, there were other big changes in the wind. Ben's company had been in the process of being sold for a year. He was trying to determine his professional future. His job had been central to his life, and he had excelled his entire professional career. He was at a crossroad with an important decision to make. He could continue with the new owners or take an early retirement package. He was only fifty-three and was fully vested in his retirement plan. Ben had worked for the same company since graduating from college and had loved it. He saw the new owners as harbingers of change that he didn't like.

We discussed it at length and concluded that retirement was the right move. In January 1999 Ben was officially retired. I thought he might find leaving the world in which he had thrived a disconcerting event. It was not. He embraced retirement and never looked back.

In February 1999, Mike was out on a break from work at the TV station with his pal Jack. They got stopped by the police with a box of nitrous oxide containers they had been using in the car. It was another way to get a quick high—one that I had never heard of just like the huffing of air freshener in his high school days. Undoubtedly they were also smoking pot.

He was late getting back to work and knew he was probably going to get fired because the station would get the police report, so the next day he turned in his resignation. Most likely they would have drug-tested him, and he would not have been clean. He was leaving a job he claimed to love. Once again, substance abuse was the hole he kept falling into. And once again we fell into the same hole of trying to pull him out of *his* hole. Just when things seemed to be going well, the rockslide had started again. At least Mike was in school and would continue there. He was still my smart and considerate child ... most of the time. I had to hold on to the positives.

In September, Hurricane Floyd paid us a visit and dumped over thirty inches of rain. Not long after that hurricane, storm clouds gathered over our son again. He and Conner had moved from the apartment into a house near the university, and Conner had walked in on a "drug party" and was very angry with Mike. Mike and Conner had gotten into a physical fight. Only later would I find out the disagreement had been over Mike's drug use. Then he was picked up again for possession of marijuana. Mike was ordered by the court to go to a counseling program. Ben and I were asked to join him for some sessions, which we did.

He was also supposed to be going to AA or NA meetings to work a twelve-step program, but I don't think he was doing that on a regular basis. He had a sponsor, but Mike wasn't really committed.

He was still in school, but was not employed, so he moved back in with us. Once again we drew up a contract. I had hopes this would be the last time we had to do that. It was wishful thinking on my part.

MIKE'S CONTRACT—FOR THE LAST TIME Dec. 1999

1. There will be no drugs or drug paraphernalia in this house or on this property. Zero tolerance. PERIOD!
2. Do all that is expected of you with court mandated counseling.
3. Staying clean and succeeding in school are your two top priorities. That comes first above all else.
4. Do not borrow money or incur debt. Pay as you go. If you don't have the money, you can't do it. In an emergency talk to us about finances and we will work something out. Your debt is our debt, as you have no other source of income, so it is our business.

Common courtesies and expectations:

5. You are expected to be home close to midnight on school nights.
6. Call if you are not coming home for dinner.
7. Your room will be kept straight and dirty dishes returned to kitchen promptly.
8. Keep up all the good things you are doing. They are noticed and appreciated.

We were housing Mike, paying for school, and giving him an allowance for incidentals. We were no longer an empty nest. Ben had retired and was home, Mike had moved back in, and my mother still would have loved to come live with us. *Please God, help me keep my sanity and my sense of humor.*

Chapter 19

The Helpers in Gingham Dresses

*M*om was in the hospital again. She had COPD and a multitude of other issues. It was not unusual for her to end up in the hospital about every six to eight weeks with pneumonia. My little brother, Russ, bore the brunt of dealing with getting her to the hospital and all that surrounded her illnesses.

My brother called to say things were not looking good this time, and she had been immediately admitted to the intensive care unit. As we talked, it was obvious I should pack a bag and fly home. I arrived later that same day. I flew into St. Louis and caught the shuttle service to Jefferson City. The driver took me directly to the hospital. People in Missouri can be very nice, and I was very grateful.

When I walked into her room, she looked terrible, but then I had seen her look bad before. However, this time she seemed to be hooked to more machines and graphs and lights and beepers. I've often thought if you put a well person in intensive care and hooked them up to all that equipment, you might just scare them to death.

My brother and I spoke with her doctor the next morning. He did not give us much encouragement. Her oxygen levels were low, the pneumonia was not responding to the IV antibiotics and congestive heart failure was wearing her down. On the third day, when I got to Mom's room she was very agitated. She insisted she was in the wrong room.

"I'm not supposed to be here. This isn't the right room," she said as soon as I walked in.

"This is the same room you've been in since you got here, Mom," I tried to reassure her.

But she would have no part of my explanation. "No! No, the other place was so beautiful. There were lots of flowers and beautiful lights and colors and music. That wall wasn't there, none of this stuff." She indicated the machines she was hooked up to. "I'm not supposed to be here, I'm supposed to be there. This is not the right place."

She was adamant and could not be persuaded. I was puzzled, but thought I should try to calm her if possible. "Well, maybe they took you to another room for some tests, Mom." She was not buying that idea either. "Some of the medication may make you sleepy. Maybe you were just having a dream."

"No, it wasn't a dream. I was there in the other place where I'm supposed to be. Jesus was there and so were his helpers. They were wearing gingham dresses. There was beautiful music. It was wonderful. That's where I'm supposed to be, not here. This is not right! Why am I here?"

I was stunned. And I had goose bumps. Maybe it had been a dream and maybe it was something else. You would have to know my mom to understand how out of character this was for her. She was not outwardly spiritual and would never have been comfortable talking about seeing Jesus.

"Go tell somebody I'm in the wrong place, please."

"Okay, Mom. I'll see what I can do. Just relax. Are you feeling all right?"

"Yes, I feel fine, but I'm not supposed to be here." She was totally coherent and determined.

"I understand," I reassured her, though I wasn't sure I understood at all. "Let me go check with the nurse, and I'll be right back." I went to the nurse and gave her a brief idea of what was going on. She said Mom had a bad night and probably had a bad dream.

"Well, if it was a dream, it wasn't bad," I said. I couldn't help but smile. *Did Mom get one foot into heaven for a brief moment during her bad night?* We'll never know, but it gave me comfort to think it was possible.

She was moved out of intensive care that evening. Mom's doctor and the intensive care nurse explained they could do nothing else to help her that couldn't be done in a regular room. My brother and I took turns sitting with her around the clock. The nurses were very attentive, and she was further sedated to keep her comfortable. Her lungs were filling with fluid. On the second night she had a stroke and was in a coma. I called Ben early that morning after the stroke and told him it was time for him and Mike to come. Mom was probably not going to live through the day, according to her doctor.

It had been an exhausting week, but I was so glad I had come home to be with my mother. I held her hand and told her it was okay to go to the place where she was supposed to be, that the helpers in gingham dresses were waiting for her. I hoped that she could hear me and that she felt at peace. And then she was gone.

Chapter 20

The Worst Day

*O*ur family left the hospital, and I went home with my brother and sister-in-law to wait for Ben and Mike to arrive from the airport later that day. We had some details to tend to, and we moved through those first duties you have to do when you are the next of kin like we were in a fog. None of us had had much sleep for a week or more.

Finally I heard a car in the driveway, and it was Ben and Mike in the rental car. I needed them to be there with me. They walked into the house and Ben immediately came to give me a hug. I looked up to see Mike, and I nearly gasped out loud.

"Are you okay, hon?" He looked emaciated, and the dark circles under his eyes were scary. Had it only been a week ago that I last saw him? Had he looked that bad then?

He put his arms around me and gave me a hug. "I'm so sorry, Mama. How are you doing?" His voice was filled with love and compassion. I thought I was too tired to cry. I would find out how wrong I was in a few short hours.

They took their suitcases upstairs, and I heard Mike greeting his cousin, Hunter. He loved that eleven-year-old like a little brother, and Hunter thought the world of Mike. He was not aware of the depth of

Mike's issues in the past few years. I was about to find out none of us knew the depth of the problem.

My brother had the guys go with him to move some of Mom's furniture out of the assisted living facility. And then I did something I had never done before. I went upstairs into the bedroom where Mike would be staying, and I started going through his bag. He just looked so bad, but, honestly, I can't tell you what pushed me to go through that duffel. I have no idea what I thought I was going to find, but I assure you I was not prepared for what I did find.

Several small packets, not much bigger than the size of a stamp, were folded, and they had a symbol of some sort on the top. I held them in my hand. *What was this?* I'd never seen anything like this before. *God, was this some sort of drug?* I took a packet into the bathroom, closed the door and carefully unfolded it. A whitish powder was inside. I sat down on the commode lid and just looked at the opened packet. *Was this cocaine? Was this the stuff people snorted up their nose? Yuk, surely not. But what the hell was it?* I was eaten up with dumb. I was at a loss for a matter of minutes, and I just sat there on the commode. I couldn't make my brain function.

And then I decided I would have to ask my brother who was in law enforcement. I actually put the packets back in Mike's bag. My hands were shaking, and I felt as if I had to work hard to just function. Breathing was difficult.

The guys came back, and I had Ben come upstairs. I told him what I had found, and I planned to ask my brother before I confronted Mike, who was still downstairs. Ben had me show him the packets. He didn't know what they were either. We rummaged around in the bag some more and found something that just blew us away.

There in his bag were needles—hypodermic needles wrapped separately in cellophane packages. *Why would Mike need needles? He was the most needle phobic kid I had ever known! He couldn't be using needles to do drugs. No way!* I looked at Ben, and I knew he was thinking the same thing. Any time Mike had ever had to have a shot, it was a major ordeal. I flashed back to more than once in the doctor's office when he did anything to delay getting a shot. A few times he had to call Ben on the phone when he was younger and talk to him while he was getting the shot so he could be distracted talking to his dad.

"No way," was all I could say. I still wasn't sure what the powder was, but I had to assume he was injecting it. I don't remember what Ben said at that point. I think part of me went on auto pilot.

I went downstairs and managed to get my brother away from Hunter and Mike.

"I found something in Mike's bag, and I don't know what it is."

"What do you mean? What does it look like?"

"I think it's some kind of drugs."

"Sis, I can't know this. I can't have drugs in my house. You know that." He held up his hands as if to ward off any more information about anything illegal. I needed my brother, not the deputy, but they were one in the same. I should have never put him in that position.

"But there are needles there too. I don't know what to do!" I felt myself starting to crumble. My wonderful sister-in-law knew something was going on and tapped on the door. She came in and knew instantly this wasn't about losing Mom. "It's Mike," I sputtered. He has drugs, and I don't know what it is."

"Go tell him to get rid of them now," Russ said. "I can't have drugs in this house. I can't know they're here." My brother was adamant.

I left the room and asked Mike to go upstairs with me. Ben was still up there.

"Why? What's wrong, Mama?" He looked worried as he put his hand on my arm.

All I could see were the awful dark circles under his eyes. And all I could hear was the loving voice of my precious little boy. "Just come upstairs with me, please. We need to talk." He followed me up the stairs and into his bedroom, where Ben was waiting. He looked at his dad, and it began to sink in. Ben held some packets in his hand, and the needles were on the bed.

"What the hell is this?" Ben was so angry. Mike looked at me and put his hands on his hips and then looked down at the floor. I had seen Ben do the exact same thing so many times. "Damn it, answer me Son!?"

Mike would not look at him. "Well, what do you think it is?" he said quietly.

"This isn't some God damn guessing game, I asked you what it is, and I expect an answer *now*!" His face was beet red.

"It's heroin." Mike lifted his head, but could not look us in the eye.

I was trying to remain standing, but I felt like I had been slammed against a wall. In fact I was leaning against the wall, and I don't know how I got there. I felt like I might hit the floor any minute. "You put that in your arm with a needle? How could you? I mean how can you do that?" I sounded a little crazy even to myself. "You have to get rid of it, Mike. What were you thinking? You can't use that stuff, and they can't have drugs in this house."

"I can't do that." I could hear real panic in his voice.

"Well, I can." I reached for the packets, and Mike intercepted me.

"*No*, Mom, you can't. You don't understand. I'll die without it." He was desperately serious.

"No you won't," I thought he was being overly dramatic, and I needed this to go away because my world was spinning out of control.

About that time Jackie, my sister-in-law, came into the room. Mike screamed at her, "Get out; you're not part of this family." She looked like she had just been slapped.

"I wanted to try to help." She had always been so close to all of us, and I loved her like a sister. She turned and left the room.

This could not be happening. My mother had not been dead for twelve hours when our only son was screaming that he was going to die without his drugs. I had to have some help. I went downstairs and confronted my brother. "You *have* to help me. I don't know what to do. It's heroin, and he says he'll die without it. Can that be true?" *Am I shouting? Am I making sense? Why won't he help me? Oh God, he has to help me! Did he ask me a question?*

"How long has he been using and how much?" Russ was asking.

"I don't know! Until an hour ago I had no idea about any of this! I would have bet my life he would never stick a *DAMN NEEDLE IN HIS BODY!*" Now I knew I was shouting. More quietly I pleaded, "Will you *please* go up and talk to him? Please."

My wonderful, strong little brother looked me in the eye and said one word. "No."

I just stood there, and then he put his loving arms around me and said, "Send him downstairs. I need to talk to him, but I cannot see those drugs."

I heard Jackie in the background on the phone with her sister asking her to come pick up my nephew. That was a good idea. Our mess was spilling all over them like a nasty sludge.

I went back up the stairs. Mike was sitting on a chair with his head in his hands. Now Ben had his hands on his hips and was staring at the floor. "Mike, your uncle wants to talk to you downstairs."

Now he looked me in the eye and said one word. "No."

"Look, you won't destroy your drugs, and he can't have them in his house, so just what do you propose we do?" Honestly at that moment I really had no idea what to do. I knew that sounded weak, but I was at the end of my mental and emotional rope.

"Well, I guess if he has to have the drugs, and we can't stay here, we'll just have to go to a hotel," Ben said with an air of flat logic.

I don't know why that struck me as so bizarre. "Go to a hotel? So our son can take his drugs? Are you serious?" I felt like I was going to laugh or cry or both. That's when I knew I was about to have a major meltdown. And my last ounce of strength kicked in. "Mike, get your ass down those stairs right now, and you talk to your uncle. *Now!*" I grabbed him by the collar and moved him toward the door. My brother was waiting at the bottom of the stairs. By some miracle, Mike walked down the stairs.

"We're going for a ride," my brother said. I didn't know if he was directing that at me or Mike or Ben, who was right behind me.

I just shook my head in the affirmative. Mike turned around and looked at me and his ashen face was filled with absolute fear. My brother outweighed him by about 150 pounds, and he was obviously in no mood to put up with any crap. He had just been through the same grueling week that I had plus a few days before I got there.

He took Mike's arm and moved him toward the garage. At the moment they disappeared I literally collapsed on the stairs, and I started wailing like I had never done in my entire life. Giant sobs were coming out of me from a place deep inside that I had never accessed before or since. It was inhuman. I had absolutely no control.

Neither Ben nor my sister-in-law could console me, and I know I scared them with my hysteria. It was like a giant dam had broken, and I could not stop it. This avalanche had finally devastated me, and I could not get up. I think there was finally some point where I just felt like I was relieved to be buried, and I just wanted to lie there under the rocks in the dark hole. I don't know how much time passed.

Then the phone rang. It was my brother, my wonderful little baby brother, who could shine a light into my darkness. He had talked to

Mike to find out how much he was using and all the other necessary facts that I would have never known to seek out. He had called a doctor who knew how to deal with this problem, and he was going to write a prescription. Mike was going to feel bad, but he was not going to die without the heroin.

"Now, Sis, flush all the packets down the toilet and put the needles in the trash can outside. Do that as soon as you hang up." That big old bear was so gentle with me.

I had to ask, "Are you sure he will be all right if I do that?"

"He's gonna feel bad, but with this medication, he will be all right. He is not going to die. He's agreed to do this. Do you want to ask him yourself?"

I only had one word left in me at that moment. "No." *Breathe. Now stand up.* I got up off the steps and relayed the conversation to Ben and Jackie. We proceeded to flush the packs of heroin down the toilet, and we took the needles to the trash.

My brother and Mike returned with the prescription in hand. I was to hold the medication and dole it out to Mike at the proper intervals. He got in the shower and stayed there for a very long time, and then he went to bed. While I remember so much of that day in wretched detail, I do not remember going to bed or to sleep that night.

We were all beyond exhaustion. I apologized to Jackie for Mike's cutting remark and for turning her household into such chaos. I thanked my little brother, but thanks would never be enough for what he did for us on that worst day of my life. And now we had an evening of funeral home visitation the next night followed by a funeral the next morning to look forward to. I think it took everything in me to just make it one hour at a time. At that point, maybe it was one minute at a time, but at least I was off the steps, and our son was alive.

Chapter 21

The Funeral

The day following my mother's death there were so many things to do, as anyone who has gone through this ordeal knows. My mom had actually kept in a notebook what she wanted for her funeral service, and we followed her wishes. It made it much easier. She even had the clothes with accessories she wanted to be buried in all together on a hanger. I don't know if that was because she was trying to be helpful, or she just didn't trust us to do it right. Perhaps it was her final act of control. Whatever the reason, I was grateful. Ben remained at my brother's house during that day, keeping a close watch on Mike and doling out the medication that was keeping his physical pain level barely tolerable. I don't think they exchanged two words.

Ben had thought about the events of the previous day enough to realize he had flown with Mike and his carry-on baggage with the drugs into the St. Louis airport, which was regularly patrolled by a policeman with a drug dog. Mike had even left him with the carry-on while he got the other bags. The realization of the jeopardy Mike had put him in, whether intentional or not, made Ben beyond angry. He took it very personally as a sign of ultimate disrespect. I think that incident shut a part of his heart that would be very difficult for him to reopen to Mike.

While my son and my husband were suffering, each in his own way, I was just trying to keep my sanity and do what had to be done. I assumed I would have time to grieve for my mom later. I went back to get dressed for the early evening funeral home visitation.

I have never liked the ordeal of the funeral home visitation, and you can imagine my absolute dread of that evening. Mike didn't want to go. *I didn't want to go either*! But sometimes you just do what you have to do. He looked like walking death himself, and I supposed he knew it. However, I insisted he get dressed and go with us. Honestly, I was afraid for him to stay at home by himself. Reluctantly he went. He spent most of that dreadful evening in the room the funeral director provides for family members who need to take a break. I remember, ironically, that a plate of chocolate chip cookies sat on the table. I also remember wishing I could just stay here and hide in this room and eat cookies too.

My aunts, uncles and my cousins all wanted to know what was wrong with Mike. They had no idea of what we had been dealing with and certainly no idea of our discovery the day before. I just couldn't face telling them the truth at this point, so I calmly lied and said he was feeling really bad (that part was true) and might have the flu. They were filled with sympathy for poor Mike and hoped he would feel better for the funeral in the morning. *God, just let us all make it through tonight!* Some of our old high school classmates came to the funeral home, and I had to speak to them. When they asked about our son, I again said he wasn't feeling well.

After the funeral home ordeal, we all went back to Russ and Jackie's house as did all the rest of the family. Jackie's family had brought in tons of food and helped serve it and do those things that needed to be done. I will always be so grateful to them. Mike immediately went upstairs and closed the door to his bedroom. I knew he was feeling miserable both physically and emotionally.

I felt like I was being pulled in a million different directions. My perception was that my entire family had an expectation of how I should be handling all of this. After all, I was the older daughter—the controlling, take charge person of the family. Poor Ben was hurting, and I suspect he needed me, though he can put on a stoic front even when he has been wounded. And Mike was in a world of pain. I remember being downstairs with my family, and for brief moments I would forget how fractured my whole world was. I even laughed a time or two, but then reality would race back into my mind like a runaway train crashing into a canyon. I checked on Mike, and he was in bed with his light out. Ben excused himself and went upstairs before the crowd had thinned. Later, when I checked again, Mike was standing in the hot shower, where he stayed for over an hour. Ben was in bed reading. Again, I don't remember going to bed or to sleep. It's possible I was asleep before I hit the bed.

Inevitably the sun rose on the morning of my mother's funeral. It was February 29, 2000. It was leap year. It would have been just fine with me if we could have just leaped right on over this year because what had gone on so far was pretty devastating.

We got up because we had to. We got dressed, because we had to. Mike pleaded to not have to go to the funeral. But I told him he had to.

"Mike, this is your grandmother's funeral. Nanny loved you very much. You know that. You can't just not go to the funeral." I couldn't believe he wasn't going to go.

"I know, Mom, but I just can't. I can't go."

"Yes, you can! I need for you to be there." I really did need for him to be there in more ways than one. Who was going to stay here with him if he didn't go? I needed Ben with me. I just could not go through this funeral without Ben beside me. I played the guilt card. "Mike I need you to be there. If nothing else, please, just do this for me." The unspoken message was there.

He started to move toward his clothes. *Thank God.* He pulled on his suit pants I had laid out on the chair. And then he headed for the bathroom. I heard him retching. Ben appeared and asked, "What's wrong?" I wanted to scream. *Everything is wrong! Our son is a heroin addict, my mother is dead, I am a wreck, and for once in my life, I don't know what to do! And we need to leave here in fifteen minutes for her funeral. Help me!*

"Mama, I'm sick," It was Mike moaning from the bathroom. I just looked at Ben.

"Just let him stay here," he said.

"But we can't leave him alone. I just can't do that." He heard my unspoken fear of what Mike might do if we left him alone.

"Do you want me to stay here with him?" He had his hands on his hips as he looked at the floor.

I thought for a minute. *Maybe.* "No, I need you with me."

Mike came out of the bathroom. He looked so awful. Have you ever wanted to strangle a child and hug him at the same time? How could he have done this to us on this of all days? How could he have done this to himself?

"Mama, I'm so sorry. I'll try to go if you really want me to, but I just don't think I can do it."

"Will you promise me if you stay here you won't do anything stupid?" *Well, now that was a stupid question. What do you think he's going to say?*

"I promise, Mama. Just let me get back in bed." He was already taking off his suit pants. Before I could answer, he had pulled the covers over his head, and I heard a muffled, "I'm sorry. Tell everybody I'm really sorry." I heard the tears in his voice.

"Dad or someone will be back to check on you. You can take another pill in two hours. I have them with me, and Dad will be back to give it to you. Did you hear what I said?"

"Yes. Thank you." He still had a polite answer. "I love you, Mama."

I was going to lose it right then and there. The lump in my throat was insurmountable. I couldn't breathe, and the tears were filling my eyes. *Just breathe.*

"Sis, we need to go." It was my brother calling from the foot of the stairs, the same stairs where I had melted into a pile of hysteria only night before last. *I will not do that again. I simply can't. I need to go to my mother's funeral now. Breathe, just breathe. That's better. Now move ... one step at a time, but you have to move.*

"Be right down." I managed to answer. *I love you too, Son.* I don't think the words came out of my mouth.

I went to our bedroom, picked up my purse, ducked my head into the bathroom, and swiped some lipstick on and tried to dab some powder under my eyes. It didn't help. Ben was waiting at the top of the stairs. He took my hand firmly, and we went to Mother's funeral while our son lay huddled under a blanket in the middle of the bed, upstairs in my brother's house in the peaceful Midwestern town where I grew up ... and made that wonderful plan about how my life would be, as I played with paper dolls. ... in the middle of my bed.

My mother's funeral is pretty much a blur to me now. I do remember looking at my watch several times and wondering how Mike was doing. My focus was much more on my living son than my dead mother. Looking back, I don't think I have ever really given myself time to mourn for my mother. Certainly on the day of her funeral I was trying to just keep my emotional head above water. If I had let my guard down, I feared the floodgates would open again, and I was not going to let that happen. Being out of control was totally out of my comfort zone.

Ben took our car from the church to the cemetery, and I rode in the limo with the family. We did that so he could go straight from the cemetery to check on Mike and give him the medication. The limo took us back to the church, where the ladies auxiliary prepared a lunch. That's when the questions started.

"Where is Mike? Is he really sick? Gosh, he must be bad to have missed his Nanny's funeral. Did you take him to the doctor? Does he have a fever? I bet it's the flu!"

I think I smiled as I fielded the questions and threw back my evasive answers. Mostly I wanted to see Ben coming through the door to give me an update on our son. When I finally did see him, he looked calm and unruffled. But then that was Ben's nature. He headed straight for me and quickly reported before I started pounding him with questions. Obviously that need to ask a multitude of questions runs in my family, as I had just been reminded by the mini-inquisition from my relatives.

"He's doing fine ... well as good as you'd expect under the circumstances. He was standing in the shower when I left."

"How was he when you first got there?"

"Standing in the shower."

"He was in the shower the whole time you were there?" That sounded so strange. "What's the deal with the shower? Did you talk to him?" As usual, I was firing questions faster than he could answer them.

"Yes he was in the shower the whole time I was there. I wasn't there very long, and, no, I didn't talk to him. I just gave him the pill and a glass of water, and he took it and then I rushed back here to check on you." He sounded tired and frustrated. I knew he was trying to be helpful, but I wished he had tried to talk with Mike, but that was expecting a little too much.

"Thanks, Ben. I guess we should try to eat something." I wasn't hungry but that never stopped me from putting food in my mouth.

Happy, sad, or frustrated, I was one of those who sought food whatever the occasion or mood. If I had been the type that stops eating when upset, I would have looked anorexic by now. The only physical symptom I had noticed from all the turmoil for the past few years was that my hair was thinning, on top especially. *Great, in a few more years I can get a job as the fat bald lady in the circus. That's not funny! Hey, anything to tap into your sense of humor is a good thing, right?* I felt so totally miserable. And so I ate.

Chapter 22

We Need Help

There was so much left to do. We needed to finish cleaning out Mom's house and the storage building, which was a total disaster the last time I looked, especially in the basement, which had been a "catch-all" for years. It was damp and moldy. There were lots of loose ends to be dealt with, including the closing on the sale of Mom's house. I dumped all of it in my brother's lap.

We knew we had to return home and get Mike some help. The prescription would only last a few more days, and, quite frankly, he was a mess. Ben and I could also fit that same description, as we were emotionally drained and looked and felt like we had been hit by a train. I made a phone call back to the court-mandated agency Mike was working with, due to previous infractions. He was still on probation for something. We had even done a few sessions of family counseling there. I made an appointment for the morning after we were getting home. We needed help.

We packed our bags and left for the airport, without any drugs in Mike's carry-on this time. I carried his prescription with me. When we got to the airport, Mike went to the phones. *What's this about? Who was he calling, and, more importantly, what the hell was he calling them for?* I marched to the phone bank and confronted him. I was in no mood to soft pedal my concerns.

"Mike, who are you talking to?" I demanded.

He tried to wave me away and turned his back and continued on the phone. That made me angry. After all he had just put us through, he owed us some respect.

"*Mike!*" I was in his face now. *You're shouting. Remember you're in a public place. Don't let your anger get the best of you. Calm down.* "Mike, I'd like to know who you are talking to." *That was better.*

He turned to me with a scowl on his face that betrayed his frustration with me. "Mom, can't you just leave me alone for one minute?" he asked.

"Obviously not," I said in a very even tone that was filled with implications, but I didn't care. "Either tell me who you are talking to or hang up the damn phone. *Now!*" He knew I meant business.

"I'm talking to Missy. Do you mind? I needed to talk to a friend. Here, you want to check?" He held the receiver out to me.

I had finally wised up to the fact that Mike could bluff his way through anything with me, and I was not going to be the sucker this time. "Yes, as a matter of fact I do," I said as I took the receiver out of his hand. "Hello," I said into the mouthpiece.

"Hello." It really was Missy. Obviously she had heard my demands through the phone. I noticed she hadn't used the familiar greeting "Mama Hen" like all of Mike's peers, usually including her.

"Hello, Missy. I just needed to check. Thanks." I handed the phone back to Mike feeling a little silly. After all, Missy was the girl he had dated all through high school and who remained his good friend. I assumed it would be harmless for him to talk to her on the phone.

"Satisfied?" he said as he took the phone back. I knew he was feeling bad, but he needed to curb that attitude. *Don't push me, not now!*

I raised my eyebrows, turned and walked away. Where he had been quiet and repentant, he now seemed to be taking on a different attitude, one that I definitely didn't like. He hung up the phone and shortly after that we boarded the plane for the final leg of our trip. He leaned his head against the window of the plane and slept, or kept his eyes and mouth shut and pretended to sleep.

We pulled into the driveway of our home. How long ago was it when I left here to go see about Mom? It felt like a very long time ago. In reality it had only been nine days, but nine days in which my world had changed. I was now an adult orphan with neither a living mother nor father. Our son's decent into the hell of addiction had escalated beyond what I thought was possible. We would have to deal with that tomorrow. My energy was at rock bottom.

We unloaded the suitcases and began to unpack. Mike came into our room and announced that Missy was coming over. *Really.* This was our home, and he was there due to our generosity. And he was there in part because I didn't trust him out of my sight. I had a gut feeling he was not ready to give up his drugs yet, and the medication he was being given was not satisfying his need. He was physically hurting.

It was just Missy. What could that hurt? Maybe he just needed to talk to a friend, after all this had been pretty traumatic for him too.

"I guess that's all right, but it would have been nice if you had asked first," I responded. There was a definite edge in my voice. He just turned and left the room.

Very soon, Missy arrived and went straight upstairs to Mike's room. She stayed for less than an hour and left. *That was pretty harmless.* I congratulated myself for not having made a big deal over her short visit.

We went to bed, and I think I slept with one eye and one ear open. It had occurred to me that Mike could leave the house during the night and get drugs, and I knew that was an honest possibility. Little did I know I could have slept soundly relative to Mike leaving the house that night, because he had no need to leave. I found out years later that Missy had brought him the drugs he so desperately wanted. That's what he had arranged with the phone call. I had been the "sucker" again.

The next morning we got up and prepared to go to the appointment with the counselor. The three of us sat in the waiting room like patients waiting to find out if they had cancer. None of us knew what to expect, and we were all dealing with our own emotional fear of what was to come. When our name was called, we went in and sat in the office. My first question concerned the privacy policy. Could what we said here be legally used against Mike? The counselor looked a bit puzzled but assured us there was a counselor-client privilege, and unless what we told him meant someone's life was in danger, it would be confidential. *Mike's life was in danger. Did that count?* I was still protecting my son. From what … the law? The biggest danger to Mike was Mike.

We hit the high spots of what we had discovered in Missouri. He asked Mike some questions and decided to speak to him privately for a few minutes. *What else could Mike tell him? Wasn't our finding heroin and needles in his bag enough?* They came back into the room, and he had two suggestions. One was the DART program. It was a ninety-day residential drug treatment program in Goldsboro, run by the state.

"It has helped some people, but I'll tell you they got some pretty tough guys up there. I can make some calls if you're interested. Usually there's a several-week wait to get in," he said with a grim look on his face.

Several weeks? What were we going to do with him in the meantime? I knew I couldn't watch him twenty-four seven. He was on such a self-destructive path, and I was scared to death! I didn't think we could wait for the help he so desperately needed.

"What's the other suggestion?" I asked.

"The other option is for him to go on a methadone maintenance program. That has some good things and some bad things about it."

I looked at Ben, and he looked as dumbfounded as I was. "What's that?" I finally asked. I had heard of methadone, but, honestly, I really didn't know anything about it. The counselor gave us a brief explanation. Methadone is a legal treatment program subsidized by the government to help heroin addicts be able to function and not have to commit crimes to get the money to support their addiction. Supposedly methadone is not as hard on your body; however, he told us it's probably as difficult to get off methadone as it is heroin. We found out later it was even more difficult.

We asked about other treatment programs, and the counselor had no information. Mike said he didn't want us to spend money on a private rehabilitation facility and he wasn't ready to do that. The wait to get into the DART Cherry program was at least a month.

Mike opted for the methadone program. Reluctantly we went with him to the clinic to get further information. This did not sound like a great treatment program, but we were at a loss for what to do that could go into effect immediately, and it appeared Mike was not ready to make the commitment to stop the drugs. He didn't want to go to a residential treatment program. The counselor there explained that methadone attached to the opiate receptors, had some of the same effects but on a more time-released basis. And, of course, the key factor—it was legal. He would also be required to go to the clinic every morning to get his dosage. He would be drug tested regularly and receive counseling. It had some benefits.

"Mike, this is your decision. We can look into some other alternatives. There has to be other treatment programs out there." We were caught off guard without adequate information and a need to get him help immediately. We honestly felt so lost in a world foreign to both Ben and me, and we were so tired, so very tired.

"This sounds like something I can do," Mike said. "I don't think it's a good idea for me to wait for weeks to go to another kind of program, and I'm not ready to go off somewhere. I just can't do that, but I know I need help." At least he recognized he was in deep trouble with his addiction. So the decision was made, Mike would go on methadone maintenance. He filled out all the papers and agreed to have a physical exam.

Again we had a written agreement. If he had clean drug screens and was passing his classes, we would let him live at home for now and give him a living allowance, with the idea he needed to start looking for a job. If he had any bad drug screens he would have to move out and be on his own. We were paying for his methadone. In fact, we were paying all his expenses.

The methadone seemed to work for Mike. At least things were improving. He lived at home, and he was doing well in school. Mike found a church and invited us to attend with him. That was definitely a step in the right direction. The road seemed to be smoothing out, and, trust me, we needed a break. The calm didn't last long. But this time the scare came from a different source.

Three months later, we had a life-threatening scare concerning my little brother. A mass was discovered in his lung. He was only forty years old and, like me, had never been a smoker. Though it looked like it could possibly be lung cancer, the doctor felt sure with his age and history that was not likely. We would not be completely sure until it was removed. I once again boarded the plane to Missouri with dread. I had just lost my mother in February, and now in May, it looked like Russ was in big trouble. I talked long and hard with God on the plane trip to Missouri.

I could tell Russ was really scared and that was hard for me to witness. While I was his big sister and had adoringly taken care of him before I left home for college, the roles had seemed to switch in the last few years, and he had become my "go-to" guy with all our troubles with Mike. Now here he was in a hospital bed, and I just wanted to hug him and rock him, sing him his favorite little songs, and make him hot chocolate like I had done when he was a little boy.

I waited in the surgery waiting room with Jackie and her whole family. First the word came out, it was not lung cancer. As it turned out, they had removed an encapsulated fungal mass that was very close to rupturing. It's possible it came from working in that moldy basement cleaning out Mother's house or from working around the ancient jail where he was the administrator. We will never know for sure. But he survived and thrived. *Thank you, God!*

Chapter 23

The Perils of Methadone

*M*ike reported to the clinic daily for his methadone. He was getting counseling and going to school. He really wanted to finish his associate's degree and transfer to the university. It was another of the times when things were looking positive.

In July, Mike came by the house to talk with us. He wanted to get off the methadone and find a treatment program to help him once and for all conquer his dependence on drugs. We were elated. He told us how he felt God had spoken to him as he sat outside a church on his way home from the clinic, and he knew it was time. He wanted to finish his summer school session, where he was excelling. That sounded like a great plan to us. We assured him we would support him totally in his efforts and he assured us he was ready to do whatever it might take to get off any kind of drugs once and for all. He called his probation officer to apprise her of his plans.

I set about seeking information on treatment centers. There was no source of centralized information or a person I found to talk to for advice. I felt such frustration with the lack of direction when we wanted to move forward on a positive path.

The first big piece of information I was able to ascertain was a bit of a shocker. Treatment programs would not take someone in unless and until they had been through a detoxification from methadone. We found a treatment program in Canaan, Connecticut, that sounded like a good fit for Mike, with a lot of outdoor elements in their protocol, but like other places we had talked to, they would not take him unless he was off the methadone. *Really?* We were talking to detoxification programs, and they didn't detox methadone? So now where would we go? How could we get Mike off methadone so he could get the help he wanted?

After several more phone calls and researching resources, we were convinced it would not be safe for us to try to deal with getting him off methadone on our own. The methadone clinic could tell you how to get on the stuff and everything about it, including that it was difficult to get off of. But they had *no* information on how or where to detox from methadone. I called every local source I could find, and I still found no help.

I finally found a small hospital in Laurinburg, North Carolina, with an in-patient detox program that included methadone. It was the Amethyst program at Scotland Memorial Hospital. I called Mountainside back in Canaan, Connecticut, to tell them we had the detox scheduled. They thought that was fine, but the detox needed to coincide so closely with Mike's physical arrival there that he would be under constant supervision from one to the other. They had been around the block a few times in this field and knew the proclivity for addicts to get a last hurrah high before getting help. I called Laurinburg back and matched the intake date at Mountainside to Mike's release date from detox, requiring a slight change from what we had originally scheduled. Finally after hours and hours on the phone and rearranging schedules, we had everything set. Wrong!!

Mike's probation officer called to say he had to appear in court. It was a total misunderstanding and miscommunication between the officer and an intern, but now we had to change the schedule *again*. Yes, I was upset and angry and frustrated. On top of that, we had Ben's brother and his wife arriving right in the middle of all of this mess, and

I had to keep excusing myself to make or receive more phone calls. I felt as if I was swimming upstream with circumstances standing on the banks throwing rocks on my head. *We need a break.* We were trying to do a good thing, and we really needed to get it done without any more conflicts! Mike really wanted to get on the road to recovery, and we definitely wanted that to happen. *Why was this so difficult!*

Mike was trying to do all the right things, making good decisions and taking responsibility, and once again there seemed to be obstacles in our path. I had to vent my frustration with the system this time. I wrote a letter to the probation supervisor.

August 16, 2000

Mr. Jones:

Mike told his probation officer of his plans to enter treatment in July. I also spoke to her personally and told her about his plans. On Friday, August 4, he called to speak to her to give her the details of the information on his treatment plans. She was unavailable and did not return his call. He left a message. He called again Monday and was told she was not going to be back in the office until Thursday. An intern was taking information, and indicated the phone call was sufficient. The plan was for him to go to Laurinburg on August 11, the day after he finished summer school. He had told her that was the plan earlier, to go as soon as he finished school, and she approved.

On Thursday morning she called our phone number and left a message. Mike went in to see her and at that time—one day before all the plans were in place for him to begin detox and treatment—she said he had to go to court. The intern miscommunicated.

As Mike's parents, we want what is best for him, and applaud his decision to seek additional treatment. He is making great strides. Though we have had to reschedule all plans that were in place, Mike will go to Laurinburg to the Amethyst program today, August 16, and from there we will take him to Mountainside, where he will remain for 4 to 6 weeks or whatever time further is determined by that program. I want you to be aware that this information has been conveyed to and approved by his probation officer.

Sincerely,

Obviously I was very frustrated with the probation system. I felt I had to support Mike, even if it looked like a mother being overinvolved. We were trying so hard to move forward, as he had made such a big decision to seek help. I don't know if writing a letter like that was the right thing to do. Again that was my protective instincts working overtime, but I wanted to support his positive decision at a crucial time.

He wrote this e-mail the day before he was going to detox:

August 15, 2000

Mom:

Well here it is. I'm sitting in the computer lab at school for what may be the last time. Seems weird, I've spent months in here learning, chatting, finding, exploring … This school is all right, but it's been time to move on for a while. What I will miss over the next few months is school itself. I know how weird that sounds, believe me. However, I actually enjoy school. Not so much the papers and the homework, but the learning and expanding my knowledge base and my understanding of how this world (or how I perceive it) works.

This may be (hopefully) the last time for something else as well. As my fingers pound the keys, I feel the mellow feeling of the methadone rising up from my spine as I have felt nearly every day for the past five months. It passes through me and my body accepts it. It comforts me in ways that anyone who hasn't done it could ever understand. I never anticipate it, yet every day I am silently rewarded with a subtle jolt throughout my system, a jolt that reminds me of what I am, what I have become. Tomorrow there will be no jolt, no warmth, and no comfort. I will have to make do without. Will it be hard? Will it hurt? Don't know. Ask again this time next week and I'll tell you.

It will though, I believe, be the best thing to happen to me. I'd be lying if I said that I'm not scared a bit. I am. Terrified. Not the fear of losing my daily dose, that does not scare me at all. Rather, the fear of falling short of my goals is what makes me totally scared. My goal to abstain, my goal to change my ways, this is what I fear falling short of most. This is the most time consuming, expensive, and dramatic solution that I (we) have thrown at this life threatening problem of mine yet. And all though I am mentally and physically ready to deal with treatment and work the program so that I give myself the best chance for recovery, deep down I am frightened to death by the thought that this too may not be the answer. Even worse, there may be NO answers, and that is far worse than any symptom of withdrawal.

I can't look at it that way though. I have to put blinders on to the future. I have to look at TODAY and do what I can NOW. I know well and sure that if I think I will fail I will definitely be correct. Mind-set is a tremendous part of this thing. Tomorrow will bring great pain and promise, grief and glory, fear and freedom, remorse and resolution. I will be afraid but I will use my fear as an incentive to perform. I can, and will beat this thing. I will seek it with my intellect, and destroy it with my will. Stand by me, and there is no doubt that I can, we can, defeat this torturous problem. I thank you and I love you very much.

Love,

Mike

His fear of taking on the monster of addiction was obvious in his letter. But more importantly, he had a strong desire to conquer that monster. I wrote him back an e-mail later that night.

August 15, 10:00 PM
Dearest Mike

The time has finally come when we are going to go head to head with this monster—and we will win! I say "we" because we are a team, but I realize that you and you alone can make the big choices. We are your support, your cheerleaders and the parents who love you so much. I would do anything to make this monster disappear—but I can't do it. With our support, your strong will and God's help—you can do it!

Everyone has to decide for themselves what that higher power or God is. For me, I know that God is within each of us. Sometimes we lose that connection to that inner strength and that goodness, but it's there inside. You have it too. Give yourself some time to connect with that strength. Find your God. I pray a lot. Often it is for the ability to accept what the right path is for me. Sometimes it is for help to find the path.

I know you're scared. That's natural. I'm a little scared too. Dad and I want this opportunity to be the best for you. I truly believe you are about to embark on a life changing journey. You said a big fear of yours is that there may be NO answer to your addiction. Yes there is. One day at a time you will find that path. Let God help you.

Be truthful and honest with yourself. Get to know the goodness and the strength and the kindness that is in your heart. I know the young man you may have forgotten. They say a true friend is a person who knows our faults, and loves us anyway. We all have faults. Even though you more than anyone, know all your faults, forgive yourself and be loving to yourself. Yesterday is gone. Today is a gift and an opportunity to make your dreams come true.

This monster has caused us all a lot of pain. It's time for the monster to go. He lives on a street we've been down so many times. We keep wanting to believe he'll go away and leave you alone, but he just keeps grabbing you. Well now for real WE ARE GOING DOWN A DIFFERENT STREET. SCREW THE MONSTER—HE WILL NOT WIN!

I know the next week may get uncomfortable, but it is only a matter of days and it will be so much better. Remember—One day at a time. You are so right; mindset is a tremendous part of this fight. Stick with it every day. We love you so much. You are doing the right thing and we admire your choice. We're proud of you son.

Love,

Mom

XXOOXX

Ed's brother left with no idea of what was going on, and we were able to take Mike to Laurinburg for the rescheduled, *rescheduled* appointment for his stay in the detox unit. We would return in four days to pick him up and head straight for Connecticut. We had no contact with him for those four days. He had packed his bags for Mountainside before going to Laurinburg. Ben and I were filled with hope ... and some fear.

We picked him up at the hospital as scheduled. We had a consultation with his doctor.

"He had a pretty hard time of it, but he will be all right," the doctor told us. "He may have some difficulty sleeping, and he will be easily agitated, but the methadone is out of his system."

"He will be all right to enter the treatment program at Mountainside with these issues?" I asked him.

"I'm sure they have taken in young people in worse shape than your son. If they can't deal with him, they shouldn't be in the business," he said with authority.

I wasn't feeling totally reassured, but we really didn't have any choice now, did we? Ben asked a couple of questions, and I was getting anxious to see Mike. We went to a waiting room, and he came in with his few belongings in a little bag. He definitely did not look as good coming out as he did going in, and he hadn't looked all that good going in.

He put his arms around us and said, "Are we ready to go now?" He felt even thinner.

"We just have to go to the checkout desk, and we are good to go," Ben said. We signed papers, got instructions, and left the hospital. Our plan was to spend the night in Pennsylvania with our good friends Joyce and Dwight, and then go on to Canaan the next day.

Chapter 24

Mountainside

*I*t was a long drive to Pennsylvania in more ways than one. Mike was restless and agitated in the backseat. I offered him the front seat, but he said it wouldn't help. He was like a caged cat.

We got there around seven o'clock, and Joyce had dinner waiting. Mike didn't want anything to eat. We tried to convince him he needed to eat something, but he wanted no part of it. Joyce and Dwight had not seen him for a while, and they certainly were not seeing him at his best.

We were tired and had a long day ahead of us the next day, so decided to turn in pretty early. Mike was in the family room outside our bedroom. He had the TV on, saying he couldn't go to sleep. That was fine, just as long as he kept the volume down enough not to disturb anyone else.

I tried to go to sleep, but sleep was not coming. I finally dozed off only to have Mike come into our bedroom in a state of complete agitation.

"Mom, you have to do something. I can't stand this. I haven't slept for four days. I'm so tired, I'm just so tired," he grabbed his head with his hands and sat on the edge of our bed. Ben stirred, and I suggested we go into the family room.

"Mike, what do you mean you haven't slept for four days?" That just didn't sound right to me.

"I haven't been to sleep since you took me there, but I can't go to sleep. You have to do something, or I'm gonna go nuts!" He was up pacing now and had a wild look in his eyes.

I had witnessed the effects of sleep deprivation before when I worked in the counseling agency, and I knew how serious the consequences could be. No one told us he had not slept, if in fact that was true. All I knew was that his current behavior was not a good omen of what was to come if he didn't get some sleep. I knew Joyce might have some kind of sleeping pills in the house, but I certainly did not want to give Mike medication that might be the wrong thing to do. I did the normal thing when I was at my wit's end and went to the bedroom and woke Ben.

"Mike says he hasn't slept in days, and he is extremely agitated. I'm not sure what to do, but he needs to get some sleep."

"What time is it?" Ben asked.

"Two o'clock," I answered. "I bet Joyce has some sleeping pills. Do you think I should give him one?"

"Didn't the doctor give you a card with the phone number to call? Call them up and ask them." Once again, Ben went right to the heart of the matter.

"Good idea. Thanks," I said and left the room. Mike was still pacing. "I'm going to call the number at the hospital and ask them about giving you something to help you sleep. Hang in there, and we'll work something out."

"Just do something, please," he whined. This behavior was not like anything I had seen out of Mike before.

I called the hospital; a nurse answered, and I explained the situation. She looked up Mike's records. "Did they not give you a prescription for a sleeping pill when you left?"

"*No*, they did not," I said emphatically.

"Oh, I see. He is going to a treatment facility; it says right here in his record. That's probably why they didn't do that. Normally we do because it's so hard for them to sleep. We can call something in for you if that will help."

"It is two o'clock in the morning, I am in a strange town on the way to Connecticut, and my son is pacing the floor with symptoms of extreme sleep deprivation. You are telling me you normally give a prescription for a sleeping pill, but you didn't give him one. I have no idea if there is a twenty-four-hour drugstore anywhere near here! Please stay on the line, and let me see what is available in this house, and you can tell me if it is safe for him to take it. You will stay on the line, right?"

"Yes, ma'am," was all she said. I was in no mood to listen to anything else.

I went upstairs, woke Joyce, and asked if she had any sleeping pills. She didn't, but Dwight did, thank God. I went back downstairs, picked up the phone, and read the information off the bottle to the nurse on the phone. It took her several minutes before she came back and told me it would be okay for Mike to take two but not to repeat. I thanked her, hung up, and got a glass of water.

"Here, take these, and they should help." He took the two pills and drank the entire glass of water. I sat up with him for another hour until he was able to finally fall into a fitful sleep. As I sat there watching him, with his arm slung above his head and one knee pulled up, I couldn't help but think how, in the shadows, he looked just like he had as an innocent little boy. And again that familiar knot formed in the back of my throat. *What happened to that wonderful little innocent boy? How could we have let this happen to him? Why couldn't we see how troubled he was before it had come to this? Was he ever going to be healthy again?* I watched as he tossed and turned and softly moaned in his half sleep. I quietly slipped back into the bed beside Ben.

"Is he asleep?" he asked softly.

"I think so," I answered with a tear-filled voice. "Ben?"

"What?"

"This just has to work. I can't take too much more of this," I said.

"I know, I know." He rolled over and put his arm around me. I think we slept.

In what seemed like only a few minutes, we were up and getting ready to finish the second leg of the trip to Canaan. Mike's agitation of the night before was replaced by groggy irritation. I suppose the sleeping pills hadn't worn off.

Joyce was busy fixing breakfast and trying her best to boost our mood and energy. She was a tremendous friend through all of our ordeals with Mike. I would hate to count the hours she had patiently listened to me on the phone. She didn't judge; she didn't pretend to have all the answers: she just listened with compassion and felt what I felt.

We ate breakfast, insisting that Mike try to get something down, which he did. Once again we were back on the road headed toward what we desperately hoped would be a new beginning for our son.

We drove through the little town where Ben and I had lived so many years before in New York. We even drove up the hill to go by our old apartment, thinking it might be interesting for Mike to see where we had lived when we were exactly his age.

Here was where our quest to parenthood had started. And my life journey had almost ended in a very short story. It was a lifetime ago when that doctor came into the examining room and used the word "infertility." If I had known where this road would go, would I have started on the journey?

It was 1970, and the field of infertility treatment was just emerging. I went through numerous tests and procedures to check out all my "pipes and equipment." After several months, I was given fertility drugs, and miracle of miracles, a year after he had used the dreaded infertility word, I was pregnant! A few weeks later there was a problem, and the doctor decided I had lost the pregnancy, and I was in the hospital for a procedure.

I went back to my teaching job the following Monday. Strangely enough, every morning when I monitored study hall, I got this light-headed feeling followed by nausea. I thought, *now I'm just a total mental case that has morning sickness, and I'm not pregnant anymore.* After several weeks of this, I went back to see the doctor. He reassured me that everything would be fine, and soon we would try the fertility drug again.

"But what about this silly morning sickness?" I asked him.

"No problem, no problem."

No problem … no problem for whom? Could we at least talk about this? Why do I feel this way … why do I feel sick, and I'm so tired? Am I a mental case? That's what I thought, but I never said another word. Back then I had blind trust in doctors.

Four days later, I had my class in the library of the high school. I started having severe cramps and couldn't wait for that class session to end because I was feeling so miserable. I went to the nurse's office to ask if I could lie down for a few minutes. An hour later, I knew I couldn't teach my afternoon classes. I was in such extreme pain that it hurt to move or even breathe. The school nurse took one look at me and got her blood pressure cuff and checked me out. She calmly told me she was calling an ambulance, and she needed Ben's phone number at work in Manhattan. I feebly tried to talk her out of both calls. Her efficient stubbornness saved my life.

She knew from my blood pressure reading that something was wrong, seriously wrong. There had been no early miscarriage. I had an ectopic pregnancy, and my fallopian tube had now ruptured, and I was lying on a cot in a school nurse's office bleeding to death.

As I lay in the emergency room waiting for their gynecologist on call to arrive, and Ben to catch a train out of Grand Central Station, I started going into shock. I was getting blood transfusions but was bleeding out as fast as it was going in. I clearly recall the nurse taking my hand and saying, "Hold on, honey; you just hold on." And to another nurse, "I think we're losing her; I can't get a pulse."

What does that mean I'm supposed to do? Should I try to breathe more deeply? Oh God, that hurts worse. I wish I knew what "hold on" means I should do. I've seen this stuff on TV before. Somebody tell me what to do to hold on. Those were my thoughts. I recall feeling very calm. The more crucial the situation, the more calmly I reacted.

The doctor on call finally arrived, and they wheeled me off to surgery. My chances of getting pregnant were about to be literally cut in half. But I survived.

The boulders in my life path were looking pretty big back then. Ben sat by my bed and held my hand. We were two young kids from Missouri alone in a hospital in New York. It had been a very close call with the end of my road.

I felt like a failure at a very basic level. I was a woman, and a woman was supposed to be able to carry children and give birth. Every hormone in my body was screaming to be able to fulfill that expectation. I could not make it happen, I was not in control. I had another surgery that was supposed to help. It didn't. But I would not give up on my quest to be a mother. We had moved to Texas, decided to adopt, and became Mike's loving parents.

Now here we were several years later as the parents we had waited so long to become. But had I failed at a role I was so sure I was meant to play? I had to believe we were going to overcome the obstacles that had fallen in our path. I could not regret our choice, not for even an instant. Mike was our son, and we loved him. Even knowing the turmoil we were living, I had to keep believing the pain would eventually be replaced by happiness. I was still holding on tight, blind to the fact that I needed to let go. Mike was beginning to see he needed to take control by deciding to go to a treatment facility. And then I stepped right in and made all the arrangements for him.

We arrived at Mountainside and got Mike's things out of the trunk and handed him his paperwork. He had perked up by the time we arrived and seemed ready for this step that he had chosen. Unloading and saying good-bye took less than fifteen minutes, and we were pulling out of the driveway. I don't know what I was expecting, but it went so … fast. It was out of my hands…out of my controlling comfort zone. He had thanked us, reassured us and hugged us, and followed the administrator into the office.

We had deposited our son in a drug rehab program. This was his choice; he wanted to get totally clean, and this looked like a good program for him. I had to think positively! This could be the end of so much pain for all of us.

We drove back to Joyce and Dwight's, collapsed, spent the night, and drove the rest of the way home the next day. It had taken a huge effort and lots of planning to make this all work, but we had managed, and it should have felt good. I guess it did … sort of. I needed to have faith that this was going to work.

We received letters from Mike, and I wrote letters back to him. He indicated things were going well.

Mom and Dad,

Just a quick word of thanks to both of you. The next
time I am home I will be a completely different person. I
know for sure that I will conquer this disease. It won't be
easy, especially when I return, but I can, and will, do this.
Thanks for all of the support and love you have shown
me. I may not always show it but I honestly do appreciate
all you both do for me. I love you both very much.

Mike

After three and a half weeks, we got a call from Mike saying he
was ready to come home. That was faster than we had anticipated. He
assured us that he had gotten all he needed from this program and that
any more time there would be a waste.

I called the director and asked his opinion.

"Well, we like for our residents to stay a minimum of six weeks.
Some are here for as long as six months," he told me.

"But what about Mike? He says he has benefited greatly from your
program and doesn't feel it's necessary for him to stay any longer."

"Mike is probably one of the smarter clients we've dealt with here
in a long time. He has done very well in the program. He's obviously
extremely motivated."

Wow, that sounded very positive. "Does that mean you think he's
ready to come home?"

"Not exactly. I told you we like for all our residents to stay a
minimum of six weeks."

It was difficult for me to determine if he wanted the additional
time because he thought Mike needed it or because he was seeking the
additional money. It would have been easier for me if he had just said

without hesitation, "Mike absolutely needs to stay here at least two more weeks." But he didn't say that, and Mike was very convincing, as usual.

"Mom, I'm doing really well. I feel great, and I'm totally clean and sober. I get it. I know I have to be careful, but I'm so ready to do that. Staying here longer is just wasting your money on a paid vacation for me. You don't need to do that. I don't want you to do that. I've finished what I started." He sounded so sure and reasonable. *Should this be his decision?*

Ben and I discussed it at length, had another conversation with Mike suggesting he stay at least another week or two—and then agreed to buy his one-way airplane ticket home. The director said they could provide transportation to the airport. Again, he did not take that opportunity to suggest we were making a mistake letting him leave the program that soon.

We weren't sure we were doing the right thing, but we also didn't want to undermine Mike's positive attitude either. There weren't any books to give us the right answers along this journey.

Two days later, we drove to the airport in Raleigh to pick him up. He looked fantastic. He had put on a few pounds; the dark circles were gone from under his eyes; he was tan, and he had a big smile on his face. This is what we had prayed for, and we were ecstatic. He dropped his carry-on bag and literally threw his arms around both of us. He squeezed us tight, and we all cried right there in the airport.

"I can't tell you guys how much I appreciate what you've done for me. I know I've been such a pain in the ass for so long, but that's over now. I'm done with it. I want to get into the university and get on with my life," he said with such pride and confidence. "I'm totally ready to do this."

We had waited a long time to hear those words. Finally this constant barrage of boulders was going to ease up, and we could move forward on life's journey with happiness replacing so much fear and anger. My heart was soaring and I felt such relief. It was so good to have our son talking about his future with such optimism.

One week later, Mike's car rolled to a stop in the middle of an intersection. He was unconscious with a needle stuck in his arm. He was charged with possession of paraphernalia and DUI. His old drug buddy, Jack, was with him in the car. *Why? Why? Why would you do this?*

His probation was tightened, and he was lucky that's all that happened. He had most definitely fallen short of his goal. His worst fears had been realized.

Looking back, we didn't follow our own rule of *finish what you start*. Mountainside was a good program, but it wasn't finished. The director was trying to tell us that, but we weren't listening closely enough. We were also trying to let Mike take responsibility and make his own decisions. There were just no easy answers. Even though there is no guarantee it would have produced a different outcome, it would have been a wiser choice for him to stay longer. We didn't make that choice.

Treatment for drug abusers usually takes place during a prescribed period of time and needs to be followed by involvement and commitment to a recovery program. Something I didn't understand then, but I know now…recovery is a lifelong process.

Mike had not stayed the prescribed time and he hadn't connected to ongoing recovery. Obviously he had still not hit the bottom—if that's what it really took to turn this thing around forever.

Chapter 25

Charge Cards and Checks

We were shattered by Mike's almost immediate relapse after his return from Mountainside. This continuing pattern was wearing thin, and we felt like we were running out of options. We had decided to get away for two days in Myrtle Beach. Our good friends Rob and Beth went with us. We were going to play golf, then see the Rockettes at the Palace Theater, and spend the night. We played golf at a great course, and for a few hours we let our worries melt away and concentrated on hitting a little white ball from hole to hole. When we went to check in at the Marriott, I got out my billfold to give them my credit card while Ben was parking.

"I always put it right here," I said to the waiting desk clerk. I searched all the little slots where all my cards were, and it was nowhere to be found. This was embarrassing. We were paying for the two-bedroom condo as a sort of thank-you to our friends for all the help they had been to us, especially as we dealt with the ordeals with Mike. Beth was like another mom to Mike. She and Rob had helped move him from place to place with their pickup truck, and a lot of sweat and perhaps a few tears along the way.

I finally asked the clerk to wait while I went to get Ben's card.

"What's taking so long?" he asked as I approached the car.

"I need your charge card. I can't find mine."

"Where did you have it last? Did you check your billfold?"

"Yes, I've done all that." I think my teeth were clinched. "Just give me your card." My mind was already searching the possibilities of where my card might be. I was shutting out a suspicion that was trying to push its way in.

I took Ben's card and got us registered. We all went to the room, and I dumped the contents of my purse and searched in vain for my charge card. That suspicion was pushing harder, and I couldn't ignore it anymore. I went into the bedroom, closed the door, and called the number on the back of Ben's card to the same charge account as my missing card. I had them check the last five charges. They were definitely not my charges, but I recognized the places where they had been made. I didn't tell the person on the phone, because I knew that suspicion had just smacked me right in the face. Mike had taken my card and used it. *Damn.*

Beth and Rob knew everything there was to know about our issues with Mike. They had been a sounding board, a place to vent, and a source of encouragement along our rocky road. There was no reason to hide this transgression from them.

I went back into the living area. "Mike took my card." No preface, no softening the blow, I just let the words plop out with a thud.

"Are you sure? How do you know?" I guess Ben didn't want to believe it either.

"I called the card people and checked on the last five charges. They're not mine, but the charges are at places Mike frequents. It's actually the last seven charges. None of them are that big. I didn't tell the guy on the phone they weren't mine."

It felt like a giant black cloud descended on the room. I didn't feel angry or scared, and I definitely wasn't going to cry. I just felt exhausted.

Beth came and put her arm around me and gave me a hug. Rob just shook his head and finally said, "Well, crap!" I guess that about summed it up. We went back home without seeing the Rockettes.

We allowed ourselves to share our difficulties surrounding Mike with only a tight circle of friends. Rob and Beth were in that circle. More often than I would like to admit, the conversation over dinner would end up on Mike, and I would inevitably dissolve into tears. Ben was never comfortable discussing any of this with anyone. Frequently he would firmly suggest that we change the subject.

Ben is a man who prefers to "go to his cave" and think issues through. I, on the other hand, am a woman who has a need to talk through what is bothering me. That is a basic difference and continued to be a problem for me throughout this entire journey. Thus I sought out my closest, dearest, friends and my brother to talk with when I felt like I absolutely had to have a sounding board or a shoulder to lean on. I'm not saying Ben wasn't there to lean on. He was. He was just a more "silent" pillar of strength, and I desperately needed someone to talk to.

Sometimes late at night I would sit in front of the computer and pour out my fears and feelings. That helped, but a computer can't give you a hug when you really need it. Joyce and Dwight; Rob and Beth; Dennis and Margaret; Paula, my tennis partner; and my brother were the friends who nourished my soul in my most desperate times of need, and I will be eternally grateful.

When we confronted Mike, he readily admitted what he had done, and as always, he was sorry. Once again, we dealt with his behavior. We contemplated turning him in, but that would have been a serious offense and probably would include jail time or maybe even prison. We worked out a plan of how he would pay us back. I also visited the establishments that allowed him to use *my* credit card with an obviously female name, but to no satisfaction. One place had even taken my card to charge $200 they then gave to Mike in cash.

We forcefully told Mike he had destroyed our trust, and it would not be easy to regain. We changed the credit card and hid our checks.

He never used my credit card again, but he found the checks. I once again took to writing to him.

WINNERS AND LOSERS

It is a deadly game you are playing and there is no winner. And it is no game. This is our lives—the only one we get and it is being overwhelmed by fear and sadness. I know you must feel that fear and sadness too. I ask God every day to help me find the path to live in His light. I pray for you too, that you will find your way. I don't have answers, just questions.

You have won again in your quest. We thought we could hide our material things from you so that we could continue to share our home with you, but you proved us wrong. Your addiction is so strong that you managed to search through drawers to find what you were looking for. You won, you found the new checks, but oh my son how you lost. Now we can no longer share this safe haven of our home with you. You have betrayed our loving trust one too many times. Your defiant path of self-destruction has led you to this. You have not destroyed our love, for that is indestructible, but the trust is gone.

You need help and I think you know that. There is no magic cure. How we all wish there was, but the fact is, no one can do this for you. I would if I could—but I can't "fix" this. I still believe you can overcome this horrible addiction that has taken control of your life. Tap into that strength and beat it an hour at a time. If you want to beat this thing, YOU have to want it and do it. If YOU don't, it is just a matter of time till your problems get worse and worse and worse. I hope and pray you will stop and take an honest look at where you are headed and decide to turn this around. Only you can make that decision and make it work. For what it is worth, I'm begging you to try. I love you so much. I want my son back. He is worth fighting for. YOU are worth fighting for.

Mike moved out of the house. He moved into a townhouse on the river with Jordan, a buddy who was also a wakeboarder. And, yes, we helped him pay his rent. We knew our son was in trouble and needed help, but we also knew he was the one who had to turn his life around.

Looking back, I have to question why we were still helping pay his rent. We were still on the same street falling into the same hole enabling our son's habitual behavior. Why?

Chapter 26

Rules Is Rules

After the incidents with the checks, we knew we had to try something else with our son. He was losing the battle against his addiction. Mike had been seeing a new counselor for several weeks. He suggested some medication, and Mike was willing to give it a try, but then he didn't like how it made him feel. Mike wanted help. He knew the heroin was controlling him and as much as he wanted to turn his life around, his addiction was powerful. Without the drugs, he would get violently ill. He was caught in a terrible web and he desperately wanted to escape. As we did more research, we found the Coleman Clinic in Richmond, Virginia, that would do a naltrexone implant that would block opiate receptors. In other words, if you used opiates, such as heroin, the heroin would have no effect. After much discussion, and quite frankly out of desperation, we took Mike to Richmond, where he had to spend the first night in the hospital to detox with the aid of anesthesia before the implant could be used. He was sedated to get through the withdrawal in a short time. This was not supposed to be as difficult as it had been to get off the methadone.

Ben and I traded off sitting with him through the hellish night that he does not remember. I watched him go through a delirious agony, and I felt the pain that he could not feel. I couldn't imagine what kind of hell he had gone through for four days to get off methadone if that detox was worse than this.

The next day, Dr. Peter Coleman placed the implant and gave Mike all the information and instructions. Surely this was going to give our wonderfully intelligent and caring young man that still lived in Mike's body a chance to win out over the drug demon that possessed him.

He had been to court earlier for the DUI and paraphernalia charge and been sentenced to eighteen months of probation or forty days in jail. He had opted for probation, and was assigned to a probation officer in the county where he was living. He had failed to show up for a weekly appointment on more than one occasion, so he had to go to court. This time we were in the courthouse of the smaller adjoining county, where things were conducted in a much more informal way.

The judge suggested he voluntarily place himself in a program called DART Cherry. It stood for Drug Addiction Rehabilitation Training. I sat in court as they made some phone calls. The clerk came back in and talked to the judge, and the judge told Mike there was a wait list to get in. This was the ninety-day residential program that had been suggested earlier when we came back from the funeral in Missouri, and Mike had opted for the methadone program. Surely he would not go down that road again.

Much to my surprise, Mike decided to just serve his forty days in jail. He clarified with the judge that when he finished, he would be free of probation, which the judge acknowledged. It was Mike's decision, and we really had no choice in the matter. The judge told him his probation officer would give him the date to report to the jail. He was to call him the next day.

Mike convinced us he was ready to clear the slate with the law and start over. Once again we grasped at the hope he had finally come to his senses. He had been able to stop using heroin with the help of the naltrexone implant, and now he was ready to get straight with the law. That trip to Richmond had been three weeks before the trip to the courthouse for the probation violation. It was working. He was off drugs and alcohol. Our son was clean and sober.

So a week after we had been in court, Mike was to report to jail. He spent the night before at our house. I asked Mike what time we needed to be there. I had not seen any paperwork, and I was trying to let him take responsibility for himself, but I was going to drive him.

"Any time before noon," he answered sleepily over a bowl of cereal.

"Are you sure? Did you check? Is it written on any of your paperwork?" Obviously I wasn't succeeding at letting him totally handle this. I was also asking several questions without giving him time to answer. Old habits die hard.

"Mom, lay off. I got it covered," he replied with his usual annoyance at my controlling nature. This was the same old pattern that had been repeated over and over. It was *my* hole in the sidewalk.

I was prodding him into the car at ten thirty. He was nervous and scared. And then he got very quiet. Perhaps he was regretting his decision to trade probation for forty days in jail. I have to admit one of the things going through my mind was the forty days of the naltrexone patch that we had paid dearly to have implanted would be wasted while he was safely behind bars. I immediately scolded myself for the thought. And then I thought with sadness, *I am on the way to take my son to jail.*

"Mom, stop up there so I can get some cigarettes." He broke the silence.

"They probably won't let you take them in anyway," I said. "And this would be a great time for you to stop that nasty habit." *Another controlling comment from Mom.*

"Please, Mom, just stop. Please! I *need* a cigarette." He had raised his voice.

I suspected this was in part an attempt to delay the inevitable, but I pulled into the Quick Stop, gave him the money, and waited while he went in to buy the cigarettes. I checked the time and we were doing fine to get there before noon. In all honesty, it also repeated the pattern of me giving in to Mike. It didn't seem like a big deal to me whether we stopped or not, so I stopped.

We pulled into the parking lot of the jail. Mike took in a last puff on his cigarette and threw it out the window. He looked at me, took a ragged breath, and said, "Mom, I'm really scared."

I felt that familiar lump in my throat as I looked into the sad brown eyes of my little boy, except he wasn't little anymore. He was twenty-five years old. He had managed to get himself into big trouble, but hopefully we were on the right track now. I needed to believe that. I couldn't have been more wrong.

I put my hand on his shoulder, and I felt him shudder. "I know, Son." I honestly didn't know what else to say. It was like I had said it all before. He knew we loved him, and we wanted him to get healthy and happy and stay straight. Perhaps I could have told him I was scared too.

"Okay, let's do it." Another deep breath, and he opened the car door. We walked into the reception area of the small jail. No one was behind the counter, so we both sat down and waited.

Several minutes later a large man in a uniform walked into the area behind the counter. He didn't act like he even saw us. Mike stood up and approached the counter. "Excuse me, sir, my name is Mike. I'm reporting to serve forty days."

The officer looked at a clipboard, found Mike's name, and said, "You was supposed to be here by 'leven a.m." I looked at my watch. It was now 11:20 a.m. We had been waiting for at least ten minutes.

"I'm sorry," Mike said. "I thought my probation officer told me to be here by noon."

"Don't think he woulda tole you that. Always been 'leven o'clock."

I couldn't believe this was happening. "So what is he supposed to do now?" I could hear the frustration in my voice, and I hadn't intended to say anything. *Let Mike handle this!*

"Call your probation officer and report back here next Friday. And be here before 'leven a.m., or I'll send you on your way again." He turned his back and seemed to busy himself with some papers.

"You can't be serious! We've been sitting out here waiting for someone since eleven." I was trying not to scream at him.

"No, ma'am, you wasn't here at 'leven."

"Well, it had to be really close to eleven." *Oh, please don't make us have to go through this ordeal all over again. This was gut-wrenching.* He just gave me a look and never said a word.

"Mom, we'll just come back next week," Mike said with some obvious relief.

"Can't you just take him now?" I pleaded. I stood there waiting.

Finally, without looking up, he said, "No, ma'am. Rules is rules." And that was that.

We got back in the car, and I slammed the door. "Damn it, Mike, I told you to check the time. I can't believe this!" *If I hadn't stopped for the darn cigarettes we would have been on time. Why did I stop? What are we going to do now?*

"Mom, calm down. It's not that big a deal," Mike tried to reassure me as he pulled out a cigarette.

Yes, it actually was a big deal. Now there would be another week of waiting, not knowing what might happen. In fact it took only a few short hours for disaster to strike.

Chapter 27

The SWAT Team

Coming back home, I made the decision that Mike should stay at the house for the next week. We had made him put his truck up for sale to pay us back for the checks he had written on our account that we had covered. We felt strongly there had to be consequences for his actions, but we couldn't make ourselves turn him in to the law because we knew that would be a felony charge. We could not do that to our son. He took that situation out of our hands that very same day.

Soon after we got back to the house, Mike told Ben he had a potential buyer for his truck and asked if he could take it for the guy to see. He made it sound like a legitimate offer, so we agreed to let him go with instructions to come right back home. We obviously weren't paying much attention when he left, as he went out through the garage. We didn't see my golf clubs and some of Ben's tools go with him. He deposited our possessions at the pawn shop to get some cash.

The time for Mike to return home came and went. Once again that mother's extra sense kicked in, and I absolutely knew something was very wrong. The emotion I felt was anger, but I had learned by then that my anger was a direct result of my fear. I called his roommate at the river and asked if Mike was there. No, he hadn't been there.

145

"If he shows up, will you *please* ask him to call me?"

"Sure, Mama Hen. Is everything okay? I thought Mike was supposed to report to jail today."

I explained the events of the morning, and we hung up. I made a few other phone calls, and then I didn't know what else to do but wait. It was almost dark when the phone rang.

"Mike, is that you?"

"No, ma'am." It was Mike's roommate, Jordan. "Have you talked to Mike yet?"

"No, and I'm worried sick. Something is wrong." I didn't have any idea how wrong. And then the rocks started to fall again.

"Mama Hen, the police were just here looking for him."

My heart sank to the floor. "Why? What did they want? What did he do?" *This is not good. This is definitely bad.*

"They wouldn't tell me, but ..." There was a long pause.

"But *what?*" *Did I just yell into the phone?* Ben appeared by my side.

"They wanted to know if Mike had any weapons," he said finally.

"Well, did you tell them *no?* Mike doesn't have any weapons."

"No, ma'am, I told them that my dad's shotgun is missing."

I had to sit down. I was shaking, and I felt as if I was going to scream or cry or pass out. I felt like a boulder had smashed me in the stomach.

I finally asked, "Do you think Mike has your gun?"

"I don't know, but it's missing," he replied. "And there's something else I better tell you." *Dear God, could this get any worse?* "When the police came ... I ... uh, my girlfriend was here, and ... we were ... smoking some pot. I got charged." I couldn't believe I was actually relieved it wasn't more bad news about Mike. "I just thought I should tell you, Mama Hen."

"I'm sorry." I didn't know what else to say. "If you hear from Mike, call me immediately." He said he would, and we hung up.

I looked at Ben, and he looked as confused and worried as I felt. Mike with a gun? And why were the police looking for him? What had he done? Of all the times I was filled with worry, none compared to this. Our son was not violent. What in the world was going on inside this young man? For all the trials we had lived through with him, this just did not make any sense. *Is he so afraid of going to jail that he would …* *no I will not let myself go there. He wouldn't do that.* Though I tried to fight my own thoughts, his behavior had been so self-destructive I could not totally push away the horrible thought that he might have taken the gun to end it all. I just knew he did not have it within him to physically harm someone else. He *would not* do that.

I don't know how much time passed, but it seemed like an eternity. My imagination was filled with horrible images. I kept reminding myself that the naltrexone implant should still be working. Heroin would have no effect. *Should I call the police?* I was about to ask Ben what he thought when the phone rang, and I answered with a weak, "Hello?"

"Mom, it's me. I know I'm late, but I'm on the way home."

A calmness came over me as I spoke slowly and evenly. "Mike, where are you?"

"I'm on the way home," he repeated. *What do I tell him? Do I tell him the police are looking for him? What if that scares him away?* We needed for him to come home. We needed to know what was going on!

"Good; you come home, Son." My own voice sounded very strange. *I have to know.* "Mike, the police were at the river looking for you. Jordan told them his gun was missing. Do you have it?" I held my breath.

"No, Mom, I don't have his gun. We can talk when I get home. Okay?"

"Okay, Son. Be careful." I hung up the phone and felt a full range of emotions. I was mostly relieved to have talked to Mike. At least some of the most horrifying pictures I had conjured up in my imagination were not true.

We were literally pacing the floor. I noticed a security patrol from our gated community circle our neighborhood twice. Mike pulled into the drive. He came into the house and headed for the stairs.

"Whoa, Mike, we have to talk." I was filled with questions that needed answers.

"I know. Just let me jump in the shower, and I'll be right down."

"Why are the police looking for you? Mike, what have you done? *Where have you been?*" *Stay calm. You are shouting again.*

He was already up the stairs. Ben was by my side at the foot of the stairs. We heard the shower start. I guess this conversation was going to be on Mike's terms. I looked out the glass front door and saw the security car pass by again. *Strange.* I had a million questions, and only Mike could answer them.

Fairly quickly Mike came down the stairs in clean jeans and a T-shirt. And he was ready to talk. He came into the sunroom where we were waiting.

"I used cocaine."

"Oh, Mike, why … why would you do that?" The agony was evident in my voice.

"Mom, you wouldn't understand. I was really scared this morning and I …"

Ben exploded. "That's just great, Son. After we went through all that shit to get the Naltrexone implant, you managed to go around it by using cocaine? Great way to show you're really trying to stay clean. Just fucking fantastic." Ben was so angry. I don't know if the source of his anger was fear. If so, he must have been scared nearly to death because he was so furious.

"Pop, before you blow your top, I better tell you the rest of it."

Oh God, there was more. Was this why the police were looking for him? Can we stand any more?

"I tried to get money at a Burger Stop. I pawned some of your stuff to get money for my first buy, but I wanted more, and I didn't have money." He stated it calmly and factually. "Nobody got hurt … I wouldn't do that, and I didn't get any money. It was almost like a joke. I was just stupid. Totally stupid."

I was incredulous. This was not believable. He went on to give us the details and ended by saying that someone probably took down his license number, and he would guess that was the reason the police were looking for him. I am seldom speechless, but I couldn't find my voice, and my mind was trying to comprehend what he had just said.

I finally muttered, "What about Jordan's gun?"

He looked confused for a minute then replied matter-of-factly, "Oh, I pawned that several weeks ago. I did it before the Naltrexone implant. Mom, I swear I've been clean since then … until today. I swear."

"Son, you need to turn yourself in." My voice was dead.

This would be the felony charge we had tried so hard to avoid. Would this send him to prison? Could he possibly fight this charge? What should we do? *Oh God, give me strength.*

I was standing in the sunroom looking out into our dimly lit yard, when I saw movement outside in our shrubs. *What was going on? Were the police coming to the back door? Why would they do that?* I opened the patio door and stepped out. Out of the dark emerged a man dressed in all black with his gun aimed *at me.* I instinctively put my hands up. "Don't shoot," I croaked. I could hear my heart pounding in my ears.

"Is your son inside?" he asked in a low-pitched deadly serious voice.

"Yes, he is." I answered. *Stay calm.*

"Is he armed?"

"He is not armed." *Just breathe.*

"Are you and your husband safe?"

"We are just fine." *I would feel better if you put that gun down.* "There is no danger. He is right here." Again that calm response came from somewhere within me.

Mike was easily visible through the open door. "Place your hands on your head, and don't move," came the command to Mike as two others in black emerged from the shrubs. I think I still had my hands up.

Mike immediately complied. They entered through the patio door and handcuffed our son, right there in our sunroom. He was totally cooperative and answered their few questions respectfully. The officer said he would be arraigned in the morning, and we could post bail. Then they led our son to one of several police cars and drove him away.

Five law enforcement vehicles with their red lights blinking were on the main road of our gated community, and two neighborhood security vehicles with green lights running were parked directly in front of our home. I remember having the rather hysterical thought given the circumstances, *Gee, it looks like Christmas with all those red and green blinking lights!* It certainly didn't feel like Christmas or any other holiday. Maybe I was in shock.

I sat on our steps and put my face in my hands and cried. Our female neighborhood security officer put her hand on my shoulder and tried to comfort me. She actually apologized for the neighborhood security's role in the arrest. They had been alerted to be on the lookout for Mike if he returned home through the gates. They were warned he could be armed and dangerous, so they complied. I assured her I understood. But our son had not been armed and dangerous. He had just been scared of going to jail and had made some very terrible and stupid decisions that he would regret forever.

So there I was again, sitting on some steps feeling as if I had been punched in the gut. This was way beyond when I cried as he left on his eighteenth birthday, but it rivaled when I sat on my brother's steps and cried hysterically when I first discovered the heroin in Mike's bag.

I felt totally exhausted and emotionally drained. It had been a difficult morning with the ordeal at the jail, and then Mike not coming back home, followed by the phone calls, and topped off with the SWAT team. And once again I had the sickening fear of losing our son.

Both Ben and I moved through the house like zombies. I was beyond tears. I simply couldn't believe what had happened, yet I knew it was real.

Later that night I called my brother. He was filled with concern and overwhelming disappointment. This time it was hard for him to say anything that could make me feel any better … and my little brother was wise enough to know that. I was comforted by his love, and it didn't require words.

Chapter 28

After the Felony

*M*ike spent the night in jail. He was arraigned the next morning. We were not going to bail him out nor were we going to pay for a lawyer. He got a court-appointed lawyer. We were finished paying for lawyers and trying to keep his record free of a felony. I guess we finally figured out we couldn't prevent it. It was a horrible feeling of failure for me and perhaps even more so for Ben. Yet it was still difficult to refuse to bail him out—but not that difficult.

He could make calls from the jail, and he did. He kept asking us to come bail him out, and we kept refusing.

We did go to visit Mike a few days later on visiting day ... only to be told he had just left. "What? How could he do that?" I was incredulous. That made no sense.

"He left here just a few minutes ago in a big black garbage bag," the officer told me with a hint of a smile and a shake of his head.

That made even less sense. Then I was told he had called a bail bondsman, who had agreed to post his bail. "Why would a bondsman do that? Mike has no money to pay him."

"Sorry, ma'am, you'll have to ask the bondsman. I have to say, that's the first time I've ever seen a guy go out of here in a garbage bag. It was pretty funny."

I wasn't laughing. "How do I get hold of the bondsman?" Ben asked him, with no humor.

"There's a list of numbers posted by the booking window. Probably one of those guys," he answered with a more sober expression on his face.

The person who had taken the bail told us which bondsman it was, and we quickly called his office. We were told Mike had been bailed out with the promise of surrendering the title to his truck. We were stunned.

He had made a phone call from the jail, got the bondsman to come get him, and put on a garbage bag for clothes and walked out of the jail. They had taken Mike's clothes and put him in a jail jumpsuit the night he was taken there. I was dumbfounded to find out that he had been released and even more shocked to find out he had offered the truck title as collateral. We had already determined he would sell the truck to pay us back. Quickly Ben made the decision to stop that transaction. We phoned that office back; they gave us the bondsman's cell phone number, and we called. Mike was with him, and they were on the way to get the title. They turned around to meet us at the office.

Now what? We paid the bondsman so the truck would not be in his hands. What were we going to do with Mike? He had been bonded out, so we couldn't exactly take him back to jail. I think we would have if we could have.

He already had an answer for that too. He was to report back to jail in the other county the next day and that's what he was planning to do—go serve his forty days. He asked if he could spend the night at our house. And once again he told us how sorry he was for what he had done.

153

Which thing was he apologizing for this time ... the SWAT team, the truck ... the golf clubs ... what? His apologies were wearing extremely thin.

This was beginning to feel insane for me. We missed the first appointment time for him to go serve the forty days. He was so scared about the prospect of going to jail that he used cocaine, made a halfhearted attempt to commit a robbery, got caught, and now the end result was that he was choosing to go spend his forty days in *jail? What was I missing here when it comes to his logic? This is my extremely intelligent son again doing something so unbelievably illogical.*

A part of me was actually filled with relief. How much could he get into if he was locked up? What a horrible thought to have about your own child. But then he wasn't exactly a child anymore. He was a very troubled young man, hanging on the edge of total disaster. I had been told more than once an addict had to hit rock bottom before he would want to turn things around. *Please, God, let this be his rock bottom!* I thought I hit mine ages ago.

That afternoon before he was to go to jail the next day, he asked me to take him to see Paul, the young minister at church. He called and made an appointment, and I drove him there. I asked if he wanted me to wait in the car, and he asked me if I would come in with him, which I did.

As I listened, I heard our son be as open and honest as I had ever heard him. He readily admitted he was scared. He knew he had wronged his friends and family and himself. Paul was so good with him. He reassured Mike he would come visit him, and that seemed to give Mike great comfort.

I knew Mike was an expert at putting up a good front, and he was able to pull the wool over my eyes time and time again. But this was my son opening himself up in a way I had not seen. I don't know that I had ever seen Mike that vulnerable. While it made me sad, it also gave me encouragement, something I desperately needed.

The next day, I took Mike to the jail. This was nothing like the larger jail he had just bailed himself out of the day before. This one in the adjoining county wasn't so intimidating. After all we had been through, I was still glad this jail wasn't so bad. *Really?* Maybe he needed intimidating!

We made no stops on the way, and I made certain we were there twenty minutes early. The same jailer was there from the week before and acknowledged he was glad to see we made it on time. Even with all that had just transpired in the past week, it hurt to see Mike go through the door that would lead to his cell, where he would live for the next forty days. I smiled and waved and assured him I would come visit and write between visiting days. There was no anger left in me at that moment. I was still writing as a form of my own therapy.

We went to visit Mike on Saturday. He looks good. How unbelievably sad to visit your son in jail. My comfort is that he is alive. He could be in intensive care or dead. My heart aches with the pain of all of this. He must see the light and turn his life around now. I go crazy thinking about all the things that might happen to him. To know that I truly have no control is frightening beyond words. Strangely, there is some peace in knowing that he is safe for now. A mug shot is better than a morgue shot. When I think of the future, I can go crazy with worry, so I am trying to get through each day.

I wrote a letter to Mike that was more personal than many. I think I was beginning to deal with some of my own issues finally and working to get on my own different street, a move that was long overdue.

Monday, February 19, 2001

Dear Mike,

I still have not heard from your lawyer. I will try to call tomorrow since today is a holiday. I just want to be sure she knows you are in the other county jail so she doesn't think you will just show up on the 28th in court. We have left that message several times.

Not to dwell on negative or past but—I want you to know that if there were things that we have done that have contributed to the unhappiness that took you down the wrong street, then I am truly sorry. I will tell you that we have always loved you son. You were the answer to so many prayers.

As a parent, you do what you think is right at the time and there is no doubt that mistakes are made along the way. I don't think any parent can know what is best for their child all the time. That's just how life is. I can think of things that my parents did that were hurtful, or that I didn't understand, but I always knew they loved me and that was the key. It is strange though how we react to parents. I always knew that I had Daddy's unconditional love and I was never that sure about Mom.

One thing about growing up with my kind of parents— where they used high expectations and the fear of disappointing them as motivators, I got a big dose of guilt. Feeling guilty about not pleasing your parents is a draining emotion. In truth, I was a pretty good kid and not a bad adult. Wasting emotion on feeling guilty over mostly petty things that my mother picked on was non-productive.

It's a year ago next week that Nanny died. I miss her. Even though she did some goofy things and sometimes drove me crazy, I loved her and she loved me. I forgive her for "mistakes" I thought she made. She was a good woman trying to do her best. She loved <u>you</u> unconditionally. Even now, I'm sure she would make a thousand excuses for anything you have done—and would probably blame me. I'm not going to do that—make excuses for you, because I don't think it is helpful. I do hope however, that you will give some serious thought to getting some professional help with dealing with whatever it might be that you feel you need drugs to cover up. If using drugs is a symptom, then it is important to also address the cause.

Wishing you health and happiness with all my love,

Mom

XXOOXX

Looking back on this letter, it was interesting how I acknowledged that my mother would have made excuses for Mike and blamed me. I went on to say I would not make excuses for him. I didn't go on to say I wouldn't blame myself. Feeling guilty is a heavy burden to carry and doesn't solve anything.

Chapter 29

I Start Asking Questions

I started seeing a counselor on my own. My frustrations were reaching a point of critical implosion. I was lost and didn't know what to do. Ben was not interested in seeking counseling with me, and I knew I needed professional help with or without him. We had seen a counselor for a short time in the past, and he didn't see much value in it. I had tried going to a Naranon meeting and came out feeling more frustrated and frantic than when I went in the door. Another mother was there talking about dealing with her son's drug issues, and he was thirty-eight years old. I didn't think I could survive this turmoil for that many more years! *I had to get on a different street.* Perhaps I just hit a bad time, but I didn't give it a second chance. That was probably a mistake. Naranon has helped scores of families.

One night when I was filled with worry, I got up, sat at the computer, and started writing. I really didn't know where this story was going when I started. I just let myself write. It was a moment of enormous clarification for me.

JUST A STORY

There once was a young man I loved and I cared deeply about his happiness and well-being. It was my job to teach him how to care for himself and tend his garden. But his garden was a terrible mess. So I cut his grass and tried to tend his garden for him. He said he was sorry and he knew he was neglectful, and he went on his way. And I worked some more to try to clean things up for him. I tried to engage him in conversation or write him notes with comments about the importance of being vigilant to guard against those darn weeds.

I tried to set a good example by keeping my garden clean and tidy. How can I best help? I have done his work for him, thinking his sense of responsibility would kick in. I think if we get his garden all cleaned up, he will take pride and want to keep it that way.

I find myself doing a lot of the work or paying to have it done. He makes a stab at cleaning up the yard, and I applaud his efforts, but the weeds and brambles have taken a pretty strong hold.

I thought God wanted me to be helpful and nurturing. I realize this young man is crippled in a way because I have spent so much effort in tending to his lawn and garden that he hasn't had to learn to do it for himself and he probably never will if I continue to do it for him.

I pay for him to go to a gardening school. He comes back refreshed and ready to have a beautiful lawn.

He tells me he is sincerely sorry he let his garden become such a mess. He swears he will fight the brambles, but the very next week he's playing right in the middle of the brambles again. The sharp thorns are tearing away at this wonderful young man and yet he seems oblivious. Doesn't he know how dangerous that is?

He doesn't want my help. I will try to let him tend his own garden. I offer tools to help. He toys with the rake. He ignores the shovel. And he takes things from my garden. The brambles are growing rampant. I can't get to the porch anymore, much less inside. He comes out into the mess that surrounds where he lives. I see him and my eyes fill with tears.

The brambles have scratched him and he is pathetic and thin with dark circles under his eyes. I feel so guilty that I didn't realize he was so sick. I find a doctor and he tells him he must stay out of the brambles or he won't survive. And I know now that indeed, this young man that I have loved with all my heart may die. And I fall to my knees, broken and shattered and consumed by fear. And in that moment of unbearable pain there is a great revelation.

I know I can always love him, but I cannot save him. That is between the young man and God. As I raise my tear stained eyes, and look around me, I see ... my own garden has been neglected.

I sat at my computer and cried. I had finally acknowledged to myself that I was the enabler. That story may not have made any sense to anyone but me, but it was the moment I finally knew in my heart that not only could I not save my son, but my efforts had actually crippled him.

Chapter 30

Probation Again

$\mathcal{M}$ ike spent his forty days in jail, and indeed that took care of his obligation instead of staying on probation for his last offense. However, he now had another court date that was even more serious. The attempted robbery was a felony charge, and with his track record, there was a distinct possibility he could be sent to serve more time behind bars.

The court-appointed lawyer was very candid with us in her opinion that jail time was a distinct possibility. She also felt strongly that Mike was a very intelligent young man with a lot of positive potential.

Positive potential. That was such a good description for our son. As I look back on this journey, I never once lost faith in his positive potential. He was a wonderful young man with a heart of gold. He was clever and creative, warm and compassionate, and yet he had made some terrible choices. If he could just get off this street that kept leading to self-destruction, perhaps he could realize that positive potential.

There we were again in that courtroom waiting to hear our son's fate. When the decision was made, it was a very mixed blessing. We were relieved when he got probation but crushed that it was on a felony charge. So much of what we had done along the road was to avoid that scar that would stay with him forever. Even after all our efforts to protect him from this fate, we realized we couldn't protect him from the consequences of his awful decisions. This hole felt so familiar. We had made bad decisions too.

So Mike was on probation again. The irony of that would have been laughable if it hadn't been so ridiculously sad. He wanted to get out of probation, so he agreed to go to jail, but he was so afraid of jail that he used cocaine and committed a felony, which got him back on probation!

We walked out of court, and Mike again had great resolve to get it right this time. He was determined to get his associate's degree from the community college and then transfer to a university. Again, this sounded like a good plan, but we had heard good plans before ... several times.

Mike made the decision to move into Stone Manor, the halfway house. He could walk to classes at the college from there. He was wise enough to know he needed a structured environment and a good support team if he was to have any chance of overcoming this monster.

Would the monster addiction ever be gone? Was I ever going to be able to go to bed at night and not worry about Mike?

Through all of this turmoil and Mike's bad decisions, there was always that good and warm lovable young man inside of him. I saw it and felt it. I wanted his pain to go away. I wanted this addiction to go away. I desperately wanted our son to be happy. I wanted us all to just be happy. But I couldn't tend the garden of Mike's life. It was his garden. I finally was beginning to understand how important it was for him to become independent and strong enough to deal with his issues. That wasn't going to happen if I kept trying to "fix" it for him.

I was not in control. I could not wave a magic wand and sprinkle happiness over all of us. Intellectually, I got it. Emotionally, I could not walk away from Mike. Fear kept a grip on my heart, and, consequently, I kept a grip on his hand. He was our son, and I was afraid to let go.

Chapter 31

Homeless Shelter

*M*ike's decision to move into the halfway house was a good one. He was actively involved in AA meetings on a regular basis and was working closely with a sponsor on a twelve-step program. He had established trust and a good reputation there. He was offered the night manager position, which helped offset his rent. He had a part-time job at a nice downtown restaurant, and he was seeing a counselor. He was still in school. It was one of those times when things were looking better for him ... again. He had been clean and sober for nine months. He was sticking to his rules of probation. But once again, it did not last.

I got a call from one of his friends asking where Mike was. "He's at Stone Manor downtown," I answered. *He knew where he lived. Why would he call here with a question like that?*

"I just called, and they said he doesn't live there anymore."

"Are you sure? That must be a mistake." *Of course Mike lived there. He worked there.*

"No, ma'am, he isn't there anymore."

There was silence on the line. I had no idea what to say. I was stunned. Finally, after the long awkward pause, I quietly said, "I don't know where he is then." I hung up the phone and just stood there. I don't know how long I was frozen in place as I just kept thinking, *Not again, not again, please, God, not again.*

I told Ben about the call, and we both came to the conclusion that something had definitely gone terribly wrong. About that time the phone rang, and it was Mike.

"Mom, can you come pick me up?"

"What do you mean? Where are you? What happened?"

"I had to leave the house. They were going to drug test me, and I told them not to bother."

"Why did you do that?"

"Why do you think? Because I'm not clean, Mom. I would have tested positive." He had that edge of frustration in his voice, but it was nothing compared to what I felt.

"Oh, Mike … no. How could you. Why?" I knew I wasn't going to get an answer. But the question of *why* would never stop hounding me.

"Will you just come, Mom? Please."

I just stood there with my head down. Ben walked in. "It's Mike. He used again, and he left before they tested him," I told Ben. He just shook his head in disgust.

Mike's voice came through the receiver, "Mom, *Mom*, are you there? Will you come get me?"

I took a deep breath. "No, Mike, I'm not coming. We told you what the rules are, and if you used, you can't come home." *I said the words. I said the words. I told him he couldn't come home. Oh God, I said the words!*

"Mom, what am I supposed to do? I don't have anywhere to go." He sounded hurt and fragile.

"You will just have to figure it out, Son. You should have thought about that before you decided you could use again." I felt anger starting to boil up in me. Was it the same anger that is born of fear? I didn't know. I was just very angry and disappointed and tired of this merry-go-round.

And I finally understood my attempts to rescue him were not helping him. He had to realize the consequences of his actions.

"Thanks a lot, Mom." He hung up.

I looked at Ben, and he put his arms around me, and we just stood there for a long time. Later that night I went to my refuge, the computer, and tried to sort out my thoughts and feelings. I continued to write over the next few days. Those entries told the story as it happened.

3-10

My heart is breaking. I feel like the ceiling is falling on my head. I don't understand. I am so quiet and still like there is no air to breathe. I'm scared too. I feel helpless. I don't know what to do. Our son has taken the wrong trail again. Will this ever stop? Ever? It hurts so much. Does he have any idea how this hurts? Is he as scared as I am? He said he was scared. He always is——after the fact. Is this what his life is all about—traveling from one scared time after another, hoping each time that it will be the last. How can we shut the door in his face? Is that what we have to do to teach him about consequences of bad decisions? Is this a bad decision on our part? I need God to help me know the answer. I want to call to see if he is still at the house. I want to reach out to him. Is that just repeating the old mistakes? If he's not alive tomorrow will I ever be able to forgive myself? God please give him strength to come out of this a stronger person.

He's not at the house. Was that God's handiwork, letting me know that he is no longer there by a phone call from someone else that just tried to reach him there only to be told, "Mike doesn't live here anymore." It's going to be cold tonight. He's resourceful enough to find shelter. Will he make wise decisions now or will he just compound his troubles? *God help him, please.*

I hate this. I hate feeling helpless. But I can't feel hopeless. Can't we reach out and love him even if we hate what he does? Would we turn a sick person out into the night? He is sick and we have refused him a place to sleep. That feels so wrong.

If there is to be change, then maybe we have to change too and every time in the past we have embraced him, taken care of him and maybe that is not what he needs. God help me know what he needs us to do. I do not know. I do <u>not</u> know. I'm going to go pray now. I need help to make it through this cold night.

3-11-02

He had the lady call me from the shelter last night to say he was ok. That was very considerate of him. I was able to sleep—finally.

So I rescued him again today—sort of. I went down and picked up his clothes from the halfway house. He slept in the shelter for the homeless at a church. My child, my bright, cultured, worldly young man slept on a mat on the floor with the homeless. He's there again tonight. The Salvation Army shelter where he plans to move won't take him till he can drug test clean. And he can't—yet. It would have been so easy to let him sleep here. I wanted to—well part of me wanted to. That soft, caring, enabling Mother part. The tougher logical part ruled. It said "Just say no!" AND I DID. But I bought his dinner and he came here and took a shower and wrote his letter for a grant to go back to school in May. Was that bad? Should I have shut him out totally?

We took a walk on the beach. He told me I was his only friend, and Ben and I are the only people who care about him, except maybe Russ and Jackie and Hunter. He's a lonely, sad figure walking on the beach. My heart hurts for him.

I told him I would take him to the campus tomorrow to turn in the papers. He left them here. They would have gotten wrinkled if he had taken them with him in his book bag. Well, they would have, because he will have to use that for a pillow tonight—at the homeless shelter—on the mat—on the floor … of the homeless shelter.

They stole his billfold there last night—at the homeless shelter, so I gave him ten dollars. I hope he doesn't use it to buy more drugs. So I rescued him again—sort of. I should have had him take care of his own papers. And I shouldn't have given him the money.

3-12-02

He was here today working with Ben in the yard. It seemed so silly to put him in the car to go sleep at the homeless shelter downtown after he had been here all day. So we didn't. He slept here. How could that be so wrong? Was that the wrong thing to do? Maybe. Did we take a step back toward the same street with the hole in the sidewalk? Probably.

3-13-02

He's still trying to get into the Salvation Army. Stayed here again. He has an appointment in the morning and it will be more convenient if he is here. At least that's what we told ourselves. Tough love is so hard! We're going to leave town to go to Tahoe in two days. How can I leave him if he still has no place to stay? God this is so hard. Should we cancel our trip?

3-14-02

Left him at the Salvation Army tonight. He finally tested clean so they took him in. I had to leave to go play a tennis match. I felt an awful dread in the pit of my stomach as I drove away while he was being processed. Cried all the way to the tennis match. We are leaving on a 6 AM flight in the morning to go to Tahoe for two weeks. I actually dread this. But to stay here to try to "save" Mike is not the answer either. How many times has he said HE HAS TO BE THE ONE TO DO THIS? I cannot do this for him. This is between Mike and God.

The next morning we got on the plane and flew to Reno, picked up the rent car and drove on up to our condo at Lake Tahoe. Our friends Dennis and Margaret were coming out to stay and ski with us. My heart wasn't exactly in the trip, after leaving Mike at the Salvation Army shelter, but I knew it was important to "tend to my own garden." I felt so pulled in so many different directions by so many different emotions. I felt an awful dread, and again, my intuition was right. This was my journal entry of what happened next.

Recollections

We were on the way to pick up ski equipment with Dennis and Margaret. Something told me to call our home phone to pick up messages. Mike had left a message. He had tried to buy drugs and was hit on the head in the process and picked up by the police. He was in jail. It was bad enough when we left and he was living at the Salvation Army shelter. Now he was living in the county jail.

Now what do we do? We didn't go ski. We felt totally miserable and totally helpless. We were across the country … on vacation … and Mike was in jail. I had to try to get hold of him. I called the jail, but they wouldn't let me talk to him of course. He had used his one free phone call when he left me the message. He could call out, but it would be a collect call and I had no way to accept a collect call in Tahoe. I called Rob and Beth and she arranged to go see him and leave some money for him. What a thing to have to ask your friends to do.

We arranged for her to have him call her collect on her home phone, and then she could call me on her cell and be the go between. We were even able to have her hold her phone to her cell phone and I could actually talk to Mike. He was pathetic, sad and of course, sorry. He wanted out. Sorry! He would have to stay there at least until we got home.

What a miserable situation ... again. I had to have a day to myself. I went and sat by the lake and cried and prayed. I felt such overwhelming sadness. I was so lost. I just knew I loved my son and I didn't want him to die and I didn't want him to be tormented forever by his addiction. I was filled with fear and anger, but mostly with sadness. I knew I couldn't answer my own questions ... I had asked them so many times. Why? WHY!? What can we do? What is driving Mike to do this self-destructive behavior over and over? Did we do something terribly wrong along the way? I'm sure we have not been perfect parents. I know I cannot walk away and leave him. I can't give up.

We have to change what we are doing. So many dreams have been shattered. We honestly have only wanted Mike to be happy and healthy and self-sufficient. Is that so much to ask? I guess it is for now.

We spent the remainder of our time at Tahoe, and I was miserable. There were moments when we would forget and be able to relax and enjoy time with our friends, but it never lasted long. They were dealing with some issues with an older daughter involving drugs and alcohol. We were haunted by the knowledge that Mike was sitting in jail because he had tried to buy drugs ... *again*! I just wanted to go home, yet I dreaded going there and facing another crisis with Mike.

Beth continued to keep us posted and accepted Mike's calls. She and Rob cared about Mike and about us. They had always been there for the good times and the bad. We knew we were so blessed to have such wonderful friends.

We came home, Mike was released, and his probation was tightened. He now had a curfew, and he had to check in more frequently with his probation officer. He was very lucky that was all that happened. He had nowhere else to go, so we let him move back in with us temporarily until he could move on the campus of the university. He enrolled in summer school, moved on campus, and applied for a student loan for the fall semester. We were trying to let him take the responsibility for his future.

Again, he was sorry for his actions and readily admitted his wrongdoing. He so desperately wanted to get it right. He didn't want to be dependent on drugs, but he was.

Looking back, it shows how inconsistent we were in how we responded to Mike's actions. We refused to let him come back home when he used drugs while living at the halfway house. I had the courage to tell him no. But then we let him move back in after he was picked up by the police for buying drugs a few weeks later. However, that living arrangement was only going to be temporary because he was going to move onto campus for the summer session. It was easy to make excuses for our decisions. *I think we just fell back into the hole in our sidewalk.*

Chapter 32

The Phone Call

*P*eyton, his neighborhood buddy from high school, had gone off to Auburn University the year Mike had come home from NC State. She pledged Delta Zeta, the national sorority I had joined in college in Missouri. She was a music major and had a glorious singing voice. For several reasons, she dropped out of school and came home a year or two later. Her grades hadn't been great, and I think she missed home. By that time we had moved out of the Magnolia Hall neighborhood where she lived. We still had some contact with her parents, as Ben played tennis with her dad, and I played in a bridge group with her mom.

After Peyton moved back, she joined an acting workshop that was held at my house. She was the youngest participant, and we all felt like surrogate mothers to her. She had always held a special spot in my heart, and it was fun to reconnect with her.

Peyton was working at a local restaurant, was going to school at the community college, and had moved in with a couple of other girls. Then she discovered a troublesome boil-like growth at the base of her spine. After a trip to a local doctor, she was sent to Sloan Kettering in New York City for further diagnosis and treatment.

Mike had just started dating one of Peyton's roommates when she told him about Peyton's trip to Sloan Kettering, where she had been told she had stage four soft tissue sarcoma. The cancer had spread to other locations in her body. The prognosis was not good. It was heartbreaking news.

Mike came in one afternoon, and I knew something was on his mind. I put my book down in my lap and motioned to a chair. I could somehow sense he was in one of his rare moods to talk.

"What's up, Mike? You seem distracted."

"Peyton is up in New York in the hospital with cancer. Mom, it's bad." He dropped his eyes to the floor. "Darcy says the chemo is really making her sick, and they don't know if she's going to make it."

"I knew it was serious. The reports I've been hearing are pretty ominous."

"I think I'm going to give her a call. What do you think?"

"That's a great idea."

"I don't even know if she wants to talk to me. And I really don't know what to say. I sort of lost track of her and ...," he paused and looked down at the floor.

"I bet she would love to hear from you," I told him with a smile. I had no idea if Peyton had kept up with Mike's journey down his broken road the past few years or if she would feel like talking to him, but I was glad to see the compassion in his eyes. He went in the office and dialed the number Darcy had given him on speaker phone.

It rang several times when a quiet voice said, "Hello."

"Peyton?"

"Yes, who is this?"

"It's Mike."

"Mike Henry? I haven't seen you for ages. What's going on?"

"I've been dating Darcy, and she told me about you being in New York … and all."

"Yeah. It's been a real bummer. They keep thinking I'm on the way out, but that's not happening."

"Are you feeling really bad?"

"Some days are better than others. I get really tired, and my hairdo is … uh, like no hair. I just do what I have to do."

It was so good to hear her voice and to know she still had a sense of humor. I couldn't help hearing the conversation as I sat in the living room. I thought about going into the kitchen where I wouldn't be able to hear, but I didn't. After all, he had used the speaker phone.

"Damn, Peyton, I'm really sorry," Mike said with concern in his voice.

"Thanks. So what's happening in your world? I really lost track. Do you see kids from school?"

"No, not much." I knew he didn't want to talk about his waning friendships. "I'm going to school again, planning to transfer to the university full time in the fall. Working some. So how long will you be there?"

"Good question. Till I get better or die, and I don't plan to die. They are throwing everything at me they have. I do chemo and radiation and anything else they think might help."

"That has to suck."

"Hey, nothing sucks like the alternative. I told you, I am not going to check out … not without doing everything I can. It's not gonna happen, Mike!"

"Good for you. You hang in there. Is there anything I can do for you?"

"Yeah, pray. And, Mike, live every day like it's a special gift. Don't waste it."

Her somber and serious words must have caught him off guard as it took him an extra moment to reply.

"Yeah, uh, sure," he managed to sputter back. There was a brief moment of awkward silence, and then I heard Peyton break in with her normal bubbly laugh.

"Hey, I didn't mean to get all serious on you, but you asked. So how are things with you and Darcy? She's a trip. She got you under control?"

His tone lightened too. "Hell, no. You know me, foot loose and fancy free to the end, darlin'. I shall be harnessed by no woman."

"Not till the right one comes along, and then you'll fall, and fall hard."

"Nah, not me."

I could hear her laugh through the speaker. "Hey I hate to cut this short, but I have to do some treatment stuff. I'm really glad you called. Will you call me again?"

"You bet I will."

"No, I mean really. I really want you to call again."

"Hey, Peyton, I said I would, and I will. You can count on it. You just keep doin' what it takes so you can get back here."

"Mike, you can bet *your* life that I am doing everything I can every day to save mine. I have so much I want to do. I will never give up … never."

"I'm right there with you on that."

He hung up, and the office was quiet for a few minutes. He came out and sat down in the chair across from me again. "Holy shit, Mom. She's fighting for her very life … every day. *Every* damn day! She told me to live every day like it was a gift." He just sat there thinking for a while.

I sat quietly with my book in my hands. I somehow knew this could be a turning point for our son. I just felt it in my whole being. He was facing a truth he had avoided for a long time. I suspect he couldn't help but draw the parallel of Peyton taking drugs that made her sick in her fight to save her own life, while he had become addicted to harmful drugs that could destroy his life. It was as if a light bulb went on in his head.

"Mom, I really want her to be okay," he said very quietly.

Mike's miracle didn't happen instantly. No lightning bolt jolted him into sobriety, but a seed had been planted, and that was the beginning. I will always believe God helped him dial the phone that day, and he reached his angel. And I will be forever grateful to a beautiful young woman named Peyton.

Chapter 33

She's Okay; He's Not

Mike continued to call Peyton in the following weeks. She finally came home from New York. Miraculously she had a clean scan and was finally released after a year of gruesome treatment for her stage four cancer. She came back home with a slimmer body, a shorter hairdo, and such a passion for life. She and Mike met up at Charlotte's Web, a favorite watering hole of the twenty-something's. Mike had recently decided he could drink in moderation. We were very skeptical, but it was his decision to make. His old drug buddy, Jack, was attending meetings regularly. He cautioned Mike that his decision to drink was a bad choice. Jack had been to the DART Cherry program that had been mentioned twice as an option for Mike. Jack was now clean and sober. I wasn't sure about Mike.

He finished his associate's degree at the community college with a 3.0 grade average and had enrolled in summer school at the university. He moved out of our house into a dorm on campus. He continued to spend more and more time with Peyton. They frequently came by our house and we enjoyed having them. The summer was going well, but I had big concerns about Mike's decision to drink, even in moderation.

He had done well in summer school, gotten a loan for the fall semester, and moved into a house with two other students as the fall semester was about to begin. He was still on probation.

Even though Mike looked like he was finally getting it together, my intuition was screaming red flags at me. Once again I was up in the night writing. My gut was telling me Mike was not finished with trouble. Some of it was intuition and some was observation. But the bottom line was I knew there was trouble ahead, and I didn't know how to stop the train heading for the wreck, and I was beginning to wonder if I should even try.

Worry and fear were haunting me. And the questions, the never ending questions, kept plaguing me. What role did we play in creating this problem, and, more importantly, what were we supposed to do now?

Aug. 20 2002

> Here we go again. Something is wrong. I don't know what. I just feel impending danger for Mike and see some of the old patterns reemerging. But I can't fall in the same hole. I'm tired of being afraid. How can I leave this street with the hole in the sidewalk when our only son is still approaching the same hole? God, stay with Mike. I have to try to leave this street because I have my own hole in this sidewalk. It may be the only way to change the old pattern. God be with him always. I think I have failed to do what I thought I was here for. Redirect me. I think I am lost.

Even though I knew something was amiss, we left for a trip back to Missouri for our fortieth high school reunion at the beginning of September. We returned home, and it was still hot and humid in North

Carolina. We turned down the air conditioner and started to unpack. I decided to try Mike again. I had tried to call him the day before on his cell phone and got no answer. I dialed his number and again no answer. That was strange since he normally answered his cell.

I finished unpacking and decided to call Peyton. "Hey, Peyton, we just got back."

"Hey. How was the trip?" she jumped in quickly.

"Fine. The reunion was fun, but riding on a float in the homecoming parade was sort of lame. Lots of family stuff as usual. Lordy, it's hot here."

"I know. It's been that way the whole time you were gone."

"Do you know where Mike is? I haven't been able to reach him for two days. Have you seen him?"

"Um … yes." There was silence. I was expecting her to say something else.

"Well, is he doing okay? It's strange that he doesn't answer his phone."

"Uh, yeah, I think he's doing okay." There was a long silence. When I didn't say anything she went on. "I saw him yesterday."

"Oh good." I was waiting again for her to say something more. But she didn't. "Well, if you see him, or he calls you, tell him to give us a call. He knows I'm a worry wart when I can't get hold of him." Somehow this conversation just had a strange feel to it.

"Okay, I'll do that."

"I'd appreciate it."

"Okay, bye," she hung up before I even had time to say good-bye.

That was definitely a weird phone call. Peyton always chatted on the phone, and she couldn't get off fast enough. That old nagging feeling started creeping into my conscious level. *What's going on? Did Mike and Peyton have a falling out? But if that happened, why wouldn't he answer the phone when I called? He's been very good about doing that when it was me on the caller ID. Should I get in the car, go by the house, and check on him? Stop. Don't go running over to his house because he didn't answer his phone for two days. Just stop.*

I could tell myself to stop, but that didn't make it happen. Again, the mother radar that is tuned to trouble was giving off strong signals that I couldn't ignore. I was heading into the bedroom to share my concern with Ben when the phone rang. *See, dummy, that's going to be Mike. I bet Peyton got hold of him and told him he better call me.*

I answered the phone fully expecting it to be Mike. It wasn't. It was Peyton.

"There's something I have to tell you," she said.

Uh-oh. "What is it, Peyton?" I asked as I bit my lower lip.

"I just couldn't lie to you. I felt awful when we hung up." Her voice was very quiet.

Now the alarm bells were sounding throughout my senses. "What's wrong, Peyton? Is it Mike?"

"I hate to tell you this. He's going to kill me, but I just had to call you back." Now she sounded a little frantic.

"Okay, Peyton, just spit it out. What's going on?" I was bracing myself for what was bound to be bad news.

"Uh …" *Come on, Peyton, I'm dying here. Whatever it is, just tell me.* "Mike is in jail." Her voice fell to almost a whisper.

"Oh no! Dear God! What on earth happened?"

"It's not as bad as you might be thinking." Well, if he was sitting in jail it wasn't anything good. "He violated probation."

"By doing what?" There were endless possibilities.

"When they came by to check, he wasn't in the house, and it was after curfew. He said he was next door helping some guys move a piece of heavy furniture."

"And they put him in jail anyway? Well that seems awfully damn picky. That little old lady in tennis shoes is one tough cookie." I was referring to Mike's current probation officer. In reality, she wasn't that much older than me, but it seemed an odd job for her. She looked like she would be more at home in the kitchen with a pretty apron baking homemade biscuits. "Didn't she check out his story?"

"Well, I think she didn't have much patience."

"No kidding. I know he is supposed to be in by nine o'clock, but if he was just next door helping somebody—"

She interrupted me, "But it was the second time."

"What are you talking about?"

"I had just bailed him out the day before for the same thing. They came by, and he wasn't home after curfew. They came back and put him in jail. He called me, and I put up his bail money. Then it happened again last night. I just can't put the money up again. He's going be so mad that I told you, but I thought I really had to tell you." She sounded miserable.

"Peyton, you did exactly the right thing. I really appreciate you telling me. And you certainly should not feel bad about not posting his bail. I'm just sorry you did it the first time. He owes you that money back."

This beautiful young woman who had conquered an almost insurmountable obstacle in her path did not deserve to be put through any sort of agony or worry concerning Mike's stupidity. My anger this time didn't come from fear that I could name. I was just plain mad that he had caused Peyton to be upset, and he had put himself in dire jeopardy. Didn't he know what this meant? He would now have to go back to court and take the consequences of his original charges. He had been warned about the importance of strictly adhering to the terms of his probation. *Oh, Mike, what have you done?* My heart sank. Was this never going to end? *Why do you insist on this endless self-destruction? Why were you not in the house two nights in a row by your curfew time?* Time and again I had pulled myself up and looked for anything positive to grab on to. I did not want to lose hope, but the rope was getting so frazzled that I was only hanging by a string. *Was this it, the infraction that would land him in prison?* Was he still using drugs? Was that why he was out after his curfew?

It was September 13, 2002. Our son was once again in jail. And this time we were not going to bail him out. No way. We could not pull him out of the hole he kept falling into. That was between Mike and God. Ben and I were finally walking down a different street.

Peyton wrote him a letter while he was in jail. She obviously shared our disappointment, this young woman who was indeed his best friend in the world.

Mike,

I thought this letter was going to be easy to write, but I was wrong. There are lots of things I want to say to you, but you've heard it before. Maybe I need to say it for my sake, so here goes. When I met up with you at Charlotte's Web, I never in a million years thought in a month's time I would care about you the way I do. This would all be so much easier if I just didn't care, but that's just not me. I hate the fact that you felt you had to lie to me. I can take a lot, but I can't stand being lied to. I know you are a strong and determined person. You would have to be Mike after everything you have been through. You know as well as I do that until you make up your mind you want to change, nothing will.

I have all the faith in you, but that isn't going to help enough. When I got sick I was given two choices. I think I told you this when you called me that first time

183

in New York. I could live or die. You are no different than me Mike. Your choice, life or death. I can't help you until you truly make up your mind.

I will not turn my back on you, not even for a minute. I pride myself on being a good friend and you are no exception! I am always just a phone call away. At the same time, I have to look out for my best interest. If you <u>EVER</u> lie to me again, we have nothing. Fool me once, shame on you. Fool me twice, shame on me. Please don't put me in that situation Mike. I am a forgiving person, but I am not a dumb one.

Don't underestimate my determination to see you through all this. Sure it is harder some days more than others, but you don't give up. If my doctors had taken that attitude, I would be dead. You aren't that much different than me. We both have been put in a less than pleasant situation. That's life, take it or leave it, but it is yours!

I gain strength from you as well. I think about you all locked up every day and it helps me to remember the gift I was given. It's just one more reason to appreciate every day. It helps me focus on the day at hand and not on what could happen. In case you haven't noticed I have issues dealing with the future. I am as scared as the next person, but I am working on it.

You were always asking me what "we were." I couldn't answer you and I still can't. But it should mean something to you that I am still here. You have given me the perfect out and I choose to put both feet in. So take that for what you will and know that "This too shall pass." I miss you every day. I got very used to you being around. I just know in my heart this time is going to be different.

Keep reading, keep writing and keep learning. When this is all over you are going to have so much to offer the world. You are a wonderful teacher, despite the fact that I am not such a great learner! I have learned more from you than you will ever know. I just like to *think* I learned it on my own. I know better.

Keep your head up and your spirits high. I am here. Will talk to you soon!

XOXO

Love,

Peyton

PS—Spelling and grammer don't count!

This was the kind of steadfast support Peyton was offering Mike at a time when he desperately needed a friend. She was holding out her hand and her heart.

Mike wrote a letter of withdrawal from the university. He would not be attending. He also now owed money back on his student loan. We made it quite clear this was his debt, not ours. *We* are on a different street. While we were not withdrawing our heart, we were trying desperately to withdraw our hand. There would definitely be no bail money.

Chapter 34

The Visit

We circled the block searching for a place to park. We had all been quiet for several minutes, alone with our own thoughts. Ben found a parking space about two blocks away from the jail. Parallel parking was always a challenge for him. He wasn't very flexible, and turning to look over his shoulder to see when and how much to cut the wheel seemed almost painful. On the third try he fit the car into the space, put it in park, and turned off the engine. We all sat in silence, not moving, and then Ben finally broke the uncomfortable silence.

"Well, let's go, if we're going to do this." He jerked open his car door and stepped out.

I looked at Peyton in the backseat. She looked so miserable. My stomach did a slow roll, and I reached out my hand to her over my seat. "Are you ready?"

"I guess." She slowly opened the door and slid out. I put my purse under the seat and got out of the car. I had second thoughts about leaving it there, as this was not the safest part of town. I pushed those thoughts away and locked the door. There just wasn't any room left in me for additional worry.

We walked toward the county jail, Ben in front and Peyton and I following. It was obvious we were not anxious to go inside the ominous red brick building that took up most of a downtown block. As we pushed open the glass door and went inside, there was a distinct "people odor." A combination of sweat, urine, and something like wet dog accosted our noses. We quickly turned left and punched the button for the elevator. Visitation was on the third floor. The enclosed elevator intensified the foul odors. Peyton made a strangled sound somewhere between coughing and gagging.

"Are you okay?" I asked her. She looked pale.

"I'll be okay. God, I don't know if I can do this." I put my hands on her shoulders and tried to get her to look at me. I was concerned about her. She really didn't look good, and she was breathing fast and shallowly. "Just give me a second," she said.

"Take your time. Do you need to go back outside? Get some fresh air?"

"No, I'm fine. Really," she protested. She definitely did not look fine as we exited the smelly box.

We were in the hall outside the elevator. We hadn't gone through the door to the visiting area yet. Ben had his hands on his hips and was staring at the floor. I knew this was killing him too. He was being very patient, but then he would have done anything for Peyton. There just wasn't anything we could do to make this any easier—for any of us.

Peyton had never visited anyone in jail, much less a close friend like Mike had become. Ben and I had visited Mike at the smaller jail in the other county but had not been in the visiting room of this larger jail, and it was on different terms this time. We all knew how serious the consequences could be when it came time for Mike to go to court.

"Are you ready?" Ben asked quietly.

Peyton took a deep breath, "Let's do it." She put a brave smile on her face and quickly took a swipe at the corner of her eye.

Ben pushed the door open, and we stood in front of a gray steel desk with a uniformed officer behind it. "Sign in here," he said dully, "and take a seat."

There were four rows of folding metal chairs. On two walls there were cubicles with thick glass separating visitors from the inmates. There was a black phone receiver in each space. That was how we would communicate. We took three chairs and waited. The current batch of visitors was just finishing their time. There wasn't much privacy as we sat in the chairs in the middle of the room. We could hear parts of the conversations as wives, mothers, and girlfriends talked into the phones. I noticed there were almost no men visiting. I knew Ben was dying inside, but I was so grateful he was there. How in the world had we ended up here in this brightly lit, dingy room waiting to speak to our only son on a phone, seeing him through heavy glass filled with fingerprints and grime? This was so much worse than the other county jail, where he had gone by his choice to serve forty days.

"Time's up. Return to your cells, and visitors need to vacate," came the announcement. "Next visitors, you are allowed thirty minutes." He then called out ten names. Mike was one of them. The inmates who had been sitting in the cubicles reluctantly said their good-byes and started clearing the area. Their visitors left the room. The next ten men were allowed into the narrow area on the other side of the glass. Mike was the fourth in line. The air caught in my throat when I saw him. *I will not cry. I will not cry.*

Peyton was trying to smile, and she waved her hand. Mike took his seat in the fourth cubicle and motioned for us to come. Only then did I realize we hadn't moved. I think I had been concentrating on just trying to breathe. Ben was the first to stand up, and we followed him. He reached for the phone and said, "Hello, Son."

"Hey, Dad." It felt like a lifetime ago when we had moved here, and that southern greeting of "Hey" was so unfamiliar. "It's great to see you guys. Thanks for coming."

Ben handed me the phone. *I will not cry!* "You look good," was all I could croak out, and that was such a lie! He looked horrible, thin and pale with dark circles under his eyes and wearing an orange jumpsuit of a jail inmate. No, he definitely did not look good.

"Hey, Mama, I love you. I'm so sorry."

"I love you too, Son." *I will not cry.* I handed the phone to Peyton and turned sideways. I was not going to win this battle against my tears.

"Let's give them a minute," Ben said. We stepped away. He knew I was about to lose it. "Not now," he said as he put his hand on my shoulder. "That won't help a damn thing."

"I know, I know," I whispered over the lump in my throat. I tried to make my breathing even and get control. I realized we had just walked away leaving poor Peyton on her own. I looked over, and she was smiling and talking into the phone. I could tell by the sparkle in her eyes that she had conquered the lump in her throat. What a trooper. And I had been worried she was the one who wouldn't make it through this ordeal. I should have known her strength.

She had her hand on the glass, and Mike put his palm on the other side, matching hers. Once again, she was giving him strength and hope. I was so grateful to this incredibly strong young woman.

We were able to visit on Saturdays and write letters, and Mike could call from jail at appointed times. We were waiting for his date in court to see what would happen, but it was hard to believe the consequences for his transgressions this time would not be severe.

Dear Mike

I will talk to Peyton tonight. Perhaps she can come with me Saturday. I'll let you know before you have to fill out your list on Friday night. She cares and she hurts for you.

We love you so much. These next few months will be difficult for all of us. Just know we want you to get your life back and for you to experience good things. It's time for that to happen. It will with perseverance, faith, and love. You are a good person who has made some rotten decisions. Just stay in touch with the goodness, help it grow, respect yourself and be truthful. Failure is an event, not a person. You are not defeated unless you stop trying.

I'll see you Saturday. Perhaps we will know a little more about what the courts have in store for you by then. Whatever the courts decide, you can handle it. The real decision is between you and God.

Love,

Mom XXOOXX

The waiting was a difficult time … for all of us. Knowing Mike was sitting there in jail filled me with all sorts of emotions. I was afraid, yet in many ways I was relieved. Was that awful … to feel relieved that your child is behind bars? I tried to keep his spirits up and send him words of encouragement. Those words were probably as helpful to me as they were to him. He actually shared the following with the chaplain, who printed it in the weekly jail newsletter.

PRIORITIES

I ASKED God to grant me patience. God said, No.

Patience is a byproduct of tribulations; it isn't granted, it is earned.

I asked God to give me happiness. God said, No.

I give you blessings. Happiness is up to you.

I asked God to spare me pain. God said, No.

Suffering draws you apart from worldly cares and brings you closer to me.

I asked God to make my spirit grow. God said, No.

You must grow on your own, but I will prune you to make you fruitful.

I asked for all things that I might enjoy in life. God Said, No.

I will give you life so that you may enjoy all things.

I ask God to help me Love others, as much as God loves me.

God said … Ahhhh, finally you have the idea.

Stop telling God how big your storm is.

Instead tell your storm how big your God is! Anonymous

You are never alone Mike. God is with you every step of the way. Make your heart and mind be still and in the calm He will comfort you. Daddy and I love you and we will never abandon you.

I wish I had magic words to make the pain and confusion less, but I don't. I fight tears constantly and yet I know tears will not help. There is a reason we are in this battle. I believe we will be stronger for enduring this pain and overcoming it with God's help. God is definitely bigger than this storm.

Love,

Mom XXOOXX

Chapter 35

Mike's Day in Court

*M*ike had been in jail nearly three weeks. He called us frequently, and we accepted the calls. He also wrote letters.

Mom and Dad,

I miss you guys a lot. I spend a few minutes each morning thanking God for the times we've had together, the ones I've just taken for granted. I also thank Him for my current situation which allows me to appreciate what I've had and will have in the future. It is such a blessing to be able to eat what you want, when you want, choose your roommate, be free on the water and in the sunshine. But I'm thankful for what I have now too. I wake up with ten fingers and ten toes and a mind that works. I spend a good amount of time thinking about my purpose in life—where I'm headed, what I want to do, how I'm going to become successful.

… I know God has a plan for me. I just wish he would reveal it soon.

… I know when you were my age you were well on your way. As ya'll have told me, I probably won't get there the conventional way, but I am determined. Sometimes I set goals that boarder on fantasy. I don't want to just be fit, I want to run all the way across the country.

… While serving God, I want all the creature comforts like you have earned, legally. I know I've miss used a lot of time. But I will get there.

Know that I long for home cooking, playing golf with Dad, and just mowing the yard. I miss you every day and I'm so sorry for the pain I've caused. Thank you for sticking with me. One day I'll make you proud. Hopefully it will be while you're still on this earth.

Eight days till court, three till visiting day.

Love,

He was still there waiting for his court date on his birthday. I would have never dreamed this is how our son would spend his twenty-sixth birthday. Peyton send him a card with an encouraging note.

Mike,

So we both know this birthday isn't going to be the best, but that just means we can look that much more forward to next years. You just keep your chin up and know I will be thinking of you, as I always do. Just think how much you are going to grow this year. Next year just has to be better. So, you stay strong and take one day at a time. And know that I am just a phone call away. Try to make the best of a <u>very bad</u> situation. Have a good day. I miss you.

XOXO Peyton

His day in court came a few days later. Once again we were sitting in a courtroom in the county courthouse. Ben and I took our seats on the wooden pew that was much like a church pew. As I sat there I closed my eyes and had my talk with God. *Please help us get through this day. I pray that whatever is the best thing that needs to happen for Mike, will happen. He is in your hands, and I accept that I am not in charge of what happens here today. Please help Mike know that he is loved and give him the strength to deal with whatever decisions are made in this courtroom.*

I no longer asked God for specifics or tried to direct His will. I asked for what was best for Mike and the strength to accept whatever that turned out to be. I had finally come to understand in my heart and mind who was in charge, and it was not me.

The judge entered the courtroom in his distinctive black robe. "All rise. Hear ye, hear ye …," the bailiff's voice droned with the words I had heard too often in the last several years. This time, like every other, I hoped it would be the last. Mike's court-appointed lawyer had talked with us the previous week. She wanted to prepare us for what she thought was going to be the probable outcome of Mike's probation violation. After talking with "the little lady in tennis shoes," she felt relatively certain Mike would be spending some time in the prison system, based on his original charges. That was gut-wrenching news, but not totally unexpected.

As on the numerous occasions I had sat on this wooden pew, there was no specific order in which inmates would be called before the judge, so we had to be there early and just sit and wait. We sat through the entire morning, and then a lunch break was announced. We left to get a bit of lunch. As we went out the courthouse doors and made our way through the horde of smokers puffing away, we finally got a breath of fresh October air. It was sunny with just a hint of fall. It's not unusual for coastal North Carolina to stay warm and humid into mid-October. We craved the infrequent cooler, drier days like this one. Mike had been sitting in jail for almost a month waiting for this day in court. I couldn't help but think how much he would have enjoyed being outside today, but then I had to push that thought from my mind.

We walked to a little café down the block from the courthouse and shared a sandwich. We talked about how tough and efficient the judge had been throughout the morning session. We finished the soda and slowly walked back to the courthouse. There was certainly no need to get back there one minute earlier than the appointed time to reconvene. Those benches were hard.

We took our same spot on the left side of the aisle. It was just like church, where the congregation sat in the same spot on the same pews Sunday after Sunday. How many times had I been in this courtroom sitting in this same pew? We stood again as the judge entered and took his place behind his raised "pulpit."

We sat through several more cases, and my backside was feeling the hardness of that bench as I witnessed the hardness of the judge. The next case was called. A young woman under house arrest had been caught riding horses with her boyfriend. She claimed she was applying for a job at the stables. The judge was not buying that at all. Her two-year-old was in the courtroom and started crying when the mother stood at the table with her lawyer. I assume the older woman holding her might have been her grandmother. I watched as she tried to bounce her on her knee and quiet the little girl. I had to wonder if I would ever get to be a grandmother. *God, I really want to have that opportunity. Stop. You are trying to direct what happens to suit your wants again.*

My thoughts were interrupted by the judge pounding his gavel loudly. "Please remove that child from my courtroom," the judge said firmly.

"See, judge, she needs me," the mother pleaded pathetically as she pointed to the distraught little girl.

Wham! The gavel was slammed down again by the judge, and the woman stopped pleading, and the grandmother stood and carried the child out as she was screaming "Mommy, Mommy," at the top of her lungs and reaching out her arms toward her mother and wiggling her tiny fingers. Everyone in the courtroom focused on that pitiful scene, and it was as if our collective hearts were painfully squeezed. The judge, however, was not moved.

He banged the gavel one more time as the door closed behind the crying child. "This courtroom is no place for young children to be used as an emotional ploy." He then proceeded to sentence the young mother to six months in the county jail. It was obvious he was angry.

I could only hope he would have a chance to cool down before Mike was called. If there was any chance for leniency I thought it just went out the door. As fate would have it, Mike's case was called next. Ben and I exchanged a look that said we were having the same thoughts about the judge.

Mike and his lawyer took their places behind the defense table. And then from somewhere appeared the "little lady in tennis shoes." Great! The judge still had steam coming out his ears; it was late in the afternoon, he was tired, and now that lady showed up. This was not good. *This is going to be bad. Take a breath, you're working yourself into a panic, and this is not the time.*

They did the preliminary exchange of paperwork, the judge took a moment to look over what papers were in front of him, and then he nodded at the table. The little lady stood up. Why did she have to talk first? Mike had obviously gotten on this woman's last nerve.

"Your Honor, it is true that Mike has violated his probation, and the charges against him are serious." *Here it comes.* "However, he is a very intelligent young man who has a lot of potential. He had just finished his associate's degree with above a 3 point grade average. He was enrolled for the fall semester at the university. He has one problem, and that is drugs. If we can get him some help to get the drugs out of his life, I believe this young man will be an asset to this community. He has a strong support system, and his parents are here in court today,"

I could barely believe my ears. This was absolutely the opposite of what I had expected to hear from this woman who had avidly pursued Mike and put him in jail on two consecutive days. It seemed to me Mike's lawyer looked surprised too, but who knows. Frequently deals are made outside the courtroom.

The judge nodded to the lawyer, and she concurred with the probation officer in her positive statements about our son. The judge asked if there was a recommendation. Once again the suggestion was the DART program, the state-run drug rehabilitation program.

"There is one within the prison system, is that correct?" the judge asked. My heart sank. They were still going to send him to prison.

"Yes, Your Honor, that is correct." The little lady paused. "However, I don't think that would be the best choice for this young man. I would recommend the DART program at Cherry outside the corrections system. I believe that would give him the best chance," she finished. *Oh my God!* She was actually making a case to keep Mike *out* of prison!

The judge took a few minutes as he looked over papers. I saw Mike's lawyer lean over to speak quietly to him. The judge addressed the lawyer. "Would your client be agreeable to that?"

"Yes, Your Honor, he would," she said without hesitation.

"There is often a wait to get into that program. I would suggest Mike remain behind bars until an opening is available. I assume he is willing to do that," the probation officer said.

Mike shook his head in the affirmative. *Yes! He understood the importance of where this is headed. Breathe.* "Yes, Your Honor," the lawyer responded.

The judge agreed to have Mike go to the DART program as soon as there was an opening. He would stay where he was until then. And then the judge spoke directly to Mike.

"Son, on the recommendation of your probation officer, I am going to give you this opportunity. If you mess this up, you will be serving your time in the prison system. I do not want to see you in my court again. Do you understand?"

Mike stood up. "Yes, sir, Your Honor, I understand. Thank you so much. You will not be seeing me in your court again."

The judge banged his gavel. And I started to breathe again. I watched as Mike gave his lawyer a brief hug, and then he turned to the little lady in tennis shoes. They just stood there for a moment looking at one another, and then Mike put out his hand to shake hers. She had a hint of a smile on her serious face, and she was saying something to him that I could not hear. I wanted to go hug that woman. Hopefully my prayers for what would be best for Mike had been answered, and this woman and the judge had made that happen. Blessings sometimes come from the least expected sources.

The lawyer motioned for us to meet her outside the courtroom. Mike turned and gave us a wave and a smile. He would be going back to the jail to await an opening in the ninety-day residential treatment program. He had already assured us that no matter what the outcome in court today, he was finished with drugs. As hard as we wanted to believe him, we had heard it before.

In the hall the lawyer explained what we had already heard in court. She thought the wait might be as much as three weeks but no more. We left the courthouse with lighter hearts and once again with renewed hope that maybe, just maybe, this would be the last time we would sit in that hard pew.

Chapter 36

DART Cherry

$\mathcal{M}$ ike had to wait another two weeks before he was notified there was an opening in the DART Cherry program. He was transported from the jail to Goldsboro and began his ninety-day stay. We were not allowed to visit or receive a call for the first three weeks. We could communicate by mail, and as I had done so many times before, I faithfully sent him letters regularly. He wrote often also. He started out with his same intellectual approach that kept him above the others in the program ... at least in his mind. As time passed, we were encouraged by his attitude and an obvious respect he felt for those in charge.

We received a letter from Mike telling us about one of his encounters with the counselors in charge of the program:

Dear Mom and Dad,

Thanks for sending the box. I really appreciate you taking the time to do that. You have always been there for me and I am so grateful for all you've done.

This place isn't so bad, at least it beats jail. I try to just mind my own business and do what I'm supposed to. We had an assignment to write a five page evaluation of the program as we experienced it so far. I just couldn't resist using my sense of humor and Mr. Mayton, the head of the program thought it was pretty good. He called me into his office, told me I obviously had a talent for writing and that he appreciated my humor. In fact he thought it was so "clever" that I should try again and this time write 10 pages. Guess he thought that was pretty funny too. I enclosed what I wrote the first time.

We have to take a course in employment preparation. Pretty basic and boring, but that fits. I am putting on some weight, but the food here sucks. My room is the size of a closet, but it's private. Actually, I'm sure at one time it was a closet.

I don't know when I can call or when you can visit yet. I will let you know.

Love, Mike

Mr. Mayton was a match for Mike. He was not going to let him intellectualize this experience. I thought his approach to Mike had been perfect. Mike came to have a great respect and admiration for him. We continued to exchange letters.

Dear Mike,

Sounds like you have a pretty full schedule. Hopefully the employment preparation will be helpful. Part of the key is to figure out where and how you can be gainfully employed. Maybe they have some helpful hints. You may have to take a whole new look at your path in life.

We really do appreciate your letters. Dad was highly entertained by your last one. He commented again on how good a writer you are. I will try to send more stamps in this letter. I guess I will close for now with a few thoughts.

Mike, I believe you have a great opportunity with each new day that dawns. Appreciate it for the opportunity that it offers.

I believe—that either you control your attitude or it controls you.

I believe—that our background and circumstances may have influenced who we are but we are responsible for who we become.

I believe—that no matter how good a friend is, they're going to hurt you every once in a while and you must forgive them for that.

I believe—that just because someone doesn't love you the way you want them to, doesn't mean they don't love you with all they have.

I believe—that you can be strong, long after you think you can't.

I believe—that sometimes the people you expect to kick you when you're down, will be the ones to help you get back up.

I believe—that maturity has more to do with what types of experiences you've had and what you've learned from them and less to do with your age.

I believe—that it isn't always enough to be forgiven by others. Sometimes you have to learn to forgive yourself.

I believe—that two people can look at the exact same thing and see something totally different.

I believe—we can change tomorrow by the decisions we make today.

Love, Mom XXOOXX

I couldn't resist trying to constantly pump Mike up with positive thoughts and probably an overdose of my philosophical ramblings. Maybe that was just another attempt at subtle control, but it was an improvement over much of my past enabling behavior.

Dear Mom and Dad,

Well another day is flying by. My feet are nice and wet now as I am getting into this routine here. It's funny how fast it goes by with a schedule to keep. We have classes most of the day. Most of the guys here grunt and groan at having to write or sit still for fifty minutes at a time. Not me. I stay away from the negative people. I only get involved when I absolutely have to, which is too often.

Right now I am sitting in this Employment Readiness class. The instructor is lecturing on the difference between listening and hearing. You should hear the answers given by these Einsteins. Seriously! I don't raise my hand.

I wrote Peyton and told her to call you about coming up with ya'll to visit. I should get a telephone pass on Monday and I will try to call you then if that's OK. Remember it's $10 per call so get used to letters.

I assume you voted Tuesday. Please send me any relevant local news. I miss you and crave some of Dad's good cooking. I'll write again soon.

Love you guys,

Mike, XXOOXX

We finally got to make a visit to Mike. Peyton went with us, and Mike seemed to be very happy to see all of us. The facility was "interesting" and the residents a unique mix of ages. It was difficult to see Mike in those surroundings, but I had to remind myself this was better than where he might have been. At least here we could hug him. His attitude seemed very positive, and he again assured us he was finished with drugs, and he intended to turn his life around. I wanted to believe that with all my heart.

Hi

It was sooooo good to see you yesterday. You really do look great. I gave thanks on the way home that you are doing well and have a positive attitude. I was also thinking about the blessing that Peyton is. What a beautiful person. She's a walking miracle. It's so easy to take things for granted. Like we've said before, when things are going well it's easy to forget who is in charge and to give thanks.

We love you. I can honestly say much of what has happened in the last few years has been very painful and extremely frustrating, but I have learned from it. Life's road has some ruts and bumps, but God's love is the suspension system. That was pretty good, huh? Ok, Ok so a little too poetic.

Stay warm and know you are loved.

Love, Mom XXOOXX

Mike answered my letters, and it was obvious that he was still holding himself above the program and the others involved. The tone of his letter was that he was "not one of them." I feared he would not get the benefit of the program if he would not allow himself to become involved. Like his stay at Mountainside, was he deciding he was okay prematurely?

Dear Mike,

I saw a card today with a very short prayer:

GOD, GIVE ME GUTS

We all need to be able to come before God and look ourselves in the mirror and like what we see. I need to be straightforward with you.

When I hear you say this is a great exercise in patience, it sets off alarm bells. It reeks of someone sitting on the sidelines and observing rather than having the strength (guts) to confront their own issues.

Intellectual aloofness is the vehicle by which we place emotions and feelings on the shelf.

Having said that, I try to reserve passing judgment on you. My questions are these:

1. What are you doing to seek out whatever is inside you that feeds the addiction?
2. After these 90 days, what will be different inside you and in how you deal with life?
3. If drugs make you feel better, what is making you feel bad?

I love you and remain hopeful.

Love, Mom xxooxx

I thought the above was finally one of the best letters I ever sent to Mike. It was short, honest, and to the point. He told me later this letter had a significant impact on him.

He finally allowed himself to let go and truly get involved in the program. That was a sign of strength, not weakness. Mr. Mayton had a lot to do with that … an authority figure he couldn't manipulate, sidestep, or ignore.

Mike's determination to stay clean and sober seemed stronger than ever. Peyton's loyalty and confidence in Mike never wavered. She was totally positive he was going to make it this time. I desperately wanted to have that kind of optimism too, but in all honesty, it was difficult.

Chapter 37

Lessons Learned

$\mathcal{W}$ hile Mike was at DART Cherry, someone close to me had a son who got involved with the law. I had been observing his emerging behavior that signaled trouble to me. His story sounded very fishy, and his mother was making all sorts of excuses for him. I was all too familiar with that pattern. Out of love, I wrote the following letter to a mother I cared about:

Dear Friend,

If someone told me the things I am about to tell you when Mike was 16, I'm not sure how I would have responded. Probably one of my reactions might have been, "It's none of your business. You don't know MY son and he's not like THAT." I offer this to you from my heart. I don't know what it will be worth to you. I don't pretend to know how it is to walk in your shoes—I just don't want you to find out how it is to walk in mine.

I think there is a relationship between Mom and son that is just different. Moms without boys don't know this relationship. You and I do. It's perfectly normal for boys around 14–16 to pull away—especially from their mothers. I always gave Mike choices … about everything. I don't think I even realized at the time there was a control game going on. I see now how giving him so much power was a bad idea.

I remember having a great discussion with Dad about why I didn't believe in "Saying NO for the sake of—saying NO." He said you have to teach kids that sometimes the answer is NO even if there's no other reason than "I said so!" I have to admit, that I did not agree with that theory at all. If I could do one thing over it would be this: Set boundaries, have consequences and STICK TO IT. You do have the right to say NO. With hindsight, I would say you have the duty to say NO—even if your son doesn't understand why. Do not let him badger you into giving in.

When I say STICK TO IT, I do not say that lightly. Anybody can tell you that, but they don't walk in your shoes. I know how tough that is. I wasn't very good at it, but I so wish now I had been. It might not have made any difference. I will never know. I try not to beat myself up with "What if …" because I know that won't change anything. But I want you to know how deeply I feel for you and your situation. If tears would make things right, your world would be better, but tears won't do a damn thing. I know. But, your actions might.

There is a great lesson of life that we must teach. **There will always be rules in life you have to follow or suffer the consequences.** Life doesn't always offer choices or allow compromise. And you don't have to agree with or even understand the rule. And as a parent, I think we have to support the rule, whether it is ours or from the school, the sports team or the law. If you think the rule is wrong, work to change it, but don't break it unless you plan to suffer the consequences.

We tried setting boundaries. We wrote contracts with Mike that included consequences. I can't say we were successful. About the time we moved to North Carolina, the flood gates started to open. Oh not with a rush, but with a trickle. We gave him too much. Too much freedom, too much money, too much car, *too much credit for maturity he didn't have.* As I saw more signs of trouble, I tried to deal with them, but in all honesty there were times I really didn't know what to do. That's hard for me to admit, because I have always seen myself as pretty much "in control." Even with my degree in psychology, my experience as a counselor I had no clue that we were headed for disaster. I was a mother trying to do my best. I made mistakes.

Mike's behavior became more erratic. I was never sure which "Mike" was going to come up the stairs. Some days he was pleasant and agreeable, even very funny. Sometimes he was grouchy and moody. I tried to tell myself it was puberty, hormones or just his age. Down deep, I knew something was wrong. But I think as a mom, you really don't want to believe that there is a BIG problem with your own son.

Mike continued to party. Even though things looked pretty good on the outside, they obviously weren't. He was breaking the rules and pushing the boundaries.

On Mike's 18th birthday, he left home for a few days, claiming I was driving him nuts. I had no idea what was going on with him and he wasn't going to answer my questions … at least not truthfully. He had some more problems at school. I didn't know until much later … years … he had been drinking at school on a regular basis. *How could I have not known what was happening?*

I needed to believe he wouldn't lie to me when the chips were down. If I could impart another bit of wisdom from experience—our adorable sons LIE. Believe it. TO YOUR FACE. They will swear they are telling the truth and get very angry when you don't believe the lies they tell. If it sounds fishy, smells fishy, you can bet there is a fish … even if you can't find it. Look harder.

There comes a time to say "Cut the crap!" AND MEAN IT. And the sooner the better.

There are probably lots of things about Mike's self-destructive path that I still don't know. I do know that things started to go wrong and I didn't see disaster coming. Nothing seemed *too* bad. If someone had warned me that the signs were all there, would I have done anything differently? I don't know. My brother tried. We don't get to go back and do it again. I believed Mike would grow out of this "phase." I thought, *"If he would just LISTEN!"* Now I know, it's not so much what we say, but what we DO that has an impact.

Mike will tell you that no one can change an addict. Until the addict is sick of himself and his circumstances he will not change. What that says to me is that maybe his circumstances should have gotten a lot worse a lot earlier. I protected Mike. I even lied for him. I didn't want him to be embarrassed. I didn't want people to say hurtful things to him. We paid for lawyers so his consequences wouldn't be so bad. We paid his debts, covered bad checks, waved good-by to property he took from us. We kept hoping that his good sense would kick in before he dug such a big hole that he would wreck his life. Mike is a bright and lovable young man and I have never lost sight of that … never. For all that, look where we all are today. I am not without hope. I pray every day for Mike to find his way. But this has been a very hurtful 8 years and it all started to get worse when he was about your son's age. He was moody and defiant at times with most of his anger directed at me. Does that sound familiar? It wasn't clear to me then, the best way I could have shown my love for him was to not put up with his crap. I should have drug tested him. You can get a test at the drug store. He would have protested, but that would have told me something too.

I wish we had let him feel the sting of the consequences early on because I assure you the consequences get bigger and bigger. You have a right and responsibility, to stand your ground, make rules and enforce them with consequences. Find out where you can get help. Trust your instincts, and confide in someone who can be objective. My brother was a great help to me, but I just didn't want to hear what he was saying. He was right on target. He has a big heart and a lot of information. Call him. He will listen.

I hesitate to say this next thing because I have very strong feelings about religion being personal choice. I will just tell you that finding a church that works for you and the boys can make a world of difference. The key is finding one that the boys can relate to. Finding a relationship with God, I believe can do miracles. It has been a great comfort to us in the last few years.

I do not pretend to know your situation or what is in your son's mind and heart. I pray that he is not involved with drugs yet. I know you love him with all your heart and would do anything to make this painful situation better. I would still give my right arm … literally … if it would make Mike OK, but it won't. Sometimes a Mom can't "fix it." The unique thing about alcoholism or addiction is that it is the only sickness you cannot nurture. And that goes against every instinct of Motherhood in the world!

There is no agony like a mother seeing her child in pain. It wasn't long ago that Mike and I walked on the beach and he cried as he told me Ben and I were all he has in the world. He was so genuinely sorry for all the pain and worry he had caused. I know he meant it. He knew he had strayed so far off the path he was feeling desperately lost.

That was before he made his last series of bad choices. He will not be at the table on Thanksgiving. I don't know if he will be able to even call on Christmas day. That genuinely hurts. I love him so much and I have to believe in his goodness. I miss him.

Thank you for letting me share these thoughts with you. If you ever need to talk, I am here. Don't hesitate to lean on those who love you. It's OK to need help.

With loving concern,

Chapter 38

Christmas in Hilton Head

Mike was going to be in DART Cherry for Christmas, and I had no desire to pull out all the decorations. My heart was not in the mood for the usual holiday merriment. We had spent Thanksgiving in Pennsylvania with Joyce and Dwight and their extended family. That had been our refuge from sitting down to a turkey dinner without Mike.

Our friends Dennis and Margaret were in much the same frame of mind. They had lost a daughter that year to an overdose. She was in her early thirties with two young daughters. Somehow we decided to meet in Hilton Head over Christmas. Who spends Christmas at Hilton Head? It felt like we were surrounded by sad and lonely people, but then maybe that was just my perception mirroring my own feelings.

We managed to get through the week, took walks, and did not dwell on our misfortune and worries. But they were always there, hanging in the air like a dark heavy cloud. Their daughter had lost her battle, and we were still so afraid we would be walking in their shoes in the future, though we did not say that out loud. It was like we were all trying to think of things to say and do that would just keep each other going.

Ben was not comfortable dwelling on these subjects. I think he just felt defeated by Mike's resistance to all efforts to help him get his life back on track. It was not something he wanted or felt he needed to talk about. And though we both so desperately wanted his stay at DART to help him find his way, we had been disappointed so many times that we were reserved in our optimism.

Mike had written a letter to Ben earlier in the month. He was reaching out in what I thought was a very honest, heartfelt plea for improvement in their relationship. When I read Mike's letter it brought me to tears.

Dad,

I want to be honest. Sometimes face to face you intimidate me—not in a physical way, but I sometimes feel awkward telling you how I feel, but I want you to know, so I'm putting it on paper.

I love you Dad. I've told you that before, but there's so much more. You are hands down the single biggest influence in my life. We have more in common than either one of us realizes. Adopted or not, daily I catch myself saying something you would, remembering something you told me or conducting myself in a way I think you would condone.

Know this Dad, you are appreciated—not your wallet, or just the way you love, but the man you are. I strive to be more like you. You are compassionate, smart and resourceful. I would like to know you better. Please Dad, let me know you better. I know I have stomped on your heart, pride and wallet time and time again. I'm sincerely sorry. I pray you know that.

I am so grateful, not only that I have a father, but I have one of the most admirable people I have known as mine. We have lots of life left Dad. Let's try to enjoy the precious time we have together. I've stolen a lot of that in the past, but I pray in the end that won't matter. Dad, you mean so much to me. I just thought you should know. I love you.

Mike

It had an impact on Ben too, but he was as guarded in his emotions as Mike had been in the past with him. He wrote a sincere letter back to our son.

Dec. 7, 2002

Son, I appreciate your letter and get a heartwarming feeling that you emulate me (the good parts that is) and want to get closer and enjoy fellowship with each other.

I always thought the most effective leadership method was to do it by example. Somehow I failed to impart to you the ethics of perseverance, hard work, responsibility, and respect for others that I thought I was modeling for you. Obviously, I should have tried harder in other ways. The siren song of pop culture was too attractive. As you know I think the current pop culture has been co-opted by the ghetto, prison mentality, values, and condition. Don't get me wrong I think the above downtrodden finding a voice is in the long run a good sign that they will develop pride and become a positive culture. Unfortunately in the early part of the process they are bringing you more fortunately raised guys down in to the maelstrom. Why, do you think, that roughly 70% of students in the UNC system are female? But I digress ...

I too would like to experience more the joy of camaraderie, closeness, and interaction between two soul mates. I thought that was happening more and more and I was welcoming it as a harbinger of your coming maturity and self-reliance. Alas, the train wrecked again just as I thought it was building up a good head of steam. To be best friends with a **man** you must be a **man** yourself! You must respect yourself and be a positive factor in some way in this world of ours. The first requirement to achieve positive contribution is to be able to take care of yourself. It is hard to be on the plus side of the ledger if you suck a vacuum on others just to survive. I don't mean just financially. I mean the full spectrum of human interactions and emotions.

I'm here waiting for you. I haven't given up hope of our having that kind of relationship and time together that we both desire. Please, please come and join the fellowship of Man.

Written with love,

Your Dad

Mike was in a program, and it appeared to be good for him. He was opening up and seeming to know himself better. He reassured us he was finished with his old ways, but how many times had we heard that before? I tried to stay optimistic, especially in my letters and conversations with Mike, but, of course, the doubts were always there accompanied by the fear. The emotion that had seemed to subside at this point was the anger. I kept turning to God for strength and guidance. I was trying to find the path where we were meant to be. I wanted the avalanche to stop, but not in the way of Dennis and Margaret's daughter. *Please, God, not that way.* I wanted our son to live!

We came home from Hilton Head and took down the few decorations I had put up earlier. At least Mike was safe for now. I desperately needed to get a more positive attitude for the new year. Mike would be coming home soon. Honestly, I had such mixed emotions about how that might turn out. His attitude seemed to have changed, and he appeared determined this time, and he had Peyton.

Peyton had visited him several times and written him letters. Her faith in him did not falter, and that had a very positive impact on him. She told me more than once in those months while he was away that he was going to make it—she knew it! And I knew when I looked into her eyes she had absolute faith that he would indeed make it. *Oh, Peyt, how I hope and pray you are right.*

I had to hope that 2003 would be the year we all could leave the painful road of addiction and move on to a happier path for the future of our little family. Mike had been clean and sober since September 12, 2002.

Chapter 39

Coming Home. Where Is Home?

*I*n January 2003 Mike came home from DART Cherry. He had already arranged to move into another halfway house off of Independence Avenue. He didn't even spend one night in our home. He felt very sure he needed the structure of the "house." We didn't argue with him.

We were again filled with hope. Mike had been so positive this time that he was walking on a different street. I prayed this would be the time that he would turn his life around ... *Uh, if that's your will, God.* I was really trying to understand that I was not in control. He looked so good after being clean for almost four months. He could now look us in the eye, and there was some peace there.

He would again be under the supervision of a probation officer, and he was expected to attend meetings every day. He did all of that. His priority was staying clean and sober. And that made a difference. He finally accepted that he needed "the program." He found hope and encouragement from others who had been in recovery for many years.

Peyton spent time at the halfway house watching TV with the guys or making popcorn or cookies. They all loved her like a little sister. And

Mike loved her too. Their relationship was growing into something very special.

She knew all his faults, and she loved him unconditionally. He could make her laugh, and after the horrible year in New York, she needed to laugh. They were a strange match. Peyton loved her single strand of pearls and was a little preppy at heart. Mike and his friends at the house were recovering addicts. It was no wonder her dad did not approve of her growing relationship with Mike. But she had stood by him and visited him at DART Cherry and faithfully written him letters. But most importantly, she demonstrated the strength of her commitment to their relationship. At a time when almost all of his friends had left him, Peyton came back from New York. She stuck by him even when he slipped and fell. She never lost sight of the loving person with the good heart. She believed in Mike, and she needed him to push her, and she adored his sense of humor. And just maybe both of them needed to be needed.

Peyton and I talked a lot. She was the one who got me interested in watching *American Idol*. Sometimes we watched it together and just talked. "I hate it when people feel sorry for me. I need to feel normal," she laughed, "whatever normal is. I just can't stay feeling down when I'm around Mike. Some of my friends don't get it, and they don't get Mike either, but I don't care. I just love him."

It was approaching our annual trip to Tahoe in March. Mike couldn't leave the county and was sad that he was going to miss the family vacation. Peyton teased him by telling him she was going in his place. We went along with the gag for several days, and Mike was starting to buy into it. That may sound cruel, but the teasing and joking was a big part of their comfortable relationship. She actually wasn't going but vowed the next year we would all go together. That sounded like a fine plan to me. I prayed Mike would still be clean and sober in a year, and Peyton would stay healthy, and we could actually all go to Tahoe. That would be heaven.

We went to Tahoe, and there were no horrible phone calls concerning Mike. That was definitely a step in the right direction. I was beginning to let myself hope.

Two days before April Fool's Day, Mike hid in the bushes in front of the house, and when Peyton came, he jumped out and scared her so badly that she wet her pants. Retribution was in order.

On April Fool's Day, Peyton worked hard with some of the guys at the halfway house and managed to "reassemble" Mike's room in the front yard. It was a great prank, and they all shared a laugh. I got a call to come see the handiwork before it got put back inside. Both Peyton and Mike were laughing as he gave her a big hug. I knew I was seeing what real happiness looked like.

He kept telling us he had to focus on himself, and his only priority was to stay clean and sober. He worked with his sponsor and attended meetings—lots of meetings. My urge to control started to kick in again accompanied by the nagging. He had some part-time jobs and seemed to stay very busy. Ben was convinced he had to have transportation so he could find a job. I made a case for a bicycle, but Ben was not in agreement. I was trying to be so careful not to fall back into the hole of enabling. Mike didn't have a full-time job for a full year following his time at the DART program. Several times I had to fight back the strong urge to push him hard to go get a job, but he knew his top priority was to do whatever it took to stay clean and sober. He finally totally understood how AA worked. I was learning I needed to stay out of his way, a lesson long overdue.

Peyton celebrated her birthday on April 15 with a group of friends and Mike by her side. She told everyone it was the happiest birthday of her life. I could see something changing in their relationship. Mike got involved with the theater company I was affiliated with and volunteered to set up their web page. He also took a part in a production. Peyton went to see the play in June and at the end of the play, he walked into the audience and presented her with flowers. She was surprised and delighted that he would acknowledge his feelings for her so publicly.

He was the love that she feared she would never experience when things looked so dim the previous year. She confided in me her love for Mike long before he realized the depth of her romantic feelings for him. To him, she was his best friend, and he would have done anything for her—and I have no doubt he loved her. It reminded me how Ben and I started as best friends all those years ago.

Peyton and I were sitting in our kitchen when she opened her heart. "When I thought I might not make it, what made me so sad was that I've never known real love. I don't mean like the love of your family. I know they love me so much, and I love them. And I have friends that mean everything to me. But I had never felt the unconditional love of a man. You know what I mean?"

"Of course I know, Peyton." I had to smile.

"I think God gave me more time to come back here so I could find Mike. Please don't tell him I said that, but I just wanted you to know. And I know he loves me too, maybe just not the same way exactly. But I know I can always count on him, and he'll be there for me."

I looked into those big beautiful eyes and saw the tears brimming there, and one slid down her cheek. "Oh, Peyton, you mean the world to him. You two have something so special." I couldn't say anything else for the lump in my throat.

Then she flashed her big smile and said, "He just doesn't want me for his Trivial Pursuit partner." They had lost the last time we played when they were partners. Peyton had a way of deflecting the conversation if things got too serious.

We frequently played Trivial Pursuit at our house. Usually Peyton would partner with Ben, and Mike and I would take them on. That made pretty evenly matched teams. We had such great fun on those occasions, and there was a lot of laughing and teasing and love that filled the room. Peyton had a way with Ben from that first meeting in the marina years before. He wasn't one to play games usually, but Peyton could coax him into it.

Things were better, but not perfect by any means. Mike had to follow rules and change behaviors and stay off the old street. The transition was not going to happen overnight—for either of us. I was struggling with my urge to "mother" him in an effort to control the situation. I had to keep working to keep myself out of the middle of his life. I was getting better, but the urge was always there.

Mike and his friends who were in early recovery needed other outlets to socialize that didn't revolve around alcohol or drugs. Many of the people in the program got together to play poker. I grew up playing poker at family gatherings, and I loved it. Ben was not a gambler, and though he was a good poker player, he didn't play. I let Mike host poker games at our house frequently, and I played with the group. Peyton learned to play too and became very good at Texas Hold 'Em. We mostly played Texas Hold 'Em tournaments for a low stakes buy-in. None of these young people had much extra money, and this was a way to be entertained for an entire evening on very little money. Endless pots of coffee, pitchers of lemonade, and chocolate chip cookies were consumed … and the bottoms weren't burned most of the time. I was learning!

Our family life seemed to be getting happier and more normal all the time. We got through the summer with no major incidents. Mike was spending more and more time with Peyton. She was such a breath of fresh air for all of us. God had sent a special angel into our lives.

Chapter 40

First-Year Chip

*P*eyton was working at a local restaurant and going to school. She wanted to get into nursing school. Her cancer was staying in remission, and she was feeling fine. Mike was approaching his first year of sobriety. It was a time for them of "I'm okay; you're okay." Peyton was there when Mike received his chip for being clean and sober for a year. She wrote him a note for the occasion.

September 12, 2003

Mike,

You are right baby, we are so blessed. Not only do I have a friend I cherish to no end, I am able to watch you smile on days like today. I know you can relate, because you make me smile all the time. I guess the only thing I can compare it to is you being able to spend my birthday with me—a birthday I really wasn't sure I would ever see. Now you know what it feels like for your feet to never touch the ground. Enjoy baby, you've earned it! I am so proud of you and proud to call you my best friend. No doubt this has been a long year, but worth every tear and heartache. You have beaten the odds and then some.

I may not be able to understand everything you go through, but I will never stop trying. I figured that every one year old needs a new pair of shoes to help them learn to walk. It just so happens that you like to walk on water so I got you new bindings for your board.

Never stop believing in yourself. I know I never will. Thank you for all you do! I am so glad I get to see you pick up your chip. I love you.

Love, Peyt

They were both in their own kind of recovery. There were some curves in their road too, but for the most part all was well. Peyton's dad was still not a fan of Mike. Actually her friends at the restaurant also couldn't understand why she wanted to hook up with a guy in recovery with a bad track record.

But Peyton and Mike thrived in spite of the adversity that surrounded them. Mike kept her laughing, and she kept believing in Mike, and Mike was clean and sober. I remember meeting him for lunch at the restaurant where Peyton worked. She was tired and grumpy until Mike squirted mashed potatoes through his teeth. *Give me a break!* I hadn't raised this young man to do that in a restaurant! It totally cracked Peyton up. *Don't encourage him!* And then I would find myself smiling just seeing her joy. He would do some crazy and immature things, just to make Peyton laugh. And the important thing to Mike—Peyton did laugh—and she loved him for making her laugh. He filled a space that no one else could. She needed him, and he thrived in that role. Whatever it was, it was magic for both of them. And it was such a joy to observe that special thing they shared.

It was difficult for them to find a common group of young people to socialize with. Her preppy friends liked to party and drink, and his circle of friends in the program could *not* do that at all. So while Peyton could come into Mike's group, Mike couldn't go into hers.

As fall came, the relationship between Mike and Peyton was becoming strained a bit. Peyton was wanting more from Mike socially than he was willing or able to give. He was still primarily focused on himself and his recovery. She was really pushing him hard to move more into her social circles. I suspect Peyton was getting a good bit of pressure from her friends and her dad to move on past Mike. I think she just wanted to show them more of the Mike she knew so well so perhaps they would understand why she loved him.

And then along came Kathy. Kathy was in the program and started playing poker with the group. She was a cute, petite blonde who was a skilled gymnast, working as an instructor at a local facility. In fact she had trained with some of the gymnasts who made the Olympic team. It appeared she wanted to be on Mike's team at the moment.

When both Peyton and Kathy came to poker, the tension was always there. Sometime that fall it all came to a head, and Mike asked for more space from Peyton. She knew she was pushing him. Once again, Peyton came to talk to me.

"I don't know what to do. I know he wants me to back off, but I'm so afraid if I do that, Kathy will just push right into the void. I see it every time she looks at him." I could sense her pain. I had also observed Kathy's attention directed toward Mike.

"Peyt, sometimes we have to let the bird fly. If it's meant to be, he will fly back to you, but holding him in the nest won't work."

"But what if he doesn't fly back? What if he just keeps going away from me?"

"Is that what he said he wanted when he asked for some space?"

"No, he keeps telling me how much our friendship means to him and that he doesn't want to destroy that, and he will always be there when I need him. I value that too, but ... but ... I want ..." she stopped and looked at her hands.

"I know you want more. But you can't force it right now." This wasn't what she wanted to hear from me. I was in such an awkward position. I knew both of them so well and what each wanted and needed, and it wasn't exactly the same thing.

Peyton did back off, and Kathy did jump in and fill the void. Peyton was still his best friend, but Kathy was the girl he started dating. It wasn't Kathy's fault, but it was painful for me to watch.

He would do anything *for* Peyton, but I think he was doing everything else *with* Kathy.

Chapter 41

Finding Melody

*A*fter he had returned from DART, Mike expressed a desire to start a serious search to find his birth mother. We had always told him we would support that effort. He had mentioned it a few times in the past but never pursued it. This time he was serious, but it still took him a few months to start his search in earnest. Mike was very computer savvy. Shortly before Thanksgiving in 2003 he was getting close to finding answers. He actually accessed a list of births in Houston on his birthday with the birth mother's names listed by the birth certificate numbers. Those kinds of files are no longer accessible today.

With diligence he had narrowed it down to some very strong possibilities with the name he found beside his birth certificate number. He was in our home office showing me his latest information. He was even able to pull up a picture of one of the women in the right age range with the same name listed on the birth certificate.

"Oh my God, Mike, that has to be her," I said with utter shock.

"Why do you think so?" he asked rather surprised.

This had to be his birth mother, as I felt as if I was looking at the female version of him. "Do you not see the resemblance?"

"No, not really." He sat there looking at the picture for a long time.

I was filled with such a mixture of emotions at that moment I had to leave the room. This was the woman who had been so unselfish as to allow us to have our son. We had always made a point of telling Mike how grateful we were to the young woman who had the courage to not have an abortion. And now I was sure he was looking at a picture of that woman twenty-seven years later. How would she feel about being contacted? Did she have other children? Would she accept Mike? *Please, God, don't let her reject him. He doesn't deserve that.*

I went back into the office, and he was still looking at the picture. "What do you plan to do?" I asked him.

"I don't really know. First I have to confirm that it's really her. If I have the right name, do you think the agency where you got me would confirm it for me if I contacted them?"

"I don't really know. Adoption has changed so much over the years. I know they have a policy of open adoption now, but back then it was very secretive. You can call and ask."

Over the next few days he made phone calls, and the agency was not going to be of any help. What he really wanted was for them to be the go-between to ask her if she was agreeable to being contacted. He wasn't sure how to proceed. The agency refused to get involved. I didn't understand that. He finally found her phone number and called. The first time a man answered, and Mike just hung up. Finally she answered, and he asked if she had lived in Houston in 1976. She said yes, and he went on to ask the crucial questions that determined that indeed she was his birth mother.

The first conversation was awkward and short. There were other conversations to follow. She was very happy that Mike had found her. She and her husband had tried for years to start a family and never had success. What an irony! This woman who had been so generous in her youth by giving up her baby was never able to conceive again.

I finally sat down close to Christmas and wrote her a letter. It seemed like the right thing to do.

December 15, 2003

Dear Melody

May the holidays find you well and happy. I have been writing this letter in my head for a long time and decided it was time to try to put it on paper. First and foremost, please know how grateful we all are for the unselfish gift you gave 27 years ago. Every Mother's Day and Mike's birthday I have thought of you and said a little prayer. I am so happy you have accepted contact from Mike openly. My only fear was that it might not work out so positively. I was sitting with him at the computer when we found your name by his birth certificate number. It was such an overwhelming feeling, to actually see a name.

As he continued his search and found the picture of you, I had no doubt that you were his birth mother. I truly see a resemblance. He has known his adoption story since before he can remember us telling him. As you can see from the pictures, he was a beautiful little boy with blond hair and big brown eyes. Ben's hobby is photography, so we have lots of pictures, especially when he was young.

He was a very good baby and slept through the night from the day we brought him home. He has always been a very bright and outgoing person. He started talking very young and never stopped. He has a great sense of humor and delights in making people laugh, a trait that has gotten him in trouble more than a few times. He loves all kinds of music ... a trait I suspect he got from you ... and plays the guitar. I know you have talked frequently and he's probably told you much of this. I just want you to know I am completely willing to share any information from a mother's perspective.

I'm so sorry you and your husband were unable to have children. I know the agony of waiting every month with anticipation. We tried everything available at the time, but to no avail. Getting a baby was such a blessing. We had been married almost ten years and were totally ready. Our friends and families were overjoyed. My parents are both gone now, but they loved Mike so much. My Dad was especially close to him. Mike wrote and delivered a eulogy at his funereal that touched my heart. He is very good with words and has a talent for writing.

We still stay in close touch with our friends in Texas who were there when we brought Mike home. We moved to Corpus Christi when he was 8 months old. Though he loves it here, I believe part of his heart will always be a Texan. He has his boots and cowboy hat.

As Christmas is just around the corner, I want to thank you again from the bottom of my heart for the greatest gift you could have ever given. God bless you. There is no way to repay you, but I am totally willing to share Mike with you. You and your husband are welcome to come here to visit any time. We would welcome the opportunity to get to know you both. Please feel free to call or email me anytime.

Sincerely,

Finding his birth mother was something he needed to do, and I totally understood that. She had been living in Texas with her father and stepmother and stepsister when she got pregnant as a senior in high school. She had gone on to college, married, and had been teaching vocal music in the same school in Texas ever since.

We found out her sister and niece currently lived in Fulton, Missouri—only twenty-five miles from Jefferson City, our hometown. Truth can sometimes be stranger than fiction.

Chapter 42

Two Women

$\mathcal{M}$ ike had moved back home, and we were all managing well. He was trying to save up enough money to be able to afford a place of his own, but he still didn't have a full-time job. He had stayed clean and sober for over a year, and that was his priority. He was working part time at a bed store, and they told him they would put him on full time when they opened their second store on our side of town

He was spending time with Kathy, and he was also available for Peyton. Peyton was not feeling as well as she had. She was living in a small apartment a few blocks from her parents' house in Magnolia Hall. When she was having a bad night, she would call Mike, and he would go keep her company and bring her out of her bad mood. Their friendship was still strong and solid. There were nights they would meet on the beach at the gazebo and just sit and talk until the sun came up. It was a deep and abiding friendship filled with love.

Now it was Kathy who was becoming more demanding and who felt threatened by his fierce loyalty to Peyton. It was painful to watch this love triangle unfold, but I knew there was little I could or should do. One night when the poker game was at our house, it finally exploded. I watched as Mike was nearly "pulled apart."

Peyton had not felt well all night, so she quit playing early. She went to sit in the sunroom, and I asked her what I could do for her.

"Nothing. I just feel a little queasy and dizzy." She looked a little pale.

"How about a cup of tea?"

"No, I just need to sit here for a minute. I'll be fine. Just go back to the game." She closed her eyes and put the footrest up on the recliner.

I went back into the adjoining dining room to the game, but I wasn't sure what was going on with Peyton. She didn't look well.

"Is she all right?" Mike asked with concern.

Before I had a chance to answer, Kathy chimed in with, "She'll be fine."

Her pointed comment took me by surprise. Kathy had expressed her opinion to Mike that much of Peyton's not feeling well was a ploy to get his attention. I wasn't so sure about that. Mike was out of the hand, so he left the table and went to check on Peyton.

"Hey, baby, are you gonna be okay?" I heard Mike ask.

I couldn't miss the look on Kathy's face as she rolled her eyes.

When the tournament was over and everyone was leaving. Peyton was still in the sunroom. Kathy came in and said to Mike, "You *are* coming over to my place aren't you?"

"Yeah, later. You go ahead. I want to be sure Peyton is okay."

"Well how long do you think that will take?" she asked with impatience. Her body language spoke volumes.

"I don't know, Kathy, but I'll be there later." His voice conveyed the message that she should leave now. She did, in a bit of a huff.

Peyton started to get up, but she felt dizzy and sat back down on the couch. "It's okay, Mike, you can go on if you want to," she said with a pained look on her face.

"No, baby, let's get you feeling better. I'm in no hurry." And with that he sat down on the couch beside her. She put her head on his shoulder. I was putting stuff away going from the dining room to the kitchen.

Shortly the phone rang, and I grabbed it on the first ring. Ben was already asleep, and I didn't want it to wake him. "Hell-o."

"Is Mike still there?" It was Kathy.

"Yes, he is."

"Could I speak to him please?"

I handed the phone to Mike. "It's Kathy." I think he already knew that.

His end of the conversation basically let her know he was still planning to come to her place later, but, no, he didn't know when. After all, she had just left our house not ten minutes before. He handed the phone back to me.

I put it back on the receiver and left the room. This was a time for Mike and Peyton to be left alone. I went into the office to check my e-mails. It wasn't ten minutes later when the phone rang again. I grabbed it at the same time Mike did. I heard him say into the phone loudly, "I told you I would be there," and he hung up. So did I. This was escalating into a battle. I could hear Mike and Peyton talking more loudly, and then they were both in the entry hall outside the office.

"If you won't come stay with me, don't worry about driving me home. I can drive myself." Peyton sounded angry and hurt.

"Don't be silly. You said you were dizzy. Let me drive you home. I'll stay for a while to be sure you're okay."

"Oh, sure, and then you're going over to Kathy's for the rest of the night?" The hurt in her voice was unmistakable. "Just go on now. I'll be fine. Really. I'm not dizzy anymore. I just needed you to be with me."

"And I said I would stay," Mike told her patiently.

"Yeah, but for how long?" she said.

"Peyton, I will be there for as long as you need me. You know that. Have I ever let you down?"

There was silence. It was broken by the phone ringing again. "Oh crap!" Mike exclaimed as he dashed for the phone. He picked it up and said loudly, "Seriously, Kathy? What the hell is the deal?"

There was such frustration in his voice. I heard the front door close quietly as Peyton left.

"Well, let me just make this simple. I will be there when or if I get there. Don't call again, please." Quiet followed. Then I heard him putting the poker chips and cards away.

Mike came into the office knowing I had heard most of what had gone on. He sat down and put his head in his hands. "I don't know what to do. I can't be in two places at once. This is crazy. They're both mad, and I don't even know what I did wrong! What the hell am I supposed to do?"

I didn't know if that was a rhetorical question or if he really expected an answer. Sometimes mothers don't have the answers to every question, and this seemed to be one of those times. He looked at me as if he wanted an answer. "What do you want to do, Mike?"

"Honestly? I just want to go to bed." He looked back down at the floor.

I just sat quietly. I had finally learned that was okay.

He picked up the phone and called Peyton. "Hey, Peyt, are you okay?" There was silence while he listened to what she was saying. "It's okay, baby. I know you didn't feel good. Do you want me to come over?" He listened again. "If you're sure you're okay. I'll check on you tomorrow then. Night."

He hung up the phone and dialed again. "Kathy, I'm really tired, and I'm going to bed." Silence as he listened for a brief moment. "No,

I'm at my house. I'll talk to you tomorrow." And with that, he hung up. He looked at me and shrugged his shoulders. "Mom, I can't keep doing this." And with that he went upstairs to bed.

I sat there for a long time thinking. I hated to see him under so much pressure. This was becoming an untenable triangle, and Mike was caught right in the middle. Could he handle this much emotion without turning to … *Stop thinking that way!* He had to be able to deal with conflict, and there were worse things than two women fighting over you.

He had a lot going on in his life, and he was working hard to do the next right thing. As I watched from the sidelines, I knew disaster was coming, but I didn't know the form it would take.

I had to hope Mike could stay on the positive recovery path he was currently on. And I knew I needed to let him make his own decisions. Mike was about to take an important journey with Peyton, one he would not forget.

Chapter 43

The Trip to New York

It was time for Peyton's checkup at Sloan Kettering in New York. She told her parents she was fine to go by herself this time. In reality, she wasn't fine at all, and she wasn't going by herself. She asked Mike to go with her, but I didn't know until later she didn't tell her parents. She knew her dad wouldn't approve.

Off they went to New York in Peyton's little blue Volkswagen Beetle to stay at the Ronald McDonald House. The test results showed the cancer had returned. She later admitted it was just what she suspected. As they walked through the streets of New York that December afternoon, it must have been very hard to know what to say. I'm sure somehow Mike kept her talking about other things and again made her laugh, even though it was through their tears.

Mike had called to tell us the bad news. He didn't elaborate, and the conversation was short. He just said they would be heading back the next day. It was heartbreaking to hear the cancer had returned, and I told him I was so glad he was there with her. He sounded calm and strong as he replied, "Me too, Mom, me too. This is exactly where I am supposed to be."

The following evening I was expecting them back soon when the phone rang.

"Mom, we're not coming home," Mike said with a little lilt in his voice.

"What? What do you mean, you're not coming home?" Had she taken a sudden turn for the worse? I didn't think so, because he sounded lighthearted. Did the doctors want her to stay in New York? My questions were dancing around my head, when Mike explained a totally different kind of "turn."

"We just passed where we would have turned off for home, and we're headed to Atlanta to see the babies." I could actually hear Peyton laughing in the background.

"I don't understand. You mean you're going to Atlanta instead of coming home?" That's exactly what he had said, and he didn't mumble. But I was confused.

"Yup, that's what we're doin'. Peyt wants to see the babies and get some hugs, and that's exactly what we're gonna do."

"But … but what about …" The questions were about to start tumbling out.

He interrupted me quickly, "No buts about it, Mama. I just wanted to let you know so you wouldn't worry. I'll call you when we're headed back from Atlanta."

"But … uh … when … I mean did she call her parents? Do they know? Are they …"

"We've got it covered, Mama. Don't worry. We're just cruising down the road to happiness right now, and that's what we need to do. Understand?" He was telling me something, and I needed to listen— and trust his judgment. This was something Peyton needed to do.

"Okay, Son. I really appreciate that you called. Have a safe trip and keep me posted."

"I will. I love you so much, Mama."

"I love you too, Mama Hen!" I heard Peyton shout in the background.

"Love you too, Son. Tell Peyton we love her too." I hung up the phone, and I smiled through my tears.

Peyton adored her niece and nephew, her older sister's two beautiful children. Mike could make her laugh, and the kids could draw her into their world of fun and fantasy, and I supposed that was not a bad place for her to be heading right now. And she had Mike right there by her side so I had to assume they would be all right. I didn't really have a choice. They were traveling down the road—together. I knew that felt right.

Chapter 44

The Seesaw of Recovery

After three days in Atlanta, Mike and Peyton drove back home. She had to check in with doctors and determine the protocol for her treatment. It was going to be a "wait and see" if anything would work this time as they had given her everything previously. But we all had hopes that again this demon called cancer would spare her.

Christmas was approaching, and we all got busy with holiday plans and shopping and tried not to dwell too much on the "What if?" question. We still played Trivial Pursuit and poker and enjoyed our time together. I sometimes felt guilty that her parents were missing so much of her good times that were being spent with us at our house.

Mike was working full time at the bed store now. He was showing more signs of maturity and taking responsibility for his life. Kathy was still in the picture, but he was devoted to Peyton.

The news after Christmas was not good. The treatment was not working, and the cancer was not shrinking. Peyton returned to her doctors in New York only to be told everything they could try was not working. It was devastating news.

She was still determined to go to Lake Tahoe with us in March. From the time we had joked with Mike the year before about her going when he couldn't, we had agreed she would go with us this year. That was before we knew where the road would lead us. Now we had to pray she would still be with us in March. Only a year ago I had prayed so hard we would still have Mike with us.

The seesaw of recovery was slowly tipping the other direction. Now Mike was so much better, and Peyton was worse. How could this vivacious, beautiful young woman who loved our son be dying? She had done so much to bring him back from the edge of total disaster or maybe even death, and now we were going to lose her. I loved her like a daughter. *Please, God, don't take her.* The lessons I had learned about not being in control were going to be tested again.

On Valentine's Day her little car was covered in magnetic hearts placed there overnight by her friends. She had a group of wonderful young people she worked with at the restaurant that cared deeply about her. Her parents and family had many friends that said lots of prayers and surrounded them with love. Peyton was loved by so many people.

Mike was still trying to treat Peyton as a "normal" person as she had so wanted him to do and had so appreciated. She told him to keep pushing her, but her energy was slowly ebbing. He was still keeping her laughing as much as he could, and he was available whenever she needed him. There were nights she would call, and he would go and slide into her bed and just hold her until she fell asleep. Other times, they would still meet at the gazebo on the beach and sit and talk all night until sun came up. She needed him to reassure her that the sky was not falling, not yet.

A huge surprise party was held for her at the restaurant where she worked. They closed the place down for the event. Her brother came from Colorado, and her sister's family was there from Atlanta with "the babies." Ben and I were talking with Jane and Dan, people we played tennis with that were very close friends of Peyton's parents.

"She looks so happy and healthy," Ben said quietly with love and concern. But we all knew she wasn't healthy. Peyton was radiant as she made her way around the room, but it felt like a farewell party. It was a bittersweet night.

Chapter 45

The Trip to Tahoe

The time had come to go to Tahoe. We had owned that time share condo on the north shore of Lake Tahoe since Mike was about ten. He always swore he would live in that area someday. It was a special place for our family.

Peyton's situation was not getting any better. She had to get fluid drained as the edema would build up in her lungs, and it would get difficult for her to breathe. There was some concern about the change in altitude involved with going up to Lake Tahoe. But Peyton was determined she was going to the mountains. She had been looking forward to the trip for a year, and nothing was going to stop her. <u>Nothing</u>!

Her mother talked to the doctors, and they warned of the possible complications. I think they also suggested that if this was something she really wanted to do so badly, perhaps she should do it. Don't wait. Liz called to tell me what the doctors had said and to reassure me the trip was so important to Peyton, and even though there were some risks, she had no doubt that it was the right thing and "meant to be." She gave me the doctor's phone number—in case. I could not let myself think about the "what if?" possibilities. Ben and I certainly were not going to

246

deny Peyton something she wanted so badly. The doctor's message had been pretty clear. <u>Don't wait.</u> I had to believe nothing bad was going to happen in Tahoe. It just couldn't. *Please, God, let her have this trip.*

Peyton was going to see family in Florida and then fly to Reno, where Mike would pick her up. When they were driving up to the lake from the airport, it was dark. Mike wanted to see her expression when she first saw the lake in the daylight. He wanted that to be a little gift he could give to her.

The next morning she got up before he did, but had us close the curtains so she wouldn't see the lake without him. He got up, and they walked out hand in hand. He had her close her eyes till she was standing in the perfect spot with the spectacular view of Lake Tahoe.

We watched them from the deck of our condo. She squealed in delight and threw her arms around his neck, and he swung her around in a circle. I felt such joy as I watched our wonderful son with his special angel. For that beautiful moment, we pushed back the anguish of what we feared was to come. I reached for Ben's hand, and he grasped mine. We couldn't talk. But then, we didn't need to. She had made it to the lake! They both had. And it was heaven.

We went to all of our favorite places. Steamers Pizza was one of our favorite spots to eat. The little broken-down theater in downtown King's Beach was where the same guy that sold you your ticket, sold the popcorn and then went upstairs to run the projector. We had to search around for four seats together that weren't broken down. We laughed a lot! We spent several evenings at our favorite casino up at the top of the hill where we played in small poker tournaments. The dealers fell in love with Peyton too. I was amazed at how well she was managing.

One afternoon, Mike got a call from Ann, the anchorwoman at the TV station back home asking him if he would be interested in coming back to work there. She knew of an opening coming up and wanted to recommend him. He was so thrilled at the possibility. Peyton was delighted for him and told him how proud she was. We were all happy about the possibility of Mike being able to return to a profession he loved. It was nice to have a little good news.

We had a glorious time and were careful to try not to do too much in one day. Most afternoons were spent in front of the fireplace, and frequently Peyton would take a short nap. Mike went snowboarding a couple of days, and she went to watch for a while from the lodge before coming back to nap. As I watched her sleep in the big chair by the fireplace, she looked so peaceful with her legs curled under her, and I felt the inevitable lump in my throat. How could something so awful be happening to this beautiful young woman who we loved so much? *Don't go there! Be grateful for today.* I was grateful because I knew Peyton was peaceful and content at that moment, and I knew we were so blessed to be able to share the lake with her. This was the heaven we had prayed for the year before, that the four of us would be here together.

We went to Emerald Bay and took lots of pictures. The sun was shining so brightly and the sky was Carolina blue as was the water in the lake. The wind was blowing Peyton's hair, and she just looked so beautiful. *Please, God, don't take her away! I will not cry. Breathe.*

"Oh, Mikey, the sky is not falling," she said with her radiant smile. It was her pet name for him, and no one else ever used it.

"Right, Peyton, the sky is not falling. Not today, baby, not today," he answered as he put his arm around her, and they stood on top of a rock and looked out over Emerald Bay in Lake Tahoe.

The sky was not falling, not yet.

Chapter 46

God's Gift of Snow

Mike would have driven her anywhere or done anything to grant her every wish. She wanted to see San Francisco, so he drove her there, and they soaked in the view of the Golden Gate Bridge and other sights she had never seen. They returned, and she was a mixture of emotions.

"I've seen and done so many things I've dreamed about, and I'm so glad I've had the chance, but there are so many things I still want to see and do. But I'm so glad I'm here." She hugged each of us, and we hugged her back. There were no words; there were just no words.

She had another wish, something she really wanted to see.

"Just one day, just once while I'm here, I want to see a beautiful snowfall." That was a wish beyond Mike's power to grant, as he had no control of the weather. I prayed hard that night. *God, please send some snow for Peyton.* Please!

The next morning, as if on cue, God designed the most beautiful animated Christmas card and delivered it to the north shore of Lake Tahoe. As we sat by the fire in the cozy warmth of the condo, overlooking the lake, the flakes began to fall. Truly, you could not dream a lovelier or more peaceful scene. The flakes were so big they would have covered your tongue if you were to try to catch one as we did when we were kids.

Peyton's eyes were filled with excitement. There was such joy in the simple pleasure of watching the snow fall from the sky and rest on the pine boughs and cover the sharp rocks and brown grass. It turned our world into a pure white fairy land—a place of untouched beauty, a place where anything that was not perfect was covered, even if just for a while, with unflawed perfection. It was her day, just one very perfect blessed day. We didn't know it would be the last snow she would see lazily float from the sky. Perhaps she knew, as she merrily went from window to window like a little girl, in awe of the gift from God.

She went outside to feel it on her face and came in with cheeks glowing and her eyes sparkling. I wanted to fall to my knees and give thanks for this small miracle. Instead I just said my own silent "Thank you, God" prayer. I will never see a snowfall at the lake that will not bring back the sweet memory of that special day of snow in March that was God's Christmas card to Peyton, our special angel … because by the next Christmas she would not be on this earth where she could laugh out loud at the miracle of a slow, peaceful snowfall.

Chapter 47

God Blessed Our Broken Road

*I*t was not that easy to find music that all four of us liked, but the Nitty Gritty Dirt Band was going to have a one-night show at the Golden Nugget in Reno, and that sounded good to all of us.

When I went to get the tickets, the only seats left were in the back and upstairs. "Please, isn't there anything else? We really need something easy to get to," I said to the customer service lady. "I'd be happy to pay more if you could find us something better."

"Do you have someone handicapped with you?" she asked.

"Well—not exactly." My heart caught in my throat. *Whoa. Don't lose it here. Straighten up!* "We have a young lady with us who is … she won't be … she's not …" I was stumbling for words and almost wished I hadn't started this conversation. I had never used the "She is sick" excuse. I just didn't know how to say it. Somehow without me ever getting out a coherent sentence, she understood.

"Wait right here, and let me check something," she said with an understanding smile.

"Thank you," I managed to get out. *Don't cry!* The other three were out in the casino.

She returned with four VIP tickets at a stage-side table. I thanked her profusely and never told the others how we ended up with those seats. I know I had help from a higher power and a very kind lady.

We were having a great time. We clapped, we laughed, and we sang along. And then the Nitty Gritty Dirt Band introduced a song I had never heard before. I felt the words were for Mike and Peyton and the journey that each had been on that led them back to one another. When they got to the chorus, Peyton and I laughed through our tears—and they were happy tears for being in that place at that moment, the four of us together. *Thank you, God!* Our broken road had indeed been blessed.

The Broken Road

I set out on the narrow way, many years ago

Hoping I would find true love along the broken road.

I got lost a time or two, wiped my brow and kept pushing through.

I couldn't see how every sign pointed straight to you.

Every long lost dream led me to where you are.

Others who broke my heart, they were just northern stars.

Pointing me on my way into your loving arms.

This much I know is true ... that God blessed the broken road that led me straight to you.

Think about the years I spent just passing through.

I'd like to find the time I lost, and give it back to you.

You just smile and take my hand, you've been there, you understand.

It's all part of a grander plan that is coming true.

Now I'm just rolling home into your loving arms.

This much I know, I know is true

That God blessed the broken road that led me straight to you.

Reprinted with permission from Hal Leonard. Writers: Marcus Hummon, Bobby Boyd, Jeff Hanna

I had no doubt that if Mike could have reclaimed the years he had lost, he would have loved to give them to Peyton now. But life doesn't work that way. That's why it's so important to live every day like the gift that it truly is.

As the time at the lake came to an end, Mike and Peyton had planned a trip to Las Vegas. She was meeting up with some girlfriends for a couple of days, and Mike was meeting up with Conner, his old roommate, for his bachelor party. We were flying back home straight from Reno.

The side trip to Las Vegas proved to be too much for Peyton, and she was not feeling well at all while they were there. When they returned, Peyton went to her parents' house and never went back to her little apartment. She was just not strong enough.

I was amazed at how her condition had disintegrated so rapidly. Had she pushed herself so hard to make it to Tahoe and then her strength just left her? It was disconcerting. She was going to the hospital again to have the fluid drained from her lungs.

Her birthday was coming up April 15, and she was having a few friends over. Once again, her dad confronted her with not wanting Mike there. She put her foot down and insisted that if Mike couldn't come to her parents' house, she would go back to her apartment. He relented. He just couldn't see how much Peyton and Mike meant to each other. I kept reminding myself, this was his baby girl, and he was her loving father trying to protect her. Unfortunately, he couldn't protect her from the real interloper that was slowly taking her life away.

Mike asked me to go shopping with him for her birthday present. He picked out a very pretty sweater, and I wrapped it for him. We knew we were losing her, but neither of us could bring ourselves to talk about it. We had just had such a good time only a few short weeks ago in Tahoe, and she had been so much stronger then.

She celebrated her twenty-sixth birthday on April 15. Only a year earlier she had declared it was the happiest birthday she had ever had. This year was not that happy, but Mike was still at her side.

Chapter 48

Don't Let Him Forget

I went to see Peyton at her parents' house. She was in the downstairs bedroom. I had printed the pictures from Tahoe and put them in an album for her.

"Hey, I'm so glad you came," she said as I walked into the room.

She had circles under her eyes, and her face was puffy. She was retaining fluid again. Her smile was bright, but her eyes didn't have the sparkle. "I brought you something." I handed her the picture album with a dragonfly on the front.

She started looking through them. "Oh, thank you so much. You knew how much these would mean to me." Her voice was soft with a quaver. *Please don't cry, Peyton. If you do, I will cry too, and I don't want to do that.* "Here, sit on the bed with me." She patted a spot next to her.

I sat down, and she gave me a big hug, which I returned. *Breathe, just breathe.* "So how's it going, Sweet Pea?" I was trying to keep my voice and demeanor light.

"Okay, but I can't do much of anything. I get so tired. Mama Hen, I'm not ready for this."

"I know Peyton." *Oh, I wasn't ready for this either!*

"They told me when I left New York if it came back, there probably wouldn't be anything they could do. They already did it all." She bit her lip and took my hand. "I wanted to get married and have babies. I'm gonna miss all of that. I won't even see Jenny's babies grow up."

"Oh, Peyton, honey, is there anything I can do to help?" That was such a feeble question.

"Tell me what to do. I don't know how to deal with this. I try not to think about it, but it's there all the time. The only times it goes away is when Mike makes me laugh." Her voice was stronger now.

"Well, I guess we'll just have to have him move in and keep you laughing during all your waking hours!"

"Or maybe laugh in my sleep?" She smiled. "My dad still doesn't want him to come in this house. I'm sorry, I shouldn't have said that, but it's true. It makes me so angry."

"Peyton, you have to try to see it from his point of view. No daddy thinks a guy is good enough for his daughter, and you are his special baby girl. He wants to protect you. He just hasn't given himself a chance to see the goodness in Mike."

"I really hope that someday he will see it because it's there. And he needs to know how much he means to me." She was about to cry.

"He will, Peyton. Just give him time."

"But I don't have much time left." I put my arms around her and just held her. I had never heard her talk this openly about her situation. She took a shuddering breath and wiped her eyes and pulled back. "I'm sorry. I try so hard not to do this."

"Oh, Peyton, honey, it's okay. You have to let your feelings out, or they'll get you all choked up being stuck inside." *That didn't sound right.*

She gave me that look with one eyebrow raised and said with a grin, "Well, yeah, I guess you could say that. Was that a pun?"

"That didn't come out right did it?" And we both laughed a little to break the tension. We sat on her bed and talked for a long time. She told me how much she loved her niece and nephew and how she hated that she would not be there for them. We talked about her writing them letters or deciding what special things she might leave for them. She was finding that so very hard to do. It seemed so final.

"I told Mike I was going to leave him a letter, and he told me he wouldn't read it. That he would just tear it up. I think he still wants me to believe I'll be here."

"I think he's having a little trouble thinking about this too, Peyton. He doesn't want the sky to fall. You do what you feel you want to do in your heart. He won't tear it up if you write a letter."

"Mama Hen …" She had to stop. We just sat quietly for a moment. "I want you to do something for me."

"Peyton, I will do anything in the world for you. Just tell me what."

"I don't want him to forget me. On my birthday every year, I want you to remind him how much I love him. And on his birthday too!"

"It's a done deal. I promise. But, sweetheart, I don't think he will ever forget you."

"I wish everybody knew how much he has meant to me. He's been there for me, and he just knew what I needed, even sometimes when I didn't. He still makes me laugh when no one else can. I love him most when he's silly. Well … sometimes I love him most when he just holds me. You know sometimes he came in the middle of the night just to hold me when I needed him. People don't know how good he's been for me. They just don't know."

"Peyton, do you have any idea how good you have been for him? You have loved him unconditionally when he needed it most. You are the one who believed in him and trusted him and saw beyond his actions to the goodness inside."

"I just want him to always know how much I love him … forever."

"I can't promise forever, but I can promise for as long as I live."

"Well, that will just have to do." She had a little bounce back in her voice. "Makes a heck of a story, doesn't it? We both had it all, with endless possibilities, until we both hit a brick wall in our lives. I get better; he gets put in jail. He gets better, and then I … get worse."

"I think it's a story of two people God meant to put together."

"Maybe you should try to tell our story someday. Remember when we listened to that song in Reno … the one about the broken road?"

"Of course I remember."

"I think it would make a good book." She thought for a minute, and then said, "But you can leave Kathy out!" She didn't laugh.

"But Kathy's part of the story too, Peyton. And the important thing to remember, even with Kathy, is that Mike hasn't ever left you. He never stopped caring, not for a minute."

"I know. She's just a place I can put my anger. I guess you can put that in our story."

I smiled, and we picked up the picture album and started looking through the pictures again. There was the special one of her Mike took above the lake. The wind was blowing in her hair, and her eyes were laughing as the sun bounced off her smiling face. I didn't know it would be the picture they would use in the newspaper for her obituary.

Chapter 49

Just Not Today

$\mathcal{M}$ ike was working full time at the bed store that had finally opened near us. The job at the TV station hadn't become available yet, but it was still a possibility. He had called and asked if I wanted to have lunch with him. And that meant I needed to bring food to him at the store, where we would eat because he was working alone that day. I was in the middle of some other chores but said sure I'd be there soon. It would be a chance for us to chat, and I enjoyed that.

Peyton was in the hospital again. The fluid was building up, and they had to get it off.

It was supposed to be routine, but each time was becoming more difficult. That day something happened, and it was all going south. The vital signs were failing, and the situation was getting critical.

Peyton told her mother to call Mike at work and tell him to come to the hospital. She was scared. Liz made the phone call just as I was walking into the store with Mike's lunch.

"Beds Plus, Mike speaking." He was on speaker phone.

"Mike it's Liz. Peyton isn't doing well. She wants you to come to the hospital. She needs you, Mike. Things aren't looking good, and the doctors ..." her voice was faltering.

"I'll be right there. I just need to close up."

"Mike, come soon."

"Tell her I'm on the way." He had already told the store owner if the emergency call came about Peyton, and he was alone, he would have to close up the store. "We gotta go, Mama." He was already moving to turn off the lights and lock up.

"My car or yours?" I asked.

"Both. Just follow me."

"Are you sure you're okay to drive?"

"Yes. Let's go."

He locked the front door, and within minutes we were on the way to the hospital. We were almost there when I realized I looked terrible, with no makeup and shorts and a tennis shirt. I couldn't worry about that right then. I just knew that I might need to be there for Mike and for Peyton. I probably wasn't thinking about how my rushing into this situation might not be totally appropriate, especially to Mark, Peyton's dad.

We parked, and Mike knew exactly where to go, as he had been to visit the night before. We got to the room and Liz was outside. "Mike, I'm so glad you're here. She was in a panic that you might not make it."

That sounded so ominous. They went in, and I stood just inside the door. She looked so pale and fragile. Her breathing was shallow and she had that frightened look in her eyes. He walked into the room and said, "I'm here, baby, I'm here."

She reached out her arms, and he went to her, and they hugged, and we heard her raspy breath. Her breathing was labored, and there was panic in her eyes. She said, "This can't be the end. It's not time. Not yet. *Not yet!* Mikey, tell me the sky is not falling."

"It's okay, baby, it's okay. The sky is not falling." He sounded calm and reassuring.

"I'm scared, Mike, I'm so scared."

"Don't be. You're okay." His voice was strong and comforting.

"I was afraid you weren't going to get here."

"I'm here, baby, I'm here, and I'm not going anywhere."

"Don't let the sky fall, not yet."

"Hey, there is no sky falling. You hear me? It's not happening, not today!"

"Not today!" A little smile turned at the edges of her mouth, and she closed her eyes.

He took her hand in both of his and held it to his face and kissed it tenderly, and the tears fell from his eyes onto their entwined hands. She reached over with her other hand and caressed his check, and the fear left her eyes, and a bigger smile crossed her lips.

"Not today," she whispered.

I quietly slipped out the door and went down the hall where I buried my face in my hands and cried. *Please, God, don't take her. Not yet. I am so not ready for this.* I knew I had to pull myself together. I marveled at Mike's calm strength and once again felt such pride in this young man that was our son.

I asked Liz if there was anything I could do. She mentioned that she had tried to call the minister at their church but had not gotten hold of him. I told her I would keep trying. I called Paula, a close friend and my tennis partner who attended the same church, and asked for her help. She was the one who got hold of him, and he came to the hospital later that afternoon.

He did a wonderful job, and I think he was a great comfort to Peyton that day. She expressed her concerns about those around her being cheated and having to deal with her tragedy. Again Mike reassured her.

"Peyton, I will never regret in any way being a part of your life, no matter what happens. You have made me such a better person. No regrets, baby, only gratitude."

Dan and Jane came, and I know they were a great support to Mark and Liz. They had been close friends for years, and Dan was someone Mark could talk to.

Peyton's vital signs were improving and things were looking a little better. This was a time for Peyton and her family. I had probably overstepped my boundaries by being in her room so much that day. I forgot for a while they didn't know how close I felt to their wonderful daughter. But it was time for me to go. I went in to tell her I was leaving the hospital. I knew I needed to be as upbeat as possible, and this could not sound like a final good-bye.

"Peyton, I'm heading out. Looks like you are in great hands here."

"Just don't take Mike with you," she said with a hint of panic.

"No, of course not."

"Thank you for being here, Mama Hen. I'll call you in the morning. I'm not going anywhere tonight. The babies are on the way from Atlanta, and I need some more hugs from them." She smiled and squeezed my hand.

"Okay, I'll talk to you tomorrow," and I hugged her and kissed Mike on the cheek and left the room with a smile and a wave. I kept walking down the hall and out of the hospital, but my smile disappeared as soon as I left Peyton's room. This was so hard. I wanted to be strong for Peyton and for Mike, but I felt like I was crumbling inside. *This can't be happening, not yet, please, not yet.* I didn't have the strength to let go of this beautiful young woman. As always, it was in God's hands.

Chapter 50

To the Beach

*T*he phone rang bright and early the next morning. "Hey, Mama Hen, it's Peyton." She sounded much stronger and upbeat.

"Peyton! You sound great." *Thank you, God. Oh, thank you so much!*

"I told you I wasn't going anywhere, and besides Mikey assured me the sky wasn't falling."

"Well, there you have it. You really do sound much stronger Peyt."

"Yeah, we turned it around—this time. I just had to see the babies and do some things. Thanks for coming yesterday. I was starting to lose it. I really needed Mike to be here."

"I'm glad he was there too." I knew he would always be there for her, for as long as she lived.

When it was time for her to leave the hospital, she wanted to go to the beach. She knew the time was getting short, and I believe she was trying to think of a way to not leave lasting bad memories in her parents' home. Dan and Jane offered their beach house, and Peyton and her family moved out there. Again, good friends are such a blessing.

Her friends stopped by in batches at first, and then it was limited to her closest friends. Her brother and sister stayed, knowing the time was short. I was able to see her once for a few minutes at the beach house. I always called ahead, and the timing was never good for another visit. Mike tried to stop by too. It was a difficult few weeks, and one that was filled with her family.

As we knew it would, the day inevitably came. The phone rang with the news and indeed it felt as if the sky had fallen.

It was Mike. "Mama, she's gone."

"Oh no." My throat closed, and I just couldn't say a word. Mike was quiet on the other end.

Finally he said, "Mama, are you all right?"

It took everything I had just to say "Yeah ..." But I wasn't okay at all. I was having trouble breathing. "How about you?"

"This is hard, Mom. This is really hard." He was having trouble getting the words out. And then we just cried.

"Come home, Mike."

"Okay, Mama."

No matter how much I think I might be prepared to lose someone I love, when the time comes I'm not ready, not really. When Daddy died, I was not prepared at all. When Mom died, the doctor told us it was imminent, yet it was still a blow that took my breath away. When I heard Mike say the words, I felt shattered. It would take years before I could talk about Peyton without choking up. She was so young and had so much more life to live.

I don't know how long I'd been standing there when Ben came in to check on me. He knew the moment he saw me what the phone call meant. He put his arms around me, and we just stood there for a long time. I felt totally drained. We had loved Peyton so much, and now she was gone. A piece of my heart was gone. *Hold me, Ben, just hold me tight. Breathe.* I knew Mike was hurting too. I wished he had been with us at that moment. He was on the way. We needed to be together.

The next day I felt I had to do something and turned once again to writing. I started to write "Peyton was ..." and I realized Peyton would always be with us. Her spirit and love and who she was would be a part of us forever. So I wrote *Peyton is ...*

Peyton IS

Peyton is a bouquet of pink flowers ... with no carnations.

Peyton is the clean, fresh fragrance of spring ... no heavy perfume.

Peyton is the voice of every song I love.

Peyton is the mischievous planner of the best April fool's jokes ever.

Peyton is the competitor who loves having the right answer in Trivial Pursuit, and the winning hand in Poker, or better yet, a successful bluff. She is not afraid to go "all in."

Peyton is the sophistication and elegance of a single strand of pearls.

She is also the comfort of a worn pair of jeans, soft socks, and a warm chocolate chip cookie.

Peyton is the smile that bursts forth with nothing held back and laughter that is contagious. She is also that sly one sided grin with a raised eyebrow that sometimes says, "Uh Oh."

Peyton is that pouty little girl … that can "get over it" in the blink of an eye.

Peyton is the outstretched hand … never asking, always giving.

Peyton is the quiet beauty of a peaceful snow … and the silly little kid throwing the snowballs.

Peyton is the strength and grace of the snowcapped mountains.

Peyton is the promise of the sunrise and the peace of the rosy sunset.

Peyton is the "Wow" of a full moon shining on the ocean.

Peyton is the joy of a beautiful pink balloon floating on the wind.

Peyton IS and always will be with us. We are blessed.

I baked chocolate chip cookies and took them to Mark and Liz's house, along with a copy of *Peyton IS*. They asked if I would make more copies so others could have one. I was flattered and so grateful that I had found some small way to help.

Words and actions all seem so inadequate when parents have lost a child. What unbearable sadness.

Chapter 51

Pink Balloons

According to Peyton's wishes, there was no funeral service or funeral home visitation. That would not have reflected her spirit. There was a memorial service on the beach near the gazebo where she had gone on so many occasions and where Mike had met her on many sleepless nights. It was a place where I knew she had felt special peace and love.

We parked the car and walked past the gazebo and through the sand. So many people were there, young and old, to remember Peyton. Mike and Ben and I stood together saying very little. Peyton's little nephew came over to say hell-o to Mike. They had become good buddies when Mike had spent time in Atlanta with Peyton after the trip to New York. I had to hope he and his sister would remember their Aunt Peyton, who loved them so much. He was about three and an adorable little boy.

People mingled and talked. And then a quiet settled over the group, and Mark, Peyton's dad, spoke. He welcomed people and thanked everyone. Some others spoke, and a young man played a guitar. At the end of the ceremony, bunches of pink balloons were released. It was a fitting tribute to beautiful Peyton. We watched the balloons float high in the blue sky over the water, and then they were gone. *Peyton is the joy of a beautiful pink balloon floating on the wind. Good-bye, Peyton. We will miss you ... forever. But you will never be forgotten.* We quietly walked back past the gazebo, each with our own thoughts. Mike was such a stronger man for having known and loved Peyton.

Sometime later, when Mike heard about a friend whose daughter had cancer, he wrote a letter to him which summed up so much of what he felt for Peyton.

Howard:

My best friend Peyton lost her battle with a rare juvenile tissue cancer in May of 2004. She had just turned 26 years old. I had the opportunity to be with her every day for most of her last year. We traveled, we laughed and we loved. The experience gained and the lessons we learned were immeasurable. Along the way I had the choice experience of staying at the Ronald McDonald House on the Upper East Side of New York City. Peyton and I stayed there while she took tests at Sloan-Kettering. I learned so much about life and sanctity, and the blessings that we all have.

I miss her every day, and keep a picture of her on my desk, not as a reminder of who she was, but, of what she taught me. We are all blessed, and nothing in this world happens by mistake. If there is anything I can do to help, please do not hesitate to ask. Sorry we haven't been in touch, but common experience bridges time and distance.

God be with you.

Mike

Mike had indeed learned so much from Peyton, and it changed the way he lived his life. He was a young man who was truly grateful for each new day. I saw him reach out to others struggling with addiction. I have no idea how many people he has helped through AA. He was on a different street, and so were we. No loss before or since broke my heart any more than losing a beautiful young woman named Peyton. *Thank you, Peyton, for being such an important part of our lives.*

Chapter 52

Where Will the Road Lead?

he next weeks passed, and the sharp edge of the pain of losing Peyton seemed to ease a bit. Life went on, as it does when you have lost a loved one. But I could not talk about Peyton. I knew that someday I would try to write the story, but I also knew it would take a while before I could do that. A long while.

Mike got the call from WWET, and he went back to the TV station to work as a cameraman. He was thrilled to be back and so grateful to Ann for suggesting him for the job. She was aware of his past, and his ongoing recovery. She had never lost faith in Mike as a person or in his talents. She knew he was very good at his job. He worked as a "one man band," which meant he was his own photographer, reporter, and editor of stories. That was the advantage of having worked there before and doing a wide scope of jobs.

Kathy was still in the picture. We met her parents, and they were very nice. Mike and her dad got along exceptionally well. We even went to their vacation home in Pinehurst to play golf with them. Mike was spending more and more time at her apartment. I liked Kathy, but the role she had played in the triangle with Peyton was something that would not go away for me. My reluctance wasn't her fault. I had enough sense to realize this was a relationship that did not need my interference.

Melody, Mike's birth mother, was going to come to North Carolina in July. Ben and I had already planned a trip to Seattle for the exact time she could come. After thinking it over, we decided to go ahead with our plans. After all, this would be the first time for her to meet Mike, and that was what was important. By this time, I was able to see Mike as an independent and responsible young man. Though it was still a struggle to not "over manage," I think I was making progress. I somehow knew this first meeting with his birth mother was something he was perfectly capable of handling on his own. Again, I had the strength to let go and trust that we were on the right road. Before we headed to the airport. I left a letter on the entry table for them.

July 27, 2004

Dear Melody and Mike,

Please know that Ben and I are so happy that you have the opportunity to reunite. Again, we are sorry we are not here for this first momentous meeting. However, this is your time to get acquainted and share your thoughts and feelings. We know we will have time in the future to be with you together and we look forward to that.

Melody, how can we thank you enough for your generous decision back in 1976? Your unselfish choice gave us the answer to our hopes and dreams and prayers. Who knows how Betty, our adoption counselor, came to the decision to place Mike with our family instead of someone else. What a wise woman. When she came for our home visit, I fed her a quiche that had two bottom crusts with the paper in between. Now that really impressed her with my skills as a homemaker! We laughed a lot at that one.

You will find he has a mind of his own, a great sense of humor and a heart of gold. He is not perfect, he is delightfully human with some flaws and rough spots and the road has had more than a few bumps. We wouldn't have "missed the dance" for anything in the world. So Melody, we are so happy to share our son with you and we look forward to meeting you in the near future. You are always welcome here.

Mike, what an exciting time for you! You know it makes me a little crazy to not be here, but we also know I would babble on and on and truly this is **your** time with Melody. We are so proud of you and it is wonderful to see you grow and mature into adulthood. Congratulations on the way you have handled this search. It reflects your intelligence and compassion. You are a fine young man and we are sure Melody will be happy with what she brought into this world. Dad and I are confident that she will see what a good person you are.

It just wouldn't be natural if I didn't give you some advice so here goes: Make sure there are clean towels in the bathroom.

XXOOXX

Mike picked Melody up, and as they drove back to our house, he stopped at DART Cherry to speak to the residents there. It was the second time he had been invited back to speak. Though Mike had shared some of his journey through addiction with her on the phone, she got to listen to his story first hand as he told it to others that day. Mr. Mayton, the head of the program, sat next to her. She didn't run for cover, and I give her lots of credit. It was a painful journey she was hearing about.

That first visit between Mike and Melody went well. He introduced Melody to our good friends Rob and Beth, and they commented on how similar they looked as they walked down the sidewalk. He was definitely capable of dealing with situations without me hovering over his shoulder. Thank God we were all walking on a different sidewalk.

Mike excelled at his job, and in December he was promoted to full-time reporter. He received several letters of congratulations, but the following short notes probably meant the most to him.

Congratulations, Mike. I'm very proud of you!

Ann

He had not let Ann down. She had gone to bat for him, and he would always be so grateful for her support. He did his first prime-time breaking live news shot standing next to Ann. He keeps a picture of that event in his office too.

And the following letter from Peyton's mother was so heartwarming.

Dear Mike,

I am really proud of you and I have a feeling that the lady upstairs is smiling from ear to ear. You have really proved that nothing in this life is impossible. You just went off the wrong path, and I join many that say, good job, well done. Peyton always had faith in you and she was right.

You were a very good friend to Peanut, as she was to you and somehow in the twisted path that her life took, you both found each other, cared for each other, helped each other to get through the toughest of times. Stay on this path, and continue to make yourself proud. She always knew you could do it.

I saw you the other day on TV, and was so excited for you, and your folks. You have wonderful parents that have stuck by your side. You've made us all proud of your accomplishments. Well done.

Love, Liz

That Christmas, Mike bought two tiny pink angels in remembrance of Peyton and gave one to me and one to her mother.

We went into the new year of 2005 with a positive outlook. I became president of the Ladies Golf Association at our club, continued with my acting, and served on several committees. Dealing with Mike and his issues no longer needed to take center stage in my life. I was also walking down a different street, which was long overdue.

Of course, I still had my controlling moments where I had to worry about the details of his life. So many of my thoughts and actions still came out of fear. It was difficult to back off and let him find his own path and deal with decisions he made. Those old patterns are hard to break. I was still trying to protect my child, and he was no longer a floundering child; he was a capable man.

It was time to hit the road for our annual family vacation to Tahoe. It would be difficult going back where we had spent our last good times with Peyton, but we had another lady who would be our guest that year. Mike's birth mother, Melody, would be coming from Texas to spend a week with us. Ben and I were looking forward to meeting her and getting better acquainted. It turned out she was so easy to get to know, and we all felt very comfortable together.

Once again, good things were happening in Tahoe. Mike had sent a tape of his work to a Reno TV station, and they had granted him an interview for when we were there in March. They were impressed with his award-winning reporting and his outgoing personality. Just as the news director was about to offer him the job, Mike felt he had to fill him in more thoroughly on his background. He told him the truth, including the felony conviction. At that point, the news director told him he would have to think about the job offer and let him know in a few days.

Mike came back to the lake, and we could tell he was going through a bit of private hell. This was his first encounter with having to deal with his past in a job interview. At his current TV station, they knew his story when they hired him back. Now he had to wait and see what impact his revelation would have.

On the second day, he got a call asking him to come back and interview again with a larger group of management. How intimidating would that be? We all gave him words of encouragement before he drove to Reno.

He came back feeling guardedly optimistic. He had been interviewed by a group of four including the station manager, another manager, the news director, and the associate producer—who he described as a very cute blonde. He was all but pacing the floor waiting for their decision.

275

I prayed whatever was best for Mike would be the outcome from that interview, but I had to add an additional little request. *And please, God, don't make him wait too long.* While I had learned I was not the one in control, I couldn't resist pushing a little. Maybe it helped, because the phone call came offering Mike the job at the station in Reno, Nevada. He was so happy and relieved, but at the same time he hated to leave his current station. Those were the people who had believed in him, trained him, and welcomed him back with open arms. He owed them a lot. Reno was a bigger market and was the way to move up in the business. It was also an area where he had dreamed of living since he was a boy. How could he say no?

He called his mentors, anchors Jim and Ann, and gave them the news. They encouraged him to take the opportunity. He sent his resignation notice from Tahoe and set out to find a place to live when he would move there in late April. It was a busy trip indeed.

We returned home, and a month later Mike packed everything he owned into his car and a car-top carrier and set off in a new direction. The road was taking him to Reno and away from Kathy. We were both proud of his accomplishments that had earned him this opportunity. I could wish him well out of trust and love. The fear was gone—well almost gone. And we did loan him some money for the move and to get started before his first paycheck. We felt he had earned our support at that point. This was not the enabling behavior of our past, but our show of confidence in our son's recovery.

Mike was very involved with AA. Once again I expressed some motherly concern. "Mike, are you sure you're going to be okay moving so far away? You don't know anyone there, and you have such a strong support system here." I will never forget his answer.

"Mom, I will always have friends and support wherever I go in the world for the rest of my life.

Chapter 53

Reno

$\mathcal{M}$ ike drove to Reno with a stop in Missouri to visit with family. He called to tell us he got a speeding ticket just inside the Nevada border on a stretch of flat and straight road. I immediately started to worry that perhaps that was a bad omen for things to come. But then I had to remind myself to just stop. *Stop worrying. He can handle it!* It was his issue to deal with, not mine.

He settled into his rental house with a housemate and quickly fit into his position as reporter at the TV station. I could only hope he would feel secure and comfortable in his new home.

What a relief to know he would have an instant support system with AA. He immediately got connected and got a sponsor. He knew what he needed. He was no longer that irresponsible boy. He was a man who knew where he was going and what he needed to do. He wrote a letter six weeks into his move to Reno. Being completely on his own financially was indeed a new experience…and also overdue.

Hey,

Six weeks into my new life and I have yet to need your help. That's longer than I thought I'd make it. I have mismanaged some funds, playing a little poker. Not a lot, just some. The speeding ticket I got didn't get paid on time, now I owe more. This probably comes as no great surprise, but I'm learning. And I know the over use of my bank card isn't the way to handle stuff.

However, I am making money, staying sober, and learning from my mistakes. It's harder than I thought to do this, but I'm smart and I'm learning. My rent is paid, my cell phone is on and I have paid my loan payment to the Department of Education. The basics are met.

Money coming Friday, money (not a lot) in the bank, money coming your way soon. I do not want to shortchange the awesome loan Dad gave me to help with the move, and I will not. I will, no matter how long it takes or how many nights I have to eat ramen noodles and watch TV, pay it back. I'm learning what it FEELS like to live on what I make. It FEELS different than what it was like living at home rent free.

The really good news is I am making it, and I know this may be hard to believe, I am very happy here. I have connected with a few good folks in AA, and a good person or two at work. The setting for this chapter in my life is gorgeous. I wake up wondering what new adventure this day will bring. The Governor of this state knows me by name. So does the homeless guy I give a dollar to on my way home from work. And Peyton even visits a time or two a week. You have never seen pinker sunsets in your life. Is *pinker* a word?

Oh well, I guess you can tell every now and then I miss ya. Hope you liked my snow story. Today I actually had to interview the Governor. Ahhh ... this certainly beats jail.

XXOOXX

Kathy had flown out for a visit in the summer, and the relationship was not going to endure the distance. We visited him in November on our way to Sedona, Arizona. He was happy and dating a nice young lady. We noticed he still kept a picture of Peyton on his desk at work. He was never going to forget her.

Mike called home about once a week, so we had some idea of what was going on in his life. He kept mentioning the cute blonde who was now the executive news producer from the station, but she was refusing to date him. She went to dinner with him but stated emphatically it was not a date ... so he didn't pay her check. I suggested this was no way to win her over if he was really serious. But again, mothers don't always know best.

He persisted, and she finally agreed to go out with him **one** time. He bought her some running shoes and took her to Galena Creek Park to hike. She was not a runner. That would not have been what I would have thought was a romantic date after he had been trying for so long to win her favor. And again, moms don't always know best. That one date turned into several more, but they kept it secret from the people at the TV station. I knew from the excitement in his voice, this "cute blonde" was someone special.

March came, and it was time for our annual trip to Tahoe. My brother's family was coming as well as my cousin Michael and his family. We would be in two big condos. Of course Mike was coming up to the lake for several of the days we were there, and we were finally going to get to meet Emily, the cute blonde from the TV station who was his boss—sort of.

What a way to meet Mike's family—in a big batch! She was a real trooper and handled it with ease. It was easy to see why Mike had been so taken with this young woman. The whole family fell in love with her, especially Hunter, my brother's son, who was no longer a "little" boy.

About this time, Mike had been approached about joining the weekend show at the station. It would mean a raise in pay, and he would be an on-air anchor. Now he needed suits and ties. He made a decision to also start taking a few classes toward a degree in broadcasting.

Mike and Emily maintained their secret relationship at work until later that spring. Mike was filming a story about the versatility of the area where he could snowboard in the morning up on the mountain and wakeboard in the afternoon down in Reno on a lake. While they were filming him doing a flip on the wakeboard, he totally blew out his knee. He went on to work as his knee continued to swell and the pain increased. No one missed Emily's concern or that she was the one who drove him home. The cat was out of the bag. And the knee was headed for surgery early in the summer.

We flew out to Reno when Mike was scheduled for knee surgery. Emily had already planned an Alaskan cruise with her family, so she would be leaving three days after the surgery. They had decided to share a house after she returned. This relationship was definitely special.

Mike was very careful with pain medication after his surgery. He had Emily keep it, then us after she left for Alaska. He knew the dangers of letting drugs make you feel too good. He managed with a minimum of medication. It was great to see his sense of responsibility.

We helped him move his things into the house he and Emily would share. She would return just as we were leaving. It looked like things were going very well for Mike in Reno. His road had taken him to a good place. He had found his princess, and he was about to get "man's best friend" too. He was getting a dog. Life was good.

But the road is never without twists, turns, and ruts. A few months later, things were not going well at the TV station. There were some management issues and an incident where Mike remained loyal to his coworkers. He left the TV station.

He took a job with Subaru car dealership while he was looking for a better job. He excelled at car sales and was making more money than he ever had. He and Emily flew to Wilmington in October, and at dawn he took her to the beach by the familiar gazebo and asked her to marry him, and she said yes.

That Christmas we flew to Albuquerque to meet her parents, Dave and Cindy. We talked about their plans for a wedding in July. We were all delighted. As Peyton had predicted, the right woman had come along, and he had fallen hard.

It was an exciting time. Our only son was going to be Prince Charming, getting married to a beautiful Cinderella in a fairy tale wedding. But the road to the wedding was not totally smooth either. Mike was being a typical man, and Emily was a frustrated bride planning her wedding. One more time I couldn't resist giving Mike a bit of "motherly" advice.

Wedding Planning:

When it comes to weddings, women are going to think differently than men. Period! For most women, their wedding day is a fairy tale they start thinking about when they are very young. It is their day to be the BRIDE, the beautiful bride. We assume it is only going to happen once in our lifetime and we want it to be perfect.

Now that's the first problem ... Is there such a thing as a perfect wedding??? Most brides don't ever understand the key ingredient ... at least not before the wedding. The key ingredient is how they feel on the inside that day, and that doesn't have anything to do with all the little details they have stressed over and cried over and wanted to pull out their hair over ... or yours ... for the months of planning. But here is the thing ... you can't tell a bride that before the wedding. They won't get it! So the way the groom can contribute is to do the best he can to survive the planning and make the bride feel so extra special that it all <u>feels</u> perfect.

This isn't going to be an exercise in logic. Throw that out the window. All those things that don't mean a hill of beans to guys, like what flowers to use, color of bride's maid's dresses, and so on ... well those are important to most brides. So be supportive and enthusiastic and don't just say "who cares!" Because SHE cares! In our quest to have that "perfect" wedding, we have some crazy illusion that it is important to US that YOU are perfectly happy about every little detail. Women will start second guessing decisions trying to make you happy and that can really complicate things. So be enthusiastic about the details. Look at it this way ... you really DO care because if these little things make your bride feel happy ... You will be happy too!

Just know that the weeks planning THE wedding are stressful. It is a kind of test to see if you can live through the ordeal and still have any idea that you really want to spend your life with that person. She will want to talk about the wedding way more than you will. Give her some time and listen ... really listen. She will ask your opinion and hope you will agree with <u>her</u> ideas on some things and really want <u>your</u> input on other things. Now here is the trick. You have no way to know when she wants your input and when she wants your agreement. Good luck.

A secret ingredient to interject at every opportunity is a sense of humor. But frequently that can backfire too! Good luck again! Normally when all else fails, put your arms around her and kiss her on the head and tell her you love her. Men used to carry handkerchiefs to wipe away tears. Guess you have to know where the tissue box is at all times in the next few months.

As women, we never want to appear weak or weepy or indecisive. Never mind if we act that way during this planning period. Get over it! I told you, this is a test. It is very likely the bride will take out lots of frustrations on the groom. You can take it! Right? GROOM stands for Get Ready to Overcome Overemotional Moments. Your reward is a lifetime with a wonderful woman who will love you forever and never act this way again … until she gets pregnant.

Love, Mom

XXOOXX

It was glorious to see Mike happy and healthy, to watch him move on. Life was getting better and better. I loved being able to write to him for fun. On Mother's Day I sent him a special card:

Happy Kid Day!

When you were younger, you used to ask "When is it going to be Kid Day?" And I wanted to answer "Every day is Kid day," because you got pretty special treatment most of the time … or at least that was my perception.

This Mother's Day is special to me because in July you will be taking a big step in your life. While it has been pure joy to see you grow into a man these last few years, there is something extra special about you getting married. For a mother, it is that time when we really let go and put you in the hands of another woman. Because everyone knows (especially Moms) that all men need to have the nurturing care of a woman who loves them.

So this Mother's Day I honor you, The Kid, because you gave me the chance to be a Mom. I give you my love, and best wishes for all the wonderful things your future holds. I give thanks for today and every day that you are healthy and happy. I rejoice in all the memories of your youth and embrace the good times and the bad. We could have missed the pain, but then we would have missed "the dance."

When you take Emily in your arms at that reception as your wife, there will be no one any happier than I to see that dance! I believe you are exactly where God meant you to be … and that is your chance!

Congratulations son and happy Kid Day!

Chapter 54

The Wedding

he Thursday before the wedding was Ben's birthday. We reserved a room at a restaurant near the hotel for a birthday celebration. Emily spent that evening with her family. It was a special night with close friends and family who had played such an important role in the journey that brought us to this happy occasion of Mike and Emily's wedding.

Bill was there from the day we brought Mike home to that little town in Texas, and it was so special having him at the wedding with his wife. Joyce and Dwight, who had stood by us as we made the trip to Canaan, Connecticut, were there. Rob and Beth, our pillars of strength in North Carolina, were there, of course. Beth had been the one to take Mike's calls from the jail and patch them on to me in Tahoe. They had all been on this journey with us. Margaret was there, and we were missing Dennis, our captain, who had died unexpectedly the year before. Our old high school buddy Gary was there with his wife Louise. All of these people had been such wonderful friends through all these years of both good and bad with Mike. My brother, who had spent countless hours with me on the phone, was there with Jackie and Hunter. I truly don't know what would have happened had he not stepped in to help when we discovered what was in Mike's bag when Mom died. Ben's brother, Guy, and his wife were there too along with Jackie's Mom. It was a group of our closest family and friends.

We were having a great time, and I stood to say a few words. "I want to thank all of you for being here. It means the world to us to have you share this wonderful happy occasion of Mike's wedding. It has taken all of you to get us to this day. Bill, you were there the day we brought him home. It does take a village to raise a child, and you have all had a part of that." I felt myself starting to choke up, and I hadn't even said happy birthday to Ben yet. Mike came to my rescue.

He stood up, gave me a hug, and said his own thanks to everyone there, and then he turned to Ben and said he wanted to honor his dad.

"Dad, I spent years being defiant and not wanting to be like you at all, but I was being stupid then, and we all know I was making some really bad decisions. But now there's no one I could want to emulate more." He had to stop a moment as he put his hands on his hips and looked down. And then he looked up and made direct eye contact with his dad.

"Dad, I want nothing more than to live my life in a way that will make you proud. I can never repay you for all you've done and for standing by me in the worst of times. There's no one I respect more. You are my best man in every way. I love you, Dad." He ended his remarks with giving his dad a giant bear hug. There was not a dry eye there.

The following night was the rehearsal dinner. It was a fun, informal Texas-themed barbecue in the pavilion in Galena Park near the site of the outdoor wedding scheduled for the next day. There were lots of tributes, but the one that was most memorable was given by Hunter. He talked through tears about how much Mike had always meant to him and how proud he was that Mike had made it through his tough times. It was another emotional evening.

Finally, the long awaited wedding day had arrived—July 21, 2007. What a wonderful world! Mike and Emily were married in a beautiful ceremony at Galena Creek Park, where they had their first date. What a glorious day it was with the bluest sky and a breeze blowing her veil.

Mike walked me down the aisle, and we chatted all the way. There was no time to remember all the sleepless nights I lay awake thinking a day like this would never happen. He looked so very handsome! *Breathe and don't cry!*

When Mike saw Emily start down the aisle, his eyes filled with tears. She was the most beautiful bride I had ever seen! The ceremony was special and so well planned by Emily. The little glass heart they filled with the two colors of sand representing the blending of two lives into one was very touching. Mike's sand had come from the beach where they had gotten engaged—near the gazebo. Melody, his birth mother, sang "Wind beneath My Wings," in her glorious voice. It was so special to have her there and even more special to have her sing.

Ben looked so handsome and proud as he stood there as Mike's best man. I know he had to be thinking how thankful we both were that Mike had found such health and happiness with Emily. Hunter was just beaming as a groomsman. And my brother and Jackie sat beside me like the pillars of support they had always been.

The reception was perfection, all the way down to the Cinderella castle ice sculpture. Mike handled his duties with charm from the first dance to the last. He acknowledged Emily's hard work in planning the event and admitted he had contributed little, but had such an appreciation as he looked out at the room and the people there. He openly expressed his gratitude. I admired his willingness to be so open with his feelings.

That week in Reno with friends and family will always be one of the highlights of our lives. It was filled with love and joy and thankfulness.

Those are the kinds of moments we live for. To have friends and family there to celebrate with us was such a blessing. Our journey had finally led to happiness for our little family.

More than once that week I thought of Peyton and how very proud she would have been. She would have loved Emily, and Emily would have loved her. I think she is at peace with giving her Mikey over to Emily. *Rest in peace, Peyton. All is well.*

Chapter 55

The Road Back Home

The year after the wedding passed quickly. Management issues worsened, and Emily also left the TV station and went to work at the Peppermill Hotel as an event coordinator. Mike got promoted to the position of financial manager at the car dealership. He was still working sixteen hours a day and not loving his job. The money was great, but it was not his passion.

In October 2008 Emily got laid off from her job, as the economy was not helping the hotel and casino business. She was seeking an affiliation with a marketing and management company, but had not landed a contract just yet.

And then the phone call came out of nowhere ... well actually it came out of North Carolina. Would Mike consider coming back to his old TV station to be a weekend anchor and weekday feature reporter? He called to discuss it with us. It would be a big reduction in his income, but Emily was willing to make the move and the sacrifices of a lower income. She loved the beach and the North Carolina weather.

"What do you think, Dad?"

"Well, Son, I would think long and hard about taking that kind of pay cut. The economy is tough right now, and you're bringing in some darn good money."

"Yeah, I know, but this is just not what I see myself doing forever. And honestly, I really love North Carolina."

"Well, the decision is yours to make, but just think about it," Ben said.

"Thanks, Dad. I will." We talked a little more and hung up. He called back the next day.

"Mom, what do you think?"

"What does your gut tell you, Mike?" I asked him. I think I already knew the answer. I heard it in his voice the minute he called to tell us about the offer.

"I don't want to work in the car business forever, but Dad's right, about the good money."

"What is your passion, Son?"

"It's TV. I loved it, and I miss it. I was excited to go to work every day when I was in TV."

"Mike, do you know how many people never find their passion when it comes to their job? That kind of excitement is worth a lot. Just listen to what you're saying."

"Yeah, I know. I bet you wouldn't mind to have us back there either, would you?" He laughed.

"Well, of course not! But the key is what will make you and Emily happy. This is a big decision."

"She's ready to move, and she loves the beach."

"What's holding you back then?"

They decided they would make the move. Mike was coming home, back to what had become his hometown. He wrote a letter to the evening anchor who had been his mentor, and it said it all.

Hey Jim,

It was really good talking to you the last couple of days on the phone. I can't tell you how exciting the prospect of returning to WWET is for me. It seems like the place has undergone some big changes since my departure in 2005. I'm aware, as my father likes to say, "One can never return home and expect it to be the same," that the salad days of handing me a camera and saying, "go get news" may be gone for good, that the station might be different than I remember. I'm not trying to find that. What I'm looking for is the same thing WWET has given me time and again—an opportunity to grow.

You and Ann are the folks I confided in when I left TV in Reno in August 2006. I wanted to plant roots in the desert and grow. At the time I thought that I could leave TV alone and try something new. I was right, I can. Problem is I've got the bug. Bad. I didn't know it last week, but it's obvious, it's been there all along. Who am I kidding? People ask me often, "Why don't you go back into television?" Which I'd reply, "No money in it. This is better." Yeah right. I want to do television bad enough that I'm willing to leave the best job I have ever had and take a 50% pay-cut.

My Dad probably thinks I'm nuts. Some of the people I respect say I'm crazy, but I know what they don't. I lived on a third of what I make now when I moved to Reno, and I had the best time of my life. I lived on even less than that when I was back there at the station and showed up early, and smiling every single day. I guess I want what makes me happy and thank God, my wife wants that for us too.

Jim, I know you know talent. One thing that hasn't wavered a bit with me is my thirst to improve. If this works out, and I end up back there, I truly hope we can pick up where we left off. I hope that you would be kind enough still, as you were when I sent tapes from Reno, to show me things I can do to get better, ways I can master the craft. If I don't become the best, it won't be for lack of ambition.

Whatever happens, I'm glad that I've at least identified the sacrifices I'm willing to make to get back in the game. And I'm glad we've had the opportunity to reconnect. I know, I tell you this just about every time I talk with you but I am truly grateful to have people like you in my life. Thanks.

Mike

In December, they moved east and rented a three-story house in Sun Beach at the southern end of our little county not far from where Mike had that wreck so many years earlier. Emily had landed a contract just as Mike accepted the job. It was determined she could work the contract from North Carolina as well as Reno. Mike continued on his quest to get his broadcast degree. His journey had led him back home ... and, yes, I was very happy to have them here. Our son was coming back to his hometown, where he would find love and support from so many people.

Chapter 56

The Incident with the Dog

*S*ometimes life lessons come about in the strangest of ways. Mountains of books, hours of counseling, and stacks of letters could not have made this point any clearer. It took a near tragedy, but the point was made.

Mike loved his big black dog, Echo, unconditionally. Echo was a Lab/border collie mix, and Mike had trained him well. He won ribbons as a dock jumping dog in Reno. He was a Frisbee whiz, and he adored Mike.

Echo didn't like to be in the kitchen when Mike was cooking. That might say something about Mike's cooking, or just a quirk with the dog. When Mike cooked pancakes on the weekend, the dog would leave the kitchen, but Mike would call him back in to get the first pancake. It was the only "people food" Echo ever got.

On a Sunday as Mike cooked pancakes, Echo went upstairs to the third story of their beach house. When Mike called Echo to get the first pancake, he didn't come so he called him again. That was when they heard the simultaneous thump and yelp of pain. For some unknown reason, Echo had jumped over the railing of the third floor balcony and landed in the bushes just a few feet from the top of the picket fence or the hard ground in the other direction. The bushes undoubtedly saved his life, but he didn't make the leap unharmed. They rushed out to find him whimpering in the bushes with his right front leg at a horrible angle.

Mike picked him up gently as Emily called the vet. Mike cried as they rushed Echo into the clinic. He loved that dog so much, and I know it was killing Mike to know his beloved dog was hurting. He had to have surgery to insert a metal plate in his broken leg, and that would curb much of his athletic activities. It was sad news, but at least Echo was alive. However, he would have to deal with his injured leg for the rest of his life. He would have to protect it, and there were some things he could never do again. The surgery was costly, but there was no question for Mike and Emily. They would do what was necessary for the dog they loved.

We were at their house a few days later, and poor Echo was not happy about the big cone around his neck that kept him from licking the bandage on his leg. Mike looked at me with tears in his eyes as he said, "Mom, I just wish so much he hadn't done that. It doesn't make sense. Didn't he know how dangerous it was? Did he really think he could jump that far? He's such a smart dog. He came within inches of impaling himself on the picket fence! Mom, he could have died. Was it because I trained him to be a jumping dog? This hurts. I just don't understand <u>why</u> he did it." He put his hand up to his mouth and looked down at the floor.

And it hit me like a lightning bolt as I listened to Mike's sincere heartfelt questions. "I understand your frustration, Son, because I have been in your shoes." He wrinkled his brow and looked at me with a question on his face. "Now think how you would feel if the dog you love so much went up and jumped off that ledge time and time again, no matter what you did or said."

He got it. He felt it. We put our arms around one another and cried. "I'm so sorry, Mama. I'm so sorry."

Chapter 57

Thank You; Thank You

A year after Mike and Emily had moved to the house in Sun Beach, they decided to move closer into town. They were looking at rental houses, and I went with them from time to time. Mike had seen an ad in the paper, and the three of us went to look at the house.

We got out of the car, and the owner was standing on the front porch. *That couldn't be ... could it? Oh God, it was.* We walked up to the front door, and he greeted us and shook Mike's hand. I was speechless and walked into the house. I walked into the master bedroom followed by Emily. I needed a moment.

"Are you all right?" she asked.

Uh ... sure ... fine." I was just a little stunned, and I guess it showed on my face. "You don't know who that is, do you?" I asked.

"Who do you mean, the owner? No, do you know him?"

"Yes." I didn't know why I was finding it hard to breathe. Perhaps because this man had held our son's life in his hands on a very important day. "He's the judge that was in the courtroom the day Mike was sent to DART Cherry," I finally managed to say.

"Oh," she said. Though she knew Mike's history, she really had no reason to totally understand the major role the judge had played in saving Mike from a terrible fate.

Mike was in the kitchen talking to the judge when we walked in. They were discussing running or something. All of a sudden, the words just popped out of my mouth. "Judge, I just need to say something. You probably have no idea who we are but ..."

"Oh yes, I know exactly who you are," he said with a warm smile and a twinkle in his eye.

"You do?" I was caught off guard.

"Yes, indeed I do. I've been watching this young man." He put a hand on Mike's shoulder.

"Well, I just wanted to say thank you for what you did that day in court. We owe you so much for giving him a chance. I was so afraid that was going to be an awful day, and it ended up to be such a good thing."

"I thought he was going to make it. You've got a good young man here." He patted Mike's shoulder.

"Yes, we do." I felt the lump in my throat and thought I could talk over it. "And again I can't thank you enough." And with that I gave him a big hug, and the tears came. "I'm sorry, Judge. I didn't mean to cry."

"No problem. We love a success story. We don't see enough of them."

We went on to look at the rest of the house. It wasn't a good fit for Mike and Emily, but I was so grateful for the chance to express my gratitude to the judge who had given our son an opportunity to turn his life around.

We got back into the car. "Oh, Mike, I am so sorry. I didn't mean to embarrass you like that. The emotion just hit me."

"No problem, Mama. No need to apologize for feelings from your heart. He's a good guy, and he definitely deserves our thanks."

A few months later, I was shocked when I opened the morning paper and read the judge had died unexpectedly. I know there was a reason we looked at his house that day. I was so glad I had the chance to tell him "thank-you."

About a year after that, I was sitting in one of those pedicure chairs with my feet stuck in the bubbly warm water. A lady walked by going to the back of the salon. She looked so familiar but I couldn't place her. I was still thinking about it when she came back my way and looked directly at me and said, "You may not remember me, but I just wanted to speak to you."

"I'm sure I know you, but I am having a hard time remembering from where."

"I know your son, Mike." She smiled and slightly tilted her head, and I knew then immediately who this little lady was, even though she had on no tennis shoes!

"Oh yes, of course. Oh my, how many times I have thought about calling you to tell you how grateful we were that day in court." It was Mike's probation officer from the past, the one I had called the little old lady in tennis shoes. "I would love to give you a hug but ... I'm a little stuck here in this chair."

She walked over, and we had a hug, and she said quietly, "Actually I have thought about calling you also."

"Really?" *Oh dear.* What did that mean?

"I wanted to tell you a story that you might not know. A year later, after I had him arrested the last time, I was in the office when someone came back and said I had a visitor. I walked out and there stood your son, with roses in his hand. He asked me if I knew what day it was, and I said no. He said, 'You saved my life a year ago today,' and then he gave me the roses. I can't tell you how much that meant to me. He is such a fine young man, and I know you are very proud of him."

"Yes, we are. Thank you so much for telling me that," and once again I found tears rolling down my face.

"He's been back on other years on that anniversary and I always love seeing him. And now I get to watch him on TV." She had such a warm smile.

"I don't know how to thank you," I said to her over the lump in my throat.

"Watching your son succeed is all the thanks I need. He certainly seems to be on the right road. Have a nice day, and tell him I said hell-o." And she turned and walked away.

I just sat there in that big chair, wiping tears on my sleeve. My heart was so full of gratitude for this woman and the chance she and the judge had given Mike that day in court. Their actions, all of them, had played a vital role in Mike's recovery. Sometimes we don't understand the importance or have gratitude for what is happening at the time it takes place. They had both seen the goodness in our son, and that trust had paid off.

Too many young people who stumbled on their road and fell into the hole of addiction weren't given the same chance afforded our son. There is a strong need to rethink how we deal with addiction in this country. I shuddered to think what might have happened if Mike had been sent to prison instead of the DART program. His triumph was a great example of how a person can come back from the edge of total disaster by a commitment to ongoing recovery.

In 2010 for the first time ever the National Drug Control Strategy, from the Office of National Drug Control Policy focused on the importance and the need to invest in recovery.

> The millions of Americans who are in recovery are the most compelling evidence that there is hope for every addicted American. In the ongoing process of

299

recovery, individuals not only stop using substances, they reestablish friendships and family ties, become productive citizens, and very often help other addicted people begin to walk the same path. As recovery advocate and scholar William White has said, "Recovering people and their families and friends are becoming a powerful healing force in America. People who were once part of the problem have now become part of the solution."

A key to solving America's drug problem is greater support for and partnership with the huge number of our citizens who have recovered from addiction and who deserve the opportunity to fully rejoin society. Their accomplishment is both a wonderful achievement for them and their families and an inspiration to the millions of our citizens still struggling with addiction.

Office of National Drug Control Policy, 2010 National Drug Strategy, Page 35,
http://www.whitehouse.gov/sites/default/files/ondcp/policy-and-research/ndcs2010_0.pdf

Chapter 58

Hi. My Name Is Mom, and I Am an Enabler

*E*nabler—one that enables another to achieve an end;
One who enables another to persist in self-destructive behavior (as substance abuse) by providing excuses or by making it possible to avoid the consequences of such behavior

Women with strong maternal instincts are most apt to become the enablers of alcoholics and drug abusers. Most of what I felt and believed about being a good mother, in retrospect, didn't help in being the mother of an addict. My maternal instincts were to help my child through adversity, but in the process I was shielding him from learning important life lessons. My maternal need to help...wasn't helpful.

We strive in the beginning to enable our child, but then we must not enable the addict. I moved from one kind of enabler right into the next. Somehow, I missed the stop button. As mothers, we teach our little children how to button their shirt and tie their shoes, *enabling* them to dress themselves. We put the spoon back in their little hands, *enabling* them to feed themselves. We hold their hands, *enabling* them to learn to walk, but we know we have to let go at some point— and sometimes they fall. But then they learn where to reach out for support or how to get back up by themselves. If we never let them fall or if we pick them up and console them every time, we delay their ability to learn how to stand and walk on their own.

Trying to shield Mike and rescue him time and time again didn't prepare him to handle the bumps that are part of life's journey. It was a classic example of how I tried to *prepare the road for our child rather than preparing our child for the road.* I could have done more teaching and less preaching.

We tried to emphasize the positive and teach him responsibility and honesty and consequences for bad decisions. We tried to set good examples. We were unable to keep the sharp knife of addiction that cuts away health and happiness of both the addict and those who love him, out of his reach. Once he got hold of it, he wasn't prepared to handle it and neither were we. I was the overly protective enabler.

Even when I knew and understood I had to change my behavior, my fears still controlled my actions. I had to embrace the fact that I was not in control of Mike's life and living that reality was not a sign that I was giving up on him at all. It meant we were moving forward. As an enabler, I was continuing the status quo and delaying a positive future. It took time, some counseling and trust in God to have the strength to let go.

When Mike was finally ready and equipped to fight the addiction, it was his strength and determination, Peyton's love, and trust in God that allowed him to let go of the drugs and get on the road to recovery one day at a time.

It's not what you do for your children, but what you have taught them to do for themselves that will make them successful human beings. Ann Landers

Chapter 59

Coming Full Circle

his journey started with my overwhelming desire to become a mother. It was a long struggle, but in the end we got our baby boy. Parenthood was filled with such joy early on and followed by an avalanche of pain as we tried to find the path God intended for us as parents. Alcohol and drugs got a grip on our wonderful son and my fears led me down the path as his enabler.

I have learned so much on this journey and so much becomes clear in reflection. *"Life can only be understood backwards ..."* If we had taken a different fork in the road anywhere along the way, we would not have ended up where we are today. And today, we are so happy with where we are. I know other parents tried their best, asked for God's help, loved their children dearly but lost the battle and paid with the ultimate sacrifice of losing their sons and daughters.

I had so much fear that we were going to lose our son, and I didn't know where to turn. I needed direction and asked God to help. And then God sent an angel our way. Peyton came back into Mike's life at such a crucial time, when they desperately needed each other.

I still find it hard to accept that Peyton is gone. That seems so unfair, and it still makes me cry to know she was denied the life she so truly wanted. I have to believe she is in a beautiful, peaceful place without pain … maybe like that beautiful snow-covered day at Lake Tahoe. I sometimes wonder if the dragonflies I see are a little message from her. I assure you, she will never be forgotten. And here is where this story of hope and love and faith comes full circle … *because it must be lived forward.*

***

The phone jarred me awake at three o'clock in the morning. Instant panic was my first reaction always when the phone rang in the middle of the night, as those calls had never been good news. I grabbed the receiver off the headboard. "Hell-o."

"Mom, we're going to the hospital." It was Mike. "Mom, it's time. She's having labor pains, and we need to go to the hospital." Mike sounded excited and a little panicked himself.

I tried to stay very calm. This was not bad news. "How far apart are the pains? Did her water break? Is she doing okay?" *Too many questions to ask at once.*

"Emily, how far apart is the water?" he shouted.

"No, honey, how far apart are the pains?" I tried to clarify.

"I don't know, Mom, but we are going to the hospital. Can you meet us there? And bring the camera."

"Yes, of course. Slow down and breathe. You probably have plenty of time."

"Okay, I gotta go. We'll see you there. I love you, Mama. Can you believe this is happening?" And he hung up. I smiled. I was so unbelievably happy this was happening. I was finally going to be a grandma.

Ben was awake. It was a week early of the predicted due date, and that was unusual for a first baby, but babies tend to come on their own schedule. I was putting my clothes on and reminding myself to slow down and breathe, but this was tremendously exciting.

Emily had been so gracious to ask me if I would like to be in the delivery room with them. I was so moved and delighted to be asked to join them in this special time. Mike wanted Ben there too, and Ben understood Emily's concern for exactly where he would be in the room.

I was going to the hospital, and Ben would come over later. I got there while they were still prepping Emily. She had a little of that deer in the headlights look, and Mike was trying to be comforting ... and funny. She wasn't laughing a lot.

They moved us up to what is called a birthing suite. It was unbelievable to me. This was so comfortable, with a couch and TV, and this was the room where she would stay all the way through the delivery. I called Emily's mom to assure her we would keep her posted on the progress. She and Emily's dad would fly in the next week from Albuquerque.

I found myself thinking back years ago to how I had so desperately wanted to be in a delivery room. After all those years, I was finally there, and it couldn't have been a sweeter experience. I watched as our loving son comforted and coached his wife through the delivery of our granddaughter. Ben was there, armed with his book and puzzles on the couch, where he could observe but not too closely. Emily did a great job, and so did Mike. Eleven hours after the phone call, with one last very hard push, in July 2010 Peyton was born. We all cried and laughed and marveled over the little, tiny baby Peyton. She was perfect!

Emily, our wonderful daughter-in-law, was so understanding and generous in knowing how important it was to Mike to name their baby girl after the person who had taught him so much about the meaning of life. *Thank you, Emily. We love you.*

Peyton, you will not be forgotten.

Forever!

As we weave the tapestry of our lives with each tiny colored thread, it is not clear what the final picture will look like. Certainly it feels like there are flaws and knots and broken threads along the way, but perhaps that is exactly how it is meant to be. The progress of the picture in the tapestry is obvious, only as we step away and look back upon it. And by the grace of God, we keep on weaving.

Jo Henry
Johenry1445@gmail.com

Miracles Do Happen

*I*n the beginning of the book I asked a question. Do we ever really know the path our life will take, and looking back, would we change it if we could? I certainly had no idea of the path my life would take sitting in my bed playing paper dolls as a naïve little girl. At that age, no one ever does. Certainly as we were going through some of the struggles along the way I thought I would have traded the pain to be in a happier place…in a heartbeat.

But looking back now, those struggles, those boulders, those decisions we made along the way, both bad and good, brought us to where we are today. I can say with certainty, the journey has made us stronger and I have to believe Mike was right. Things do happen for a reason.

Another book could be written about Mike's success and long list of accomplishments. But for now, just know there is a positive future possible for those who fall into the hole of addiction.

To our son, I admire you more than words can say and marvel at how your journey has become so glorious. I have learned volumes as we traveled this broken road and found our way out of the shadows into the sunshine. I salute your strength, your integrity, your compassion, your wisdom, and your trust in God. We are so blessed to have you in our lives. *I love you, Son, forever.*

Updates

1. Coach Roberts, the cross-country coach, retired, and Mike helped plan his party and gave a tribute speech filled with memories. Some of Mike's old high school teammates are still his running buddies as he continues to run and coach young runners.

2. Mike's drug buddy, Jack, has been to prison more than once, and as I began writing this book, he was sober and doing very well. He has since died from complications of drug use. Many of the poker players are thriving and successful in their recovery.

3. Mike's birth mother, Melody, and her family are still a part of Mike's life and always will be. Hey, more love is not a bad thing.

4. Echo, the dog, is thriving and can still catch Frisbees and run and play. He is little Peyton's best buddy.

5. Mike and his wife started an event planning company. Ben is the CFO, and I am the CBS—chief baby sitter. It is such a joy to see Ben and Mike work together as two grown men filled with mutual respect, trust, and love. Mike got his broadcast degree shortly after Peyton was born. Ann, the TV anchor, is still a very close friend and mentor to Mike.

6. Mike has had a boulder or two crash into him with a devastating force since his stay at DART Cherry, but he has managed

to stay clean and sober for over twelve years as I write this book. He knows how to seek support through AA and, more importantly, how to give that support back to others. What a fantastic organization.

7. We all remain very close to my brother and his wife. He's still a big, lovable teddy bear and reminds me more of Dad every day. Mike's cousin, Hunter, married his high school sweetheart, and Peyton was the flower girl in the wedding.

8. Mike and Emily take little Peyton to see our special Peyton's parents from time to time. They came to a party celebrating Mike's ten years of sobriety. Peyton's dad embraced Mike with warmth and understanding a long time ago. I know that makes Peyton a happy angel.

9. I am deliriously happy with my role as little Peyton's "Mimi." I still struggle with being a controlling and worrisome mom and grandmother and mother-in-law. I'm an enabler in recovery. God isn't finished with me yet.

10. I can talk about our special angel Peyton now and remember the good times and not cry ... most of the time.

11. Mike has been asked back many times to speak at DART Cherry. Mr. Mayton, the director, has retired, but stays in touch. Mike was the speaker at the annual area AA Christmas banquet. I have watched him touch the lives of so many people in such a positive way. I believe God indeed has a plan in mind for our son, and I am awed as I watch his journey continue to unfold.

It was almost exactly ten years since the day Mike got clean and sober. He had to take a CPR course because he coaches cross-country. Just ten days later, he went on a trip to Pittsburgh to visit Emily's grandparents. That trip had almost been cancelled and was rescheduled twice. He entered a 5k race and Emily decided to enter at the last minute. After Mike finished, he circled back around to encourage and run in with Emily. As they crossed the finish line, a runner collapsed and wasn't breathing. Mike, without hesitation, administered CPR. When the EMT's arrived, they used the paddles to get the heart beating again. They told Mike he had definitely saved the man's life.

A week later, Tim, the man he saved, called from the hospital in Pittsburgh.

"Mike, I'm at the hospital," Tim said.

"Are you okay? Why are you back at the hospital?" Mike was immediately concerned.

"I'm fine. Mike, I just wanted to say thanks again. My first grandchild was just born and if it weren't for you, I wouldn't be here." And then they both cried. I believe Mike was trained and in that exact place on that day for a reason.

Mike was given The Citizen's Hero Award by our fire department and Tim and his wife flew in as a surprise. In an interview, Tim said, "He could have given up on me, but he didn't. Somewhere along the way a coach or a parent told him to complete the race, finish what you start."

How many threads in the tapestry did it take to reach that moment?
And we keep on weaving.

Acknowledgments

This book could not have been written without the help and support of so many people who are very dear to me. First and foremost, I thank our wonderful son for letting me share this story. My husband is the wind beneath my wings, always there quietly supporting me with love, and that means everything to me. We travel this road together.

To my brother, Russ, who spent hours listening to me on the phone, and to his family, who gave him to me for those hours, I owe my sanity. Ron and Barb, and Joyce and Dwight Bedsole, and Gary and Louise White—you are the most loyal friends, we are so blessed to have. Thank you to our beautiful daughter-in-law for your understanding and generosity. I love you all.

My Wednesday ladies poker group has kept me laughing and provided endless material for a new play. My book club has indulged me through this writing process and shared my tears. There are countless others out there who have been a part of this journey, and I value your friendship beyond words. You know the role you played:

Frances, Paula, Sue, Pete and Jane, Brad, Gary, Conner, Jeanie and Tom, Margaret and Dennis (we miss you), Pat L., John M., AA, the Judge, and every sponsor Mike has ever had, I thank you all.

My sincere appreciation to those of you who read this manuscript along the way and so graciously gave me your feedback. I hope I didn't forget anyone: Joyce, Penny, Christine, Gail, Barbara, Martha B., Mary, Jane, Sig, Laura, Suzanne, Susan, Martha E., Jerry, Ed, Michelle, Jeanie, Pat, Nancy, Linda, Ron, Janice and John.

My thanks to Gene and Linda Ormond for introducing us to the paradise in the North Carolina mountains that provided the perfect peaceful setting to write this story. My thanks to Mike Leach, who gave me some great technical advice while we were in the mountains. Jenn Fullagar gave me helpful ideas on cover design. And to Martha Edgerton, your kindness brought me to tears.

A very special thank-you to Penny Richards. You are the mother who gave me the courage to continue writing this book. I admire your strength and respect your wisdom.

For all parents who have lost this battle, my heart hurts for your loss.
This book is humbly dedicated to Penny and to you.

Resources

$\mathcal{E}$ach of these programs mentioned in this book are still in existence. Hopefully if you are seeking help you will find it easier than we did. The internet is full of information.

Amethyst Program, 910-291-7880, Scotland Memorial, 500 Lauchwood Drive, Laurinburg, NC 28352

Mountainside, 844-863-2466, PO Box 717, Canaan, CT 06018

The Coleman Institute, (nine locations) 877-773-3869, 204 Hamilton Street, Richmond, VA 23200
They now detox methadone.

DART Cherry, 919-731-7930, 1302 West Ash Street, Goldsboro, NC

Made in the USA
Lexington, KY
15 June 2015